OFF-ROADER'S
HANDBOOK
CONTENTS

Cover Photo: Andrew Kenny

Published by HPBooks, a division of Price Stern Sloan, Inc.
11150 Olympic Boulevard, Los Angeles, California 90064
ISBN: 0-89586-403-7 Library of Congress Catalog Number 86-81202
© 1986 Price Stern Sloan, Inc.
Printed in the U.S.A.
9 8 7 6 5 4

NOTICE: The information contained in this book is true and complete to the best of our knowledge. All recommendations on parts and procedures are made without guarantees on the part of the authors or Price Stern Sloan. Because the quality of parts, materials and methods are beyond our control, the authors and the publisher disclaim all liability incurred in connection with the use of this information.

ON THE COVER

John Cummings of California's San Fernando Valley splashes his big, mean $26,208 Chevrolet Blazer through its paces. John is a private investigator and says that the red Ferrari that was used in the *Magnum P.I.* television series stands out in a crowd, so why shouldn't his own personal transportation. Actually, John saves the heavily equipped, black-and-red Chevy for weekend outbacking and does his investigative work in a nondescript sedan. And you thought he was the *Fall Guy*. His super 4WD Blazer has a Burbank Suspension lift kit with triple-front/dual-rear shock absorbers and twin steering stabilizers, Dick Cepek Off-Roader tires, and a host of other goodies installed by Don's Off-Road Specialties of Reseda, California. The Blazer was photographed in muddy action by Andrew Kenny of—believe it or not—the California Highway Patrol. A very special thanks to both of these off-road enthusiasts.

ACKNOWLEDGMENTS

Books of this type are not possible without the cooperation of a number of people and firms. Most of the photographs were taken by co-author Spence Murray and Jim Brokaw II, although they are not so identified in the interests of brevity. Jim, by the way, when he's not getting stuck purposely for the camera, gets stuck a lot accidentally. Other photo sources are individually credited. A special note of appreciation goes to *Road & Track* magazine for the use of invaluable historical photos, to *Four Wheeler* magazine for certain action shots, and to John Lawlor whose camera work over the years has been invaluable.

Appreciation is also due photographer/desert historian Dennis Casebier and his Friends of the Mojave Road for their help on our behalf. More thanks go to Pete Condos of Con-Ferr, Inc.; Brian Chuchua of Chuchua Jeep; Tom Cepek of Dick Cepek, Inc.; and especially to John Baker of John Baker Performance Products, for allowing us full use of their facilities and many of their products.

Many vehicle manufacturers and distributors were helpful in supplying photos, vehicles and valued information. Here's a tip of the editorial hat to Mike Parris of Ford Motor Co.; Dodge Division of Chrysler Corporation; Tim Gallagher of Mitsubishi Motor Sales of America; Lou and Clay Bintz of AMC's Jeep division; Nissan Motor Corporation in U.S.A.; Toyota Motor Sales of America; American Isuzu Motors; and other representatives of the four-wheel-drive industry.

We cannot stop without saluting Mike and Shirley Dougherty who have no peers in their knowledge of our southwestern deserts, especially Death Valley, their 4WD expertise and unmatched hospitality during a rare snow storm.

Thanks to you all.

James T. Crow/Spencer Murray

Go Forth, Have Fun

If you're already a hard-core off-roader, know where to go and how to do it, this chapter is an elective rather than a prerequisite.

However, if you haven't already graduated to the off-road expert class, these introductory remarks are directed at you. First, we want to tell you that we envy you. That's because you have so much good stuff to look forward to. There's a whole new world opening up out there ahead of you. We call it the wonderful world of off-roading. Our own discovery of off-roading was a major experience in our lives.

Both authors brought backgrounds in automotive journalism to the off-road world. For Spencer Murray, this experience included being part of the early hot-rod movement in southern California and led to his being the editor of one of the early specialty magazines in this field. To this, he added an interest in boats and was the author of a pair of boating guides to the Gulf of California.

His earliest off-roading experience was so long ago that he's now forgotten the exact circumstances. He does remember that he teamed up with Ralph Poole fan in 1967 and used an ordinary passenger car—a *Rambler!*—to set a new elapsed-time record between Tijuana and La Paz, Baja California.

This uplifting experience led him to involvement with and production of more journalism on the subjects of off-roading in general and off-road racing in particular. When NORRA (National Off-Road Racing Association) was formed in 1967 as a direct result of the historic Baja record runs, they began issuing sequentially numbered competition licenses. His was No. 4 on a list that eventually exceeded 1000.

At the same time, the emphasis in his professional career shifted from ordinary vehicles to recreational and off-road machines. For a period of time, he was Feature Editor of *Wheels Afield,* a magazine devoted to RVs and off-roading.

There's a whole new world waiting for you out in the great beyond. Off-road vehicles and heads-up driving can handle terrain like this that would sink an ordinary passenger car down to its doorhandles. Photo by James T. Crow.

Later, he was Managing Editor of *Pickup, Van & 4WD* magazine, which coincidentally was founded by co-author, James T. Crow.

His work at *PV4* included not only articles about off-road travel and adventure, but tests and evaluations of all types of cars and trucks capable of off-road travel. At present, he is a free-lance writer, meaning that he chooses the magazines and the subjects he wants and this includes nearly all of the recreational and off-road publications.

Jim describes his introduction to this wonderful world as one of the three or four "watershed" experiences of his life. That is, after that point, his whole life was changed and nothing was ever quite the same again. This occurred when he went to Baja California with a group of people in dune buggies and in just over a week's time discovered a new activity

that was to profoundly affect the rest of his life.

For him, the world became a different place after that. When he discovered off-roading, he was the editor of *Road & Track,* a sports-car magazine. Over the next several years, his interest in the off-road world replaced sports cars and in 1972, he founded *Pickup, Van & 4WD* magazine for CBS Publications. Since that time, off-roading has been a major part of his professional life, as well as continuing as a major fun pursuit after working hours.

So, what the authors have experienced as a result of our interest in off-roading is a way to make a living as well as do what we'd like to be doing anyway.

You can't get much luckier than that.

Some Good Things—One of the good things that off-roading brought to us and can also bring to you is an increase in

Co-author James T. Crow (left) and Neal Allen co-drove a second Meyers Manx as a back-up to "Old Red" in an early Baja Record Run. Photo courtesy Road & Track magazine.

Off-road racing world was stunned when, on July 4-5, 1967, co-author Spencer Murray (left) and Ralph Poole (right) battled Baja and won—in an ordinary Rambler American two-door sedan. Their time; 31 hours flat. Photo by John Lawlor, from the Spencer Murray collection.

Co-author Spencer Murray at speed deep in a Louisiana swamp during a Jeep off-road rally. The idea was to run up as many off-road miles as possible between Montreal, Quebec, Canada, and New Orleans in 5-1/2 days. Naturally, he and his co-driver won! Photo by Jimmy Nylund, courtesy Four Wheeler magazine.

your horizons. It's almost fundamental that you're interested in traveling off-road because that makes it possible for you to go places you want to go and do things that you like to do.

If you're a fisherman or a hunter, for instance, your off-road vehicle can take you to places you couldn't get to otherwise. If you have an interest in geology, either as a student of the science or as a rockhound, it's your off-road vehicle that delivers you to the places you most want to go. Likewise, if you have an interest in the history of an area, an off-road vehicle provides you with the transportation that lets you visit all of the important places. Or, if you're like many contemporary urban dwellers, your primary interest in off-roading may simply be in getting away from the people-polluted nine-to-five environment.

Be Neat—Unfortunately, there are some off-roaders whose main reason for being there is to escape the restraints that civilization imposes on all of us. This group simply casts off any trace of self-restraint the moment they leave the pavement and regard the off-road as an opportunity to frolic without recognition that even in the back country we have certain responsibilities. More than once we traveled through a beautiful canyon where a group of these had been. Typically, there were at least 50 beer cans

Load up with area maps for a weekend off-road. This way, you'll keep tabs on where you are and how to get back.

Off-road driving should, in many cases, be termed off-pavement driving. There are many byways like this that a two-wheel-drive recreational vehicle can take in stride.

scattered around, many of which were riddled with bullet holes. There were also broken bottles in the trail plus empty tin cans and enough empty sacks, scraps of newspaper and food wrappers to make you wonder about the human race.

Fortunately, such inconsiderate Neanderthals make up a small minority of those who use off-road vehicles. On the contrary, we're often pleased by how much trouble thoughtful off-roaders take to leave their campsites as unmarked as possible by hauling out everything they bring in and not littering the back country with their trash.

WHERE TO GO

A Jeep dealer friend of ours, Bryan Chuchua, tells us that one question that the buyer of an off-road vehicle is almost certain to ask is, "OK, we've got the vehicle. Now, where do we go?"

One of the most efficient ways to find the best trails in your area is to join an off-road club. Dealers who are enthusiastic about selling four-wheel-drive vehicles usually keep in close touch with the local clubs and can usually put you in touch with them. Another good source for information about clubs and club activities is the people at your local off-road shop, which you should get to know in any case.

Off-Road Clubs—There are many

If you're new to off-roading and aren't sure where you can go legally and safely, join a local 4X4 club. This group is caravanning across an immense dry-lake bed in a southwestern desert.

advantages to belonging to a club, particularly if you're new to off-roading. Club members can tell you not only about the good places that are available in your area, but also organize treks that you can participate in. Traveling with an experienced group ensures that you won't be stuck there for the rest of your life if you do happen to get in beyond your level of skill.

In fact, there's no better way to learn the capabilities of your vehicle than to travel with a group of off-roaders who know what they're doing. You not only gain in off-roading know-how by observing how the experienced drivers do it, you can also pick up valuable tips about additional equipment you may want or need and suggestions about where to buy it.

Posted information at National Parks, Forests, Monuments and other scenic areas will reveal what there is to see and do. A ranger can pinpoint interesting sights off the beaten track.

Part of the fun and games of off-roading is keeping your vehicle on the move.

Other valuable information you can acquire includes tips about camping out of an off-road vehicle. There's a large variety of camping gear available, not all of which is ideally suited to off-road use. By seeing what other people are using, you can get all sorts of good ideas and also find out where to get them. In any club activity, the variety of camping skills and equipment is amazing. For some, camping is as basic as an army surplus sleeping bag rolled out on the ground. Others may prefer equipment akin to collapsible houses complete with everything, including a portable version of the kitchen sink. Between these two extremes are dozens of good ideas.

Theme Trips—One of our basic recommendations for a longer off-road adventure includes what we call taking a "theme" trip. For example, one theme trip we were involved with several years ago followed what a writer named Charles Kelly called the "outlaw trail." This trail ran from from Palomas, Mexico, and Columbus, New Mexico, all the way to Landusky, Montana, and on into Canada. The idea was to visit places between those two points that were used by outlaws at one time or another.

So we traveled the owl-hoot trail, spe-cifically seeking out those places where Butch Cassidy and the Wild Bunch had robbed trains and banks. We visited such places as Circleville, Utah, finding the house where Butch's family lived and also located the family ranch south of there. We also went to Telluride, Colorado, where Butch was involved in his first bank robbery, then duplicated the trail he must have taken from there to Monticello, Utah, after the robbery. Other out-of-the-way places we visited on the Wild Bunch Trail included Brown's Hole at the three-state junction of Utah, Wyoming and Colorado, plus Rifle, Colorado, the Hole-in-the-Wall country near Kaycee, Wyoming (wow, did we get lost there!), Dandy Crossing on the Dirty Devil River, the Robber's Roost country east of Hanksville, Utah, and many others.

By the way, this was more than 20 years ago, before the movies made Butch Cassidy and the Sundance Kid familiar to every movie or television watcher in the country.

Another theme trip we made was through the Reese River country in central Nevada. This was in connection with background for a book about prospecting in that part of the country. We never got around to writing the book, but it did give us an excuse for exploring the whole fascinating gold mining and ranching country between Austin on the north and Tonapah in the south.

Still another type of theme trip involved a long-distance off-road rally from Montreal to New Orleans that was sponsored by Jeep. The object was to drive as hard as possible over the worst possible roads for five-and-a-half days. Co-author Murray and his companion, although neither had been in any of this country before, racked up 2600 horrible miles and won the rally hands down. The key to their success was obtaining as many county and other local maps as possible well in advance, then laying out a route that covered what appeared to be the least-traveled roads.

The point is that there's no end to the variety of theme trips you can take—the trail of the Pony Express, the route of the Overland Stage, the places Jesse James and his gang did their work, the places that Pershing's troops went when they chased Pancho Villa into mainland Mexico in 1916, the Gila Trail from Texas to the California gold fields, the Oregon Trail, the route followed by the 20-mule teams hauling borax out of Death Val-

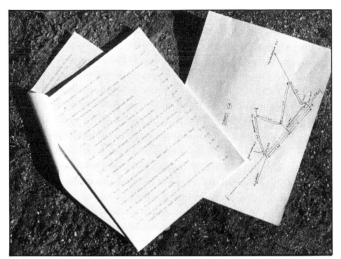

Keep a log of your travels and draw your own maps if you have to. Share these with others so they can also enjoy what you've "discovered."

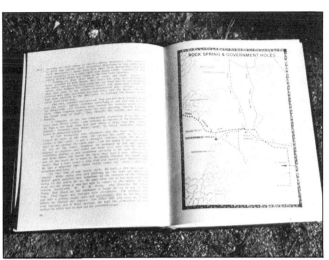

After 25 years of probing the Mojave Desert, Dennis Casebeir has authored the *Guide to the Mojave Road*. It gives a mile-by-mile description of a 130-mile 4X4 trail with detailed maps, and describes flora, fauna, cultural resources and history of the area.

ley…. The variety and length of the list is limited only by your imagination.

Adopt an Area—One of the basic problems for many off-roaders is in thinking they've been every place there is to go within a reasonable driving range. There's a way to avoid this problem. What you do is pick out an area and adopt it. Make it your own. Go there time after time. Don't just drive through it once or twice and think you know it. Instead, establish a goal of learning everything there is to know about that particular section of the country.

This includes traveling every road, trail and cow path in your chosen area and finding out where each one of them goes. To do it properly, you need to get the most-detailed maps possible—topographicals (see Chapter 16)—and deliberately set out to travel every trail that's shown, making road logs and getting to know that area like the palm of your hand. Become an expert on the roads and trails in this area, in other words.

If you have any inclination in that direction, you can also start learning other facts about your chosen area. Get the appropriate books and learn the name of every plant that grows there and what its

peculiarities are that account for its being in this particular place. Do the same with the animals and bird life. You can also expand your horizons by learning the

geology of the area, classifying the type of environment you're dealing with, becoming familiar with the minerals you can expect to find there.

A local library or an area resident may come up with an old newspaper that will reveal first-hand history about an area you want to explore. The imaginative logo of this 1908 newspaper came from Needles, California. From the Casebier Collection.

The history of almost any area can be fascinating, once you get involved in it. This is also easy to get into because almost every area of the country has its local historical society with a wealth of research information. There may be a book or an unpublished manuscript or even old diaries or letters that will help fill in the blanks in your own knowledge. Also, in many instances, the local historians can put you in touch with descendants of the original settlers and this can result in your sharing the stories their families have passed down to them.

Read Old Newspapers—Old newspapers provide another fascinating glimpse into the history of an area. There's scarcely a section of the country that did not have its own local newspaper in its early days. These are often available on microfilm and this is a marvelous way to spend a day or a weekend when the weather isn't suitable for off-roading.

Doing Original Research—You can also do your own original research into a place or an area. Let's say you've come upon a collection of old foundations and junk that you can tell used to be a town, a mining area, a farm or a ranch. If there was anything of that nature there, you may be certain that it was recorded in the tax rolls for that county. This means that records exist about who filed on that property, when it was filed, when ownership was transferred, to whom, and so on. You can begin your search at the County Clerk or County Tax Assessor's office, which is usually in or near the county courthouse. Once you've ferreted out this basic information, it's then possible to begin your search for the story of that place. Maybe it will involve phone calls to people with the same name. Or more digging through county records looking for clues in the marriage licenses that were issued during that time, or births that were recorded. Often your search will take you back to the historical society, or to the file of old newspapers.

Pretty soon, as you get to know more and more about your chosen area, the individual bits of knowledge you've accumulated will begin to come together to create patterns. The man named Hardcastle who paid taxes on that property in 1904 had a daughter who married a man named Wade and you're already

It's more fun to go off-roading with a group. There's a lot of camaraderie to be enjoyed at the campsite after a hard day's travel.

aware that just down the street from the court house there's a store named Wade Feed and Grain....

As you keep traveling and expanding your knowledge, you'll also get to know the people who live there now and this can be another source of interest and pleasure. Then you're not just another stranger blasting through the country in your off-road vehicle. You've become a friend and are able to broaden your understanding of people living in an environment unlike your own.

Become an Expert—We have a friend who has carried this process to such an extent that he's now the leading expert on the history of the Eastern Mojave Desert. He has accomplished this even though he has never actually lived there and has always worked full time at a totally unrelated job. By now he's devoted almost 20 years to this consuming interest of his and there's scarcely a road, trail, track, ranch, mine, ghost town or fallen down building in that whole fascinating section of the desert that he doesn't know the history of. In fact, there are times when we're convinced that there isn't a tree, rock, lizard or red-tailed hawk out there that he doesn't know by its first name.

This man, Dennis Casebier, has chosen to share his knowledge through

books he's written about the area. He has also been instrumental in the creation of two off-road recreation trails in that part of the country. One of these, the Mojave Road, was originally an Indian trail, then a wagon road through that part of the country and is about 130 miles long, a great weekend trip. The other, which he calls the Ivanpah Loop, is a 400-mile collection of old wagon trails, mine roads and other abandoned byways that link a large number of the most interesting places in the Eastern Mojave. He has also been responsible for the creation of guidebooks to these areas for off-road travelers. These guides include maps and detailed mileage logs so you know where you are, plus information about the history of the area as well as the flora, fauna and everything else of interest.

If that part of the country is available to you, don't miss these experiences. You can get more information by writing Friends of the Mojave Road (P.O. Box 307, Norco, CA 91760).

But our main point is that you should never find yourself with no place to go.

Go Forth, Have Fun—As we said, there's a whole marvelous world of off-roading out there. So read this book, go forth, have fun, respect the environment and be part of it.

2

Off-Road Vehicles

If you don't already own an off-road vehicle, it's fairly safe to say that you are contemplating doing so soon. Or else you wouldn't be reading this book. But in the event you don't have one waiting in the carport for another foray into the Great Weekend Beyond, then this chapter is designed to familiarize you with the great wealth of vehicles best suited to back-country travel.

No, you don't absolutely need four-wheel drive to take you far from the city's lights and into the lands of forest and desert trails. The relative merits of two-wheel-drive vehicles are explained in the next chapter. But what you do need to go stump-jumping is ground clearance.

Ground Clearance—Conventional vehicles, those low-slung coupes, sedans and sporty cars that you see zipping along the highways every day—are simply not suited to off-road travel. And they're not intended to be. Their soft underpinnings are too close to the ground. Their suspensions have limited travel. And usually there is too much front and rear end *overhang*—distance from the bumpers to the wheels—to let them safely tackle anything more severe than a graveled driveway ramp.

Park a pickup truck next to a luxury sedan and you'll immediately see what ground clearance is all about. The boulevard cruiser sits so low that you have to get down on your hands and knees to see under it. Its swoopy hood slopes out from the windshield to a low-down bumper/grille assembly which may have an aerodynamic chin spoiler, or air dam, underneath that comes within inches of Mother Earth. Around back, the decklid flows back and down to a bumper as much as four feet behind the rear wheels. As appealing as such a limo might be, it's anything but an off-roader. Such a machine simply cannot be propelled over the roads of Baja, through the swamps of Florida, or anywhere else that isn't paved.

The lowly pickup truck, on the other

There's a wide array of off-road vehicles to choose from. The 1987 Jeep Wrangler shown replaced Jeep CJ after production run of more than 40 years. Photo by Peter du Pre, courtesy of Four Wheeler magazine.

Popular for serious off-roading are pickup trucks and the wagon-like utility vehicles derived from them. These are Ford's Bronco II, left, and Ranger. Both are 4WD, though 2WD versions of both are available. Photo by John Lawlor.

As pointed out in the text, attributes for a good off-road vehicle include tall ground clearance and short overhang. The Mitsubishi Montero provides the best of these worlds.

Derived from the Jeep truck is the luxurious full-size domestic utility called the Grand Wagoneer. It is one of few utilities with four-door convenience and excellent as either inclement-weather or off-road vehicle. Photo courtesy of American Motors.

Who could not but love the redoubtable CJ-7 from Jeep whose World War II ancestors started the off-road movement over 40 years ago. For real topless motoring, try one. Photo courtesy of American Motors.

hand, sits high off the ground and with its firm yet compliant suspension, it won't squat low on its haunches after slamming hard over a rock pile. Its suspension and running gear are more brutish than a passenger car's and the average truck will outlast a car by a wide margin.

Trucks generally have little front overhang; the bumper is close enough to the wheels that it won't easily bury its nose on the far side of a gully. Rear overhang is usually more pronounced, but unless a truck is loaded down with a heavy cargo, the rearmost part is sufficiently high that the vehicle won't drag its tail end when it drops into, or clambers out of, a *wadi*—you look it up.

Some dirt roads and trails frequently used by off-roaders are marked with signs stating, "High Clearance Vehicles Only." And many maps that depict seldom-used tracks are similarly labeled. They say nothing about four-wheel drive. It's merely a polite way of explaining that conventional passenger cars dare not tread here or they'll get stuck for sure.

Low Points—Ground clearance is more than just the distance between the vehicle's underpinnings and the ground. It also works with a vehicle's *wheelbase,* the distance between the center of the front and rear wheels, to determine its suitability for off-road. One of the more critical ground-clearance points is midway between the front and rear wheels. This is often the location of the muffler or catalytic converter and, with a 4X4, the transfer case. It's easy to understand that a long-wheelbase vehicle will scrape its mid-section more readily than a short-wheelbase rig. If a rock, stump or similar projection is struck by the low-hanging exhaust system or other chassis part and the vehicle is held fast, then it is said to be *high-centered.* It follows, then, that the less the ground clearance, and the greater the wheelbase, the more easily a vehicle can become high-centered. Conversely, the higher a vehicle stands off the ground and the shorter its wheelbase, the better an off-roader it will be.

Ground clearance is a consideration at other chassis points as well. The lowest point of any potential off-roader is generally the under side of the differential; one

Toyota offers 14 models on its pickup-truck platform, including 4WDs and various 2WDs with gas or diesel engines, four-speed or five-speed manual or automatic transmissions, plus standard-cab models (shown) or the extended-cab version. Photo courtesy of Toyota.

Trooper II by Isuzu is among the imported Japanese utilities. Unlike most others, it's offered both as a two-door and a four-door.

Full-size sport utility Dodge Ramcharger is available in 2WD or 4WD. Photo courtesy of Chrysler Corp.

on a two-wheel drive and two of them on a 4X4. This can measure 7 in. or less in some cases. It's a fixed dimension because the rear axle is a one-piece affair on 4WD trucks and, as the vehicle rides up and down over undulations, the differential goes up and down with the wheels. In front, it's another story unless the vehicle also has a one-piece driving front axle.

More modern 4WDs feature independent front suspension—IFS. With IFS, the front differential is fixed to the chassis and as the suspension travels up and down, the differential's height above terra firma varies considerably—as do the distances to bottom sides of the engine, transmission and other vulnerables. And this is a consideration in two-wheel drives, as well.

Ground clearance can be increased, of course, by using taller tires and wheels or other, more extensive modifications, page 40. But this may not be your cup of tea if you're planning on becoming just a casual off-road traveler. If you're shopping for your first off-road vehicle, bear in mind that both good ground clearance and an abbreviated rear-end overhang are essential elements of successful back-country motoring.

TYPES OF VEHICLES

Basically there are really only two types of vehicles that are best suited to off-road driving: pickup trucks and the station wagon-like utility vehicles—the latter usually based on the chassis, suspensions and drive lines of the former.

Pickup Trucks—Pickup trucks are just that: light duty trucks with a pickup box in back. Some of these can carry only the driver and one passenger, and are limited by either cab width or the designer's insistence on installing sporty-looking bucket seats. Others can carry three across on a bench seat. Then, there are versions with seating for four—with a pair of rear-mounted jump seats—in what are termed stretched-cab trucks. Finally, there are trucks with four doors, just like a sedan, but long enough to have the usual pickup box in the rear.

Utility Vehicles—Utilities, as already noted, are based on the running gear of pickup trucks. The difference lies in the enclosed body with the knockabout features of a station wagon. The smallest of these will seat four folks in some degree of comfort or five in a pinch. Others can contain five and six people and there are a couple of gargantuans that can accommodate up to nine—your basic Little League ball club!

Utilities also come with a choice of either two or four doors, the latter intended for group traveling without backseaters having to scramble over a folded-down front passenger seat to get in or out.

The trend in imported pickups lately is to stretch-cab pickups. This is the Isuzu Spacecab introduced for 1986.

For 1986-1/2, Nissan upped the ante in the small-truck wars with the "hard body." Optional is 140-HP V6 from Z Car. Photo courtesy Nissan.

Finally, the off-road motoring arena includes both pickup trucks and utility vehicles from U.S. manufacturers as well as from overseas, with Japan being far and away the leading importer of these recreational rigs. So you see, there's a whole lot out there to choose from. In fact, all U.S. manufacturers—Ford, General Motors, the Dodge side of Chrysler Corp., and American Motors—and, from the far side of the pond, the Japanese firms of Toyota, Nissan, Mitsubishi, Mazda and Isuzu, have a wide array of recreational off-roaders. From this bewildering array, be assured that there's a vehicle that's just right for you and your specific purposes.

Off-Roading Array—The most important thing to consider when you're shopping for an off-roader is your planned use of the vehicle. Will it be for you and your spouse, or a friend, to use prowling the far country on a weekend cruise during periods of good weather? If so, then by all means consider the pickup truck. Of course, if you expect to venture forth during marginal or downright inclement weather, or you want to keep your camping, hunting or other equipment in a safe and lockable environment, you can always add a camper shell to protect the contents of the bed. Or, you can opt for a slide-in camper unit with bunks for sleeping, a small galley with stove and sink, and cupboard and drawer space sufficient to provide you with a small but mobile home away from home for a two or three day's stay in the boondocks.

Jeep's compact Cherokees are available with two or four doors while the companion and look-alike Wagoneer comes as a 4-door only. Such a mixture of conveniences and amenities should cause a first-time recreational vehicle buyer to carefully consider his choices. Photo courtesy of American Motors.

Either the shell or the slide-in can be left at home, of course, when these temporary conveniences are unnecessary. Pickup trucks are also eminently handy for tossing duffle—such as an ice chest, a cot and sleeping bag or two, a box of utensils, a stove, and a sack full of groceries—into the bed without the worry of scuffing upholstery or crowding your mother-in-law out of her place in the rear seat. If such uses appeal to you, then by all means let a pickup truck become your off-road rig.

On the other hand, if you've a family to consider and would prefer keeping everyone under one roof, then give the wagon-like utility vehicle some serious thought. These offer protected inside stowage for valuables, the luxuries of warmth and air conditioning in every cubic inch of the interior, and most have fold-down or removable rear seats so you can increase the inside storage area when your passengers are limited to one or two.

Because utilities are, for the most part, based upon pickup-truck chassis, neither one has a real advantage over the other in terms of ground clearance, power, or off-roadability. And because most utilities

Full-sized utilities, offered only by U.S. manufacturers, are every bit as sprightly as the smaller counterparts. Here's a diesel-powered GMC Jimmy somewhere west of Laramie.

Some folks feared that when Ford downsized the big Bronco to create the compact Bronco II, that big brother would go away. Not so, thank you. Photo courtesy of Ford Motor Co.

Dodge pickups come in Baby Bear, Mama Bear and Pappa Bear sizes. From left to right, imported Dodge D-50, mid-size Dodge Dakota and full-size D-150. Photo by Ron Sessions.

share at least the front half of a pickup's sheet metal, the front and often the rear overhang, width, height—almost every physical dimension—are shared by same-make pickup trucks and utility vehicles.

Large or Small—Perhaps just as important as deciding whether your needs will be best answered by a pickup or a utility, is choosing between a full-size vehicle and one of more compact dimensions. Another major consideration is whether you prefer a made-in-the-U.S. domestic rig or one manufactured in a foreign country.

When you stop and consider that the various types of vehicles we have talked about so far are available both with and without four-wheel drive, you can begin to realize what a tremendously broad selection there is for carefree backwoods driving.

But there's even more to contemplate. Do you want or need the brute power that comes only from a U.S.-built V8 engine? If you plan to tote a heavy trailer or carry weighty loads with any sort of regularity, you can certainly use one of these.

But then, maybe you're more economically inclined or don't foresee weighing

your rig down with mountains of gear and outdoor toys. So your needs might be better answered with a fuel-stingy four-cylinder engine. Or better, something between these two extremes like an in-line six or V6.

Do you relish top-down, wind-in-the-hair motoring? There are, if not true convertibles, removable-top models waiting for you. Some of these offer topless driving for everyone aboard. Others have removable rear roofs that keep front-seaters out of the weather while backseaters can soak up the sunshine.

Shifting Around—And what about the transmission? There are a surprising number of folks just starting off on their off-road careers who assumed that all 4X4s have manual transmissions. Not so. Jeep was first to couple an automatic transmission with four-wheel drive in their 1963 Wagoneer. Although it was an innovation at the time, the idea was quickly copied by all of the other 4X4 manufacturers.

Therefore, you're faced with another decision: choosing the transmission that not only appeals to you, but also to anyone else who'll be sharing the driving chores. Don't forget that other family members may not want to cope with an ungainly and truck-like shift lever. Or that the up and coming younger drivers in the family may not even know what a clutch pedal is for. Then, there's resale value to consider: Come trading time, is

Manufacturers are busily converting passenger cars and conventional station wagons to all-wheel drive for inclement-weather use. But off-roading prowess is limited by vulnerability of their undersides.

As late as 1986, Mazda was only imported pickup to shun four-wheel drive.

Nothing works like a Chevy truck. And that's not a bad slogan. While Ford F-series trucks are the largest single-model sellers, that's only because the sales figures for the twin Chevy and GMC models are tallied separately. Photo courtesy of Chevrolet.

Chevy Suburban with four-wheel drive will take nine passengers into the outback in living-room comfort. Photo courtesy of Chevrolet.

your rig worth more to the next buyer with a stick or a juicebox?

Other Decisions—Available on the modern off-road vehicle is just about any creature comfort and amenity optional on a passenger car. There are two- and four-wheel-drive pickup trucks and utilities that offer power brakes and steering, air conditioning, power windows and door locks, sun roofs, rear window washers and wipers, cruise control, high-tech audio systems with cassette players, power seats, reclining seats, and so on. Or, if you feel you don't need all the bells and whistles just to forage through the boondocks a few times each year, you can order up an off-roader just as plain-Jane

as you like. Most factory accessories aren't all that imperative for successful back-country travel anyway, and you might prefer paying less money up front for a new vehicle. Later, you can take the dollars saved and apply them to real essentials such as a winch, auxiliary lights, larger wheels and tires, and on down the off-roader's wish list.

Passenger Cars—We would be remiss in not mentioning the growing number of passenger cars that offer the attributes of four-wheel drive. Pioneers of this trend were the AMC Eagle and Subaru 4WD Wagon. Though the Eagle is as American as apple pie and had its genesis near the Motor City, it is now actually pro-

duced at Brampton, Ontario, Canada. The balance of the elite group comes from abroad: the Audi Quattro and VW Golf Synchro from Germany, and the Toyota Tercel, Honda Civic, Colt Vista and Subaru GL 4WD series from Japan.

There are others, of course, and even more are on the drawing boards. But while these mutations boast the tractability of four-wheel drive and are a good compromise for foul-weather travel in the security of a passenger car, they are just that: passenger cars without the so-necessary attributes of good ground clearance and limited overhang. So, while we do not deny that these all-wheel drives exist, and although co-author

Murray had a splendid weekend knifing through an Arizona outback in an AMC Eagle, we aren't detailing them here. There's no need to further complicate your recreational off-roading choices, you see.

THE CHARTS

These basic comparison charts are intended as quick reference of what's available in the off-road marketplace. We have not attempted to note every conceivable model, nor all vital statistics. Horsepower, vehicle weights, load capacities, gear ratios, and the like are very much subject to change at the manufacturer's whim. But because pickup trucks and utility vehicles are not as apt to undergo serious annual facelifts or changes for the mere sake of change, as are conventional passenger cars, there is some important data we can give you. These include the general overall dimensions, seating accommodations, types of engines and transmissions available, the all-important turning radius, and whether the models are 2WD, 4WD or are available both ways.

To prevent your being overwhelmed by the number of vehicles awaiting your beck and call, we have grouped them into convenient categories. These include full-size domestic trucks and utilities, the compact and domestically built trucks and utilities, and the imported versions of these. If you find the size and type of vehicle that most appeals to your recreational needs, then a trip to the nearest dealership for that brand of rig is in order. The dealer will have the product detail you'll want, including available options, colors and trim combinations.

Another good way to zero in on the rig of your dreams is to peruse any of the off-road-oriented monthly magazines. In nearly every issue of each, there are road tests, product evaluations and head-to-head comparisons between competing models. This way you can get at least some idea of what a specific vehicle is like and, hopefully, arrive at some basic conclusions.

First imported small sports utility based on pickup truck is Toyota 4Runner. Photo courtesy of Toyota.

Downsized version of Chevy Blazer first appeared in 1982 and has been a runaway success. For 1986, optional 2.8-liter V6 gets electronic fuel injection. Photo courtesy of Chevrolet.

Finally, go forth with an open mind. Though you might set out thinking you really need a pickup, you might choose a utility rig once you've tried it on for size. Shopping for an off-roader can be almost as much fun as pointing one toward open country. When your choice has finally been made, come on back here and finish the rest of this book. Owning an off-road vehicle is one thing. But learning how to use it is another. And that's why we've prepared this book for you.

UNDERSTANDING THE TABLES

It is important to understand that the accompanying tables are by no means complete. They are presented for comparative purposes only. Space prohibits listing all the specifications and other data for all available off-roadable vehicles. Then it would be outdated after a single model year. Data for horsepower, torque, internal engine dimensions, and so forth, is subject to change thanks to variables in emissions standards. And a given manufacturer may vary gear ratios, gross vehicle weight ratings (GVWR), and other factors without notice. So we are limited to listing seldom-changed information, though even some of this will vary in time as new models are introduced and older ones discontinued.

But if you're interested in a pickup truck or a utility vehicle as a recreational off-roader, the listings will give a rough idea of how vehicles are categorized and how the competitive makes differ in physical size and basic componentry.

This is how to interpret the various column headings:

Make/Model—Name of manufacturer given first, followed by model designation (if any). Trim levels are not listed.

Engine Type—Letter L designates inline engine, V means a Vee type. The figure gives the number of cylinders. Diesels are not so designated.

Transmission—Here are given the number of forward speeds followed by M for manual transmission or A for automatic.

Transfer Case—Obviously, 2WDs do not have transfer cases and the entries here do not apply to them. But 4X4s do and the numbers indicate the low-range gear ratio. (High-range ratio is always 1:1).

Hubs—Letter A designates automatic locking/unlocking front hubs, M refers to manual hubs. (Not applicable to 2WDs). Where the letter appears singly, the designated hub is the only type available. Where both appear, manual hubs are standard equipment and the automatics optional.

Wheelbase—Distance between front- and rear-wheel centers in inches. More than one figure in the truck categories indicates a choice of standard or extended cabs as well as various-length pickup beds.

Overall Length—Length in inches from front of vehicle to rear, usually from bumper to bumper. Variations are due to alternative wheelbases.

Overall Width—Widest cross-sectional dimension of a vehicle in inches, usually taken at the doors. This is a single measurement for a given vehicle since widths are standard regardless of wheelbase variations.

Overall Height—Nominal dimensions, given in inches, for the distance from the ground to a vehicle's highest point will vary with optional tire sizes. Most 4X4s stand taller than a same-model 2WD, as well. Our numbers are averages.

Cargo Area—Numbers represent cubic feet. For trucks, the figures give the volumetric capacity of the bed *not deducting for rear intruding wheel wells* and computed only to the height of the bed. More than one figure indicates availability of alternate-sized boxes.

Two figures are given in the utility vehicle tables. The first represents rear cargo-area volume with rear seat upright. The second is the volume with rear seat folded down or removed. NA indicates the manufacturer does not list this dimension.

Turning Circle — Diameter in feet of a circle scribed by a vehicle steered fully right or left. Some manufacturers term such a circle as being "curb-to-curb," meaning the vehicle can turn between curbs that far apart. Others list "turning diameter" as a circle scribed by other than the wheels, usually an outer tip of front bumper. Tire size variations also affect these figures. Our figures are nominal and are most often for 4X4 models; 2WDs may turn more sharply.

Ground Clearance—In inches, the measurement from the ground to lowest part of vehicle usually, but not always, under the differential. Again, dimensions will vary with the size of tires fitted but these listings are clearances with standard equipment tires. Most figures are for 4X4s, and the 2WDs will vary somewhat.

Number of Doors—Listed for utility vehicles only and designating the number of doors (not including the rear hatch). Only the Jeep Cherokee and Trooper II have a choice between two- or four-door bodystyles.

FULL-SIZE PICKUP TRUCKS

Make/Model	Engine Type	Trans- mission	Transfer Case	Hubs	Wheel- base	Overall Length	Overall Width	Overall Height	Cargo Area	Turning Circle	Ground Clearance
Chevrolet (2WD/4WD)	V6 V8	4A 4M	1.96:1 2.61:1	A	117.5 131.5	192.2 212.1	79.6	71.9	47.3 53.2	42.5 46.8	8.5
Dodge (2WD/4WD)	L6 V6	3A 4M	2.61:1	M/A	115.0 131.0 149.0	189.5 208.3 210.2	79.5	73.1	47.2 58.5	39.6 44.4 49.7	8.5
Ford (2WD/4WD)	L6 V8	3A 4A 4M	2.61:1	A	116.8 133.0 155.0 168.4	192.1 215.0 208.3 230.3	77.2	73.1 77.0	65.7 78.0	41.5 NA NA NA	NA
GMC (2WD/4WD)	V6 V8	4A 4M	1.96:1 2.61:1	A	117.5 131.5	192.2 212.1	79.6	71.9	47.3 53.2	42.5 46.8	8.5
Jeep (4WD)	L6 V8	3A 4M	2.61:1	M	130.7	206.0	78.9	69.0	77.7	44.5	8.5

COMPACT DOMESTIC PICKUP TRUCKS

Make/Model	Engine Type	Trans-mission	Transfer Case	Hubs	Wheel-base	Overall Length	Overall Width	Overall Height	Cargo Area	Turning Circle	Ground Clearance
Chevrolet S-10 (2WD/4WD)	L4 V6	4A 4M 5M	2.61:1	A	106.3 117.9 122.9	178.1 192.8 194.0	64.7	65.0	43.5 53.0	35.4	7.4
Dodge Dakota	L4 V6	3A 5M	—	—	111.9 123.9	185.9 204.4	68.3	64.2	47.0 58.0	NA	NA
Ford Ranger (2WD/4WD)	L4 V6	4A 5M	2.48:1	M/A	107.9 113.9 125.0	175.6 187.6 192.7	68.0	68.8	37.0 43.1	35.4	7.8
GMC S-15 (2WD/4WD)	L4 V6	4A 4M 5M	2.61:1	A	106.3 117.9 122.9	178.1 192.8 194.0	64.7	65.0	43.5 53.0	35.4	7.4
Jeep Comanche (2WD/4WD)	L4 V6	3A 4M 5M	2.61:1	A	119.9	195.5	71.7	64.7	48.9	41.3	7.5

IMPORTED PICKUP TRUCKS

Make/Model	Engine Type	Trans-mission	Transfer Case	Hubs	Wheel-base	Overall Length	Overall Width	Overall Height	Cargo Area	Turning Circle	Ground Clearance
Dodge Ram (2WD/4WD)	L4	3A 5M	1.94:1	A	109.4	184.4	65.5	61.5	47.5	36.8	6.9
Isuzu P'UP (2WD/4WD)	L4	4M 5M	1.87:1	A	104.3 117.9	174.4 191.5	63.0	64.8	37.3 45.7	34.8 38.7	7.5
Mazda B2000 (2WD)	L4	5M	—	—	108.7 117.5	177.6 193.7	65.7	61.9	37.8 46.1	36.8 39.4	7.9
Mitsubishi (2WD/4WD)	L4	5M	1.94:1	A	109.4	184.4	65.5	61.5	47.5	36.8	6.9
Nissan (2WD/4WD)	L4	4A 5M	2.07:1	M/A	104.2 116.1	174.2 190.0	65.0	66.7	35.3 42.2	35.4 38.0	8.3
Subaru Brat (4WD)	Flat 4	4M	2.17:1	—	96.3	174.2	64.4	56.9	12.6	31.4	8.3
Toyota (2WD/4WD)	L4	4A 5M	2.27:1	M/A	103.0 112.2 121.5	174.6 184.1 186.2	66.5	67.2	38.5 44.4	37.4 40.0	7.7

FULL-SIZE UTILITY VEHICLES

Make/Model	Engine Type	Trans-mission	Transfer Case	Hubs	Wheel-base	Overall Length	Overall Width	Overall Height	Cargo Area	Turning Circle	Ground Clearance	Number of Doors
Chevy Blazer (4WD)	V8	4A 4M	1.96:1	M/A	106.5	184.4	78.5	71.1	NA/NA	37.5	7.0	2
Chevy Suburban (2WD/4WD)	V8	4A 4M	1.96:1	M/A	129.5	218.7	79.6	74.3	40.8/167.0	46.1	8.5	4
Dodge Ramcharger (2WD/4WD)	V8	3A 4M	2.61:1	A	106.0	184.6	79.5	73.6	NA/105.8	36.9	8.0	2
Ford Bronco (4WD)	L6 V8	3A 4A 4M	2.74:1	M/A	104.7	177.6	77.2	74.0	51.8/81.6	36.5	8.3	2
GMC Jimmy (4WD)	V8	4A 4M	1.96:1	M/A	106.5	184.4	78.5	71.1	NA/NA	37.5	7.0	2
GMC Surburban (2WD/4WD)	V8	4A 4M	1.96:1	M/A	129.5	218.7	79.6	74.3	40.8/167.0	46.1	8.5	4
Jeep Grand Wagoneer (4WD)	L6 V8	3A	2.61:1	A	108.7	186.4	74.8	66.4	NA/95.1	37.7	7.2	4

COMPACT DOMESTIC UTILITY VEHICLES

Make/Model	Engine Type	Trans-mission	Transfer Case	Hubs	Wheel-base	Overall Length	Overall Width	Overall Height	Cargo Area	Turning Circle	Ground Clearance	Number of Doors
Chevy Blazer (2WD/4WD)	L4 V6	4A 4M 5M	2.61:1	A	100.5	170.4	64.7	65.0	NA/NA	35.4	7.4	2
Ford Bronco II (2WD/4WD)	V6	4A 5M	2.48:1	M/A	94.0	158.3	58.0	69.0	25.6/64.9	32.4	6.5	2
GMC Jimmy (2WD/4WD)	L4 V6	4A 4M 5M	2.61:1	M/A	100.5	170.4	64.7	65.0	NA/NA	35.4	7.4	2
Jeep Cherokee (2WD/4WD)	L4 V6	3A 4M 5M	2.61:1	M/A	101.4	165.3	70.5	63.3	35.7/71.8	35.7	7.4	2/4
Jeep CJ-7 (4WD)	L4 L6	3A 4M 5M	2.61:1	M/A	93.4	153.2	65.3	70.9	NA/16.0	35.9	8.3	2
Jeep Wagoneer (4WD)	L4 V6	3A 4M 5M	2.61:1	M/A	101.4	165.3	70.5	63.3	35.7/71.8	35.7	7.4	4
Jeep Wrangler (4WD)	L4 L6	3A 5M	2.60:1	M/A	93.4	152.0	66.0	68.6	12.5/43.2	33.6	8.1	2

IMPORTED UTILITY VEHICLES

Make/Model	Engine Type	Trans-mission	Transfer Case	Hubs	Wheel-base	Overall Length	Overall Width	Overall Height	Cargo Area	Turning Circle	Ground Clearance	Number of Doors
Isuzu Trooper II (4WD)	L4	5M	1.87:1	A	104.3	175.2	65.0	70.1	45.5/71.3	35.4	8.3	2
Mitsubishi Montero (4WD)	L4	4A/5M	1.94:1	A	92.5	157.3	66.1	70.9	14.0/35.0	34.1	8.3	2
Toyota 4Runner (4WD)	L4	5M/4A	2.28:1	M/A	103.4	174.8	66.5	66.1	NA/80.9	41.3	7.9	2
Toyota Land Cruiser Station Wagon (4WD)	L6	4M	2.28:1	M	107.5	184.1	70.9	69.5	NA/99.0	40.7	7.5	2

3

Two-Wheel Drive

There was no such thing as four-wheel drive in the early days of the automobile, yet motorists like this stalwart thought nothing of going where today off-roaders would fear to tread even with all the traction and mobility that a modern 4X4 can muster.

Do you really need a four-wheel-drive vehicle to participate in the wonders of off-road motoring? Absolutely not.

In the early days of automobile travel, even the best out-of-town roads were what we'd now consider terrible. Even so, virtually everybody got along without four-wheel drive. There wasn't any other practical way, unless you admitted defeat and hitched up Old Dobbin again.

The Case Against 4WD—Even now, there are drivers who routinely use two-wheel-drive trucks to go places you and I would fear to tread in a completely equipped 4X4. To be honest about it, there's a persuasive case that can be made against buying a four-wheel-drive vehicle. First, there are mechanical com-

plications contributed by such things as transfer cases and free-running front hubs. Then, you can factor in the extra fuel it requires to operate a 4X4 compared to a 4X2. And you can cap off your argument with the considerable additional dollars it takes to buy a four-wheel drive compared to a two-wheel drive. This amounts to roughly $1500 for a compact-size 4X4 and about $2000 for a full-size.

Nevertheless and in spite of all this, we admit that we'll take four-wheel drive when heading off-road. Four-wheel drive gives you an extra margin of confidence that you'll get there and back. There's seldom any hesitation because you figure you'll get out of most anything

you can get into. That same degree of assurance is not present with two-wheel drive.

Risk of Overconfidence—There's an old saw among off-roaders that four-wheel drive lets you go on so you can get stuck in a much worse place just down the road. And that's sometimes true. With four-wheel drive, you always run the risk of getting overconfident. You think you can go anyplace and, as a result, get into more trouble than you can get out of without expending a lot of personal energy and suffering a loss of dignity.

The four-wheeler who has to leave it there and seek help is something like the horseman who walks home after being

Short-course off-road racers don't need four-wheel drive to go jumping and charging around the course. Here, veteran racer, Walker Evans, shows that fastest way is often *two-wheel drive.*

Lack of traction of 2WD is apparent when trying to scale a hill like this, even after a run at it. A 4X4, though, could ease up this slope from a dead stop and not even spin a wheel—if driven properly.

Sometimes *downhill* is almost too tough for a 4X4. This Comanche is picking its way down a rocky Utah trail with two bystanders giving advice and a photographer to record the scene if something goes awry.

bucked off into a cactus patch. You may be able to console yourself by chalking up the experience as a character-building exercise. But what is inevitably lost is that exhilarating delusion that you and your mount can go anyplace and do anything, any time at all.

Limits of 2WD—If you have a two-wheel-drive vehicle, you're likely to be more cautious and put limits on the kind of off-pavement motoring you do. You're not as likely to give that extra ounce of challenge. You'll avoid sand dunes, for instance, unless you've specially prepared your two-wheel-drive

vehicle for that kind of running.

Nor, if you're wise, are you going to seek out rock piles where the only way through is an inch at a time, up one rock and down the next. It's no fun riding at a high pucker the whole distance while hoping you won't come down on anything that will steal that last ounce of traction or break something vital.

Also, if you live in snow or mud country, the limits of travel by two-wheel drive are much more rigidly defined than if you have four-wheel drive.

Max Fun, Min Investment—However, for the everyday kind of recreation-

al off-pavement motoring that most of us do, you can get a lot of pleasure out of a two-wheel-drive vehicle. This is especially true if your budget is modest and you want maximum fun for a minimum investment.

There are basically two different kinds of two-wheel-drive vehicles that can be satisfactorily used for off-pavement travel—4X2 pickup trucks and utility vehicles, plus rear-engine Volkswagens and the derivatives thereof. Because trucks and utilities are the most obvious of these, let's have a look at those first.

4X2 VS. 4X4

Given a skilled driver in each machine, there aren't many places a four-wheel drive can go that a two-wheel drive can't. A while back, we did an off-road comparison of Isuzu 2WD and 4WD trucks. These Isuzu pickups were identical in everything but the number of wheels that could be driven: same engine, same gearbox, same wheelbase, same tires and so on.

The younger half of the combination drove the two-by the whole time while the older half drove the four-by. Yes,

Look closely and you'll see two 4X4s stuck in the same hog wallow while a third waits unscathed nearby. Four-wheel drive obviously isn't a panacea for all stuck situations; driving prowess has a lot to do with it. Photo by John Lawlor.

Fording a stream in Jeep Wrangler 4X4 is tricky enough in four-wheel drive and would be next to impossible in 2WD. Photo by Peter du Pre, courtesy of Four Wheeler magazine.

there were a couple of places that the old guy was able to get to in his 4X4 that the young guy couldn't go in his 4X2. But in both instances, these involved a fairly unusual situation where four-wheel drive became essential for headway to be maintained.

We traveled some genuinely challenging terrain during this comparison. For several miles we worked our way up a canyon where the walls closed in, the trail became narrow and the surface changed from packed dirt to heavy rock.

2WD Requires More Skill—One of the facts that quickly became obvious was that a great deal more skill is required if you're going to do it in two-wheel drive. And this kind of skill only comes with experience. For example, in several potentially tricky areas, the driver of the 4X2 was able to sneak through only because he was well aware of the hazards before he lost headway.

In another place, he had to apply more throttle so the truck would carry itself through on momentum. He knew from experience that if he tried to motor through at a slow, steady pace, the truck would bog down and lose traction.

In another place where the tracks led straight through a rocky gully, he sneaked over to one side where he could keep two wheels on higher ground. That put more space between the ground and the vehicle and reduced the chance that the 2WD would drag its tender un-

derbelly on the rocks sticking up in the middle of the track.

Lesson Provided—Even with all his skill, however, the driver of the 2WD truck finally did get in over his head. This was a dip where, in four-wheel drive and low range, the other driver was able to crawl through the loose rock and sand at a sensible two miles an hour and reach the other side completely unscathed.

With the two-wheel-drive truck, however, it wasn't possible to crawl through. To keep his speed up and maintain sufficient forward progress, he had to hit the dip at a considerably greater velocity. So what happened? In the bottom of the dip there were these rocks. Because he had to hit them much harder than had been necessary in the four-wheel-drive truck, a rock shifted—just *one* rock.

Damaged Fuel Tank—So, instead of staying on top of this particularly innocent-looking rock, the rear end slipped off. This caused the back end of the truck to juke over to the right and then come down hard, ker-blam, and the underside of the truck made contact with still another rock that just happened to be directly under the gas tank. The result was a light trickle and the telltale scent of gasoline from the now-creased tank.

Being a wise off-roader, the younger guy borrowed a bar of bath soap from the older guy. He then slid under the truck and rubbed the soap into the crease until

the trickle stopped. The problem was solved, at least temporarily. Later, when the other driver asked why he'd borrowed his soap instead of using his own, the younger driver sensibly replied that he didn't want his own soap to smell like gasoline. Fair enough.

End of Trail—Later, up this same canyon, the stone walls closed in, hanging out over the narrow trail. With very little side clearance left, the trucks arrived at a series of rock slabs set at crazy angles to each other. It was here that the two-wheel-drive truck got a rear wheel off the ground and couldn't proceed. The spinning tire sang a little as it tried to get traction but that was as far as it was going to go.

Given open country, the driver could probably have taken a run at it and forced his way over this obstacle, too. But the canyon walls loomed mean and ominous by this time and any deviation from the one true path promised to do bad things to the sheet metal.

4X4 Crawled Through—The four-wheel-drive truck crawled over the same slabs with only a minor scramble for traction and eased its way on through.

So, we were able to prove that there were times when four-wheel drive would get you through when two-wheel drive wouldn't. And we knew that before we started. But what we didn't know, exactly, was how close you could come to going "anyplace" in two-wheel drive.

When our co-photographer Jim Brokaw II isn't getting stuck on purpose for the camera, he's getting stuck accidentally. This soft sand did-in his off-roader after he'd hung up on a rock and spun his wheels trying to get free.

PREPARING A 2WD

Most four-wheel-drive vehicles were originally designed as two-wheel drive, but with the capability of being transformed into a 4X4. Turning a two-wheel-drive truck into a four-by consists of more than just bolting in the front-drive system, however. In almost all four-wheel drives, there's a set of low-range gears in the transfer case. There are also protective skid plates for the more vulnerable parts underneath. The tires are generally larger as well and on compact pickups, they're usually on 15-in. wheels instead of 14 inchers. The final-drive ratio is often different. Even the front suspension may be of different design. If so, it's engineered to be less vulnerable to damage. So there may be a lot more that's different than upon first blush.

MODIFYING YOUR 2WD

Let's say you're determined to turn your two-wheeler into an off-roader. There are several modifications you can do to help make it more suitable for that kind of use.

Because the typical two-wheel-drive truck sits closer to the ground than its four-wheel-drive counterpart, one good thing to do is increase ground clearance. The quickest, simplest way to do this is to install larger wheels and tires. This simple bolt-on can increase ground clearance an inch and a half or more—very important when it comes to either hitting a rock or passing over it unscathed.

And when you change tires, it's a good idea to go up in section width as well as diameter. There's a finite limit to how big a tire you can get under a fender without altering sheet metal. As a general rule, we suggest using the largest tire that will go under the fender without doing any more than nipping off the inner-fender corners. And make sure the front tires clear the fenders with the steering at full lock and the suspension at full jounce!

Big Tires Practical—These larger tires not only do wonders for the macho appearance of your truck—there's nothing that looks wimpier on an off-road truck than skinny tires—they also provide a measure of flotation that can save you when there's no other way of getting through the sand.

What about a body-lift kit? We're not advocates of super-tall trucks and have serious reservations about the use of body-lift kits because of the handling and safety problems that may be encountered. We've gone into this subject, and the legalities thereof, in some detail on pages 40—51 in Chapter 7. So, you may want to check that out before taking the plunge—or should we say, taking the lift.

Consider Limited Slip—If you're really serious about running in the dirt, consider a limited-slip differential. This is a great boon when traction is marginal and may be the next-best thing to four-wheel drive.

Also, to be on the safe side, add a skidplate under the gas tank and engine oil pan. Come to think of it, the automatic-transmission fluid pan is extremely vulnerable and vehicles so equipped should be skidplate protected, too.

Modifications are Expensive—By this point, you may have noticed that we haven't said anything lately about how much cheaper a two-wheel drive is. That's because modifications such as bigger wheels and tires cost you money. Well, maybe you'd have bought new wheels and tires anyway. Most off-roaders do, it seems. But skidplates are pricey whether you buy from the manufacturer or have the blacksmith shop make them for you. Limited-slip differentials are also costly, especially if your mechanical skills don't extend to setting up differential gears with the proper lash.

Honestly now, how good an idea is it to get serious about modifying a two-wheel-drive vehicle to do what a four-wheel drive was born to do? Economically, it's a doubtful proposition. If a serious off-road vehicle is what you're interested in, it's better to start with a vehicle that's designed for that kind of use. Which is what a four-wheel drive was built for.

4

Buying A Used 4X4

Buying a used four-wheel-drive vehicle may be one of the wisest investments you'll ever make, or one of the dumbest. But you can tip the odds favorably by applying some resourcefulness and patience. Be willing to crawl in, over and under the vehicle in question, have the spunk to challenge some of the seller's statements, and be able to haggle price like a veteran camel trader.

This is all common-sense stuff, of course, applicable to purchasing any type of vehicle. So let's chat specifically about the types of vehicles with which this chapter concerns itself: 4X4 pickups and sport-utility wagons. Used ones.

Sources—Used 4WDs can be located from a variety of sources: used-car lots, the back lots of new car/truck agencies, classified ads and the infamous private party. Be aware that the prices of comparable vehicles will probably be higher at a dealership's lot because he's more apt to offer a good warranty program. And if the used vehicle you buy there is the same make as his new cars and trucks, good service and parts availability are assured.

The Once-Over—The purchase of a used 4X4 is often based more on impulse than on need. There are regions where a 4WD is absolutely essential during inclement-weather months. But more often than not, the fun and games of recreational off-roading is the real basis of the purchase. That high-riding, he-man off-roader you found at a dealership, used-car lot or through a private party, may be exactly what you want, or think you want. But, as the saying goes, *Caveat Emptor:* let the buyer beware.

Once you've gone through the motions of tracking down what appears to be the perfect 4X4 through the sources suggested, your work is really only just beginning.

Check out the fit and finish of the outside of the vehicle, but do it in daylight instead of under artificial lighting. Is the paint worn and faded? If it is, rub a small

Buying from an established dealer may cost more, but many offer follow-up service. Never select the first vehicle you see. Shop around. Photo by John Lawlor.

Rolled Blazer is probably good for parts only. If sheet metal is bent this badly, it's a good bet internals were abused, too. Photo by Ron Sessions.

spot with compound or a cleaner and see if it can be brought back to its original luster. Look for blotches of mismatched paint indicating past body dents or the cover-up of something sinister like rust. Check door and fender alignment: Are the gaps reasonably constant and do the exterior trim strips come pretty close to

On the other hand, buying from a private party may bring you a better price and a chance to check the vehicle with the owner along. Photo by John Lawlor.

Look the subject vehicle over carefully. Check the condition of the finish and see if the trim strips align. Make a mental list of any superficial problems and try and get the seller to reduce his price by the cost of repairs—even if you don't plan to make the repair. Photo by John Lawlor.

See if the doors open and close smoothly and if, when they are closed, the gaps around the edges are even. A misfit here could indicate a bent or wracked frame. Photo by John Lawlor.

These are bubbles in the paint caused by rust coming through from underneath. Check the vehicle thoroughly for such signs and, if there are many of them, go shopping somewhere else.

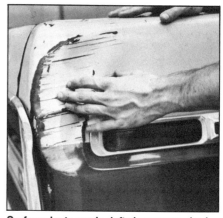

Surface dents can be left alone or repaired—it's up to you. Just be sure something mechanical hasn't been injured in the vicinity. Photo by John Lawlor

aligning? If it's a truck you're after, stand behind it and eyeball the lines formed by the base of the rear window and the tailgate. Are they parallel? If not, misalignment may indicate a bent or wracked frame. Try the hood. Does it latch and unlatch properly? Shoppers for conventional cars wouldn't pay close attention to such matters. But on a 4X4, they can indicate what sort of treatment the vehicle has experienced.

Check the *rocker panels*—sheet-metal strips under the doors. If they're dented or show evidence of repair, then the vehicle has likely been subjected to some pretty heavy-duty rock crawling; a closer-than-average look at the chassis will be in order. If the body has dents that have not been repaired, try and judge how serious the impact might have been and if anything mechanical behind or near the dents has also been damaged.

Books and Tools—Before going any further, check if the original owner's manual is still with the vehicle. If you're considering buying from a private party, he or she may have put the owner's manual somewhere else. See if it can be found. It will give you the recommended maintenance schedule for that vehicle along with instructions on finding the fuse panel, telling you how many gallons the fuel tank holds, and an infinite number of things you'll probably forget to ask the seller but will need to know in the future.

If the owner's manual is missing, check with the local dealer's parts counter. They probably won't have older manuals on hand, but they can be ordered from the factory. If the parts man claims he can't help you, remind him that the

Used vehicles found on dealer lots may carry a warranty, with specific guarantees spelled out. Or it may be for sale strictly on an as-is basis. Be sure you understand which you're dealing with.

Make a list of things you want to check for before you go over the vehicle up close. You may be blinded by the wonderment of 4WD and forget to look for problem areas.

owner's manual carries a regular part number just like any other part, and parts is parts.

If you plan to do your own wrenching, it's a good idea to track down a factory service manual. One is used for each year of a particular model line. They go to great lengths in explaining, and showing pictorially, the disassembly and reassembly of every component part. These are not always published by the vehicle manufacturer, but may be produced by specialty firms at the manufacturer's request. So, one of these may not have a part number and may only be available through the publisher. But the agency parts department will be able to point you in the right direction.

If you get no satisfaction from a dealership on acquiring either an owner's manual or a factory shop manual, write directly to the manufacturer as listed in the appendix of this book.

Some import manufacturers are reluctant to supply the consumer with factory shop manuals. They figure it's better business for them to let their agencies handle overhauls and repairs. Therefore, while they do publish factory shop manuals, you'll play heck getting one unless you know a friendly parts counterperson.

If the vehicle you're considering has had any aftermarket accessories added that might require special tools or other equipment, be sure these are included with the vehicle. An electric winch, for example, needs its hand controller; usually a hand switch with six or more feet of cord. Make sure you get this; the winch is useless without it. If the truck of your dreams has larger-than-stock tires and wheels, often the standard wheel wrench won't fit the lug nuts and an aftermarket jack is necessary to lift the vehicle high enough to change a flat. Check to be sure these come with your purchase.

Bed Check—The bed of a pickup truck can be a good clue as to how hard the vehicle has been used. Are there signs that it has carried heavy loads? Scratched paint is normal wear, but obviously severe dents and deep gouges indicate weighty objects may have overtaxed the suspension.

Perhaps the pickup has a plastic liner to protect the bed. Great. But before reaching for your checkbook, make sure the liner isn't hiding serious damage. Some liners trap water underneath and cause premature bed rust-out.

Underneath—If the engine and chassis have been freshly steam-cleaned, perhaps the owner/dealer has tried to make the vehicle as presentable as possible. Or

If the vehicle includes any aftermarket accessories that are mechanical or electrical, check their operation. Check all the lighting, not just the auxiliaries.

maybe he was getting rid of crud buildup near a leak. Look underneath for any signs of a drip or, worse, a small puddle. If the engine is cold, and the vehicle has stood in the same spot overnight, so much the better. The least sign of a dribble is good cause to take your shopping spree elsewhere.

Plan on spending some time under the vehicle; take along a flashlight for peering into dark crannies. Check the general condition of the frame and crossmembers, the axles and suspension parts, whatever's down there. Look for cracks, recent signs of welding, bashed flanges, and study the spring hangers for signs of

25

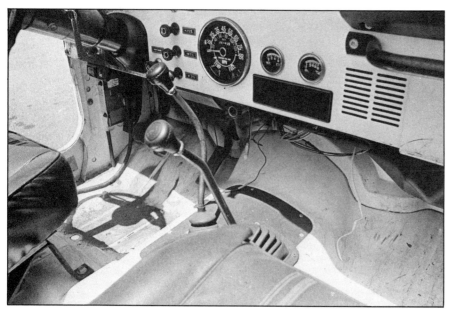

A sloppy wiring job means a pro wasn't around when something electrical was installed. We'd recommend staying away from a mess like this.

The tires, especially the fronts, are good indicators of how the vehicle has been treated, how wheel alignment is, and whether the shocks need replacing. Photo by John Lawlor.

damage. Look at the engine and transmission/transfer-case mounts. Are the rubber insulators intact and all bolts in place? Look around to see if the cab/bed body mounts and their rubber or fabric isolators are in good shape.

Grab hold of the drive shafts, one at a time of course, and twist them. What you're checking for is U-joint slop and play in the differential gears. Some play is OK, but if either shaft turns more than several degrees, an overhaul may be needed.

Try twisting or jerking on the suspension members, especially the anti-sway bars, if so equipped. If these move in their bushings or the end insulators are sloppy, they'll need attention.

Check for loose steering by pulling and pushing on the tie rods and steering arms under the truck, and by climbing aboard and turning the steering wheel back and worth with the vehicle motionless. Squat on the ground facing each front wheel in turn. Grasp the top of the tire with both hands and push and pull on it as hard as you can. If it moves at all, chances are the wheel bearings are bad.

Look for leaks on or near the shock absorbers and at each of the wheel's brake cylinders. And what about the tires? Do they show signs of uneven wear? Tires that have been run underinflated will show more wear on the outside of the tread. Overinflated tires will have worn more in the center of the tread. Cupping or scalloping of the tread may mean the shocks are bad on a vehicle with independent front suspension. On a solid front-axle vehicle, it may also mean that the owner never rotated the tires with recommended frequency.

If the front hubs are the manual lock/unlock type, twist the levers between the two positions a few times. Do they move freely? Of course, you can't tell if the hubs are actually engaging until you go for a test drive, but be suspicious if the hubs require more than thumb and forefinger pressure to operate.

Test Drive—Now comes the moment you've been waiting for: your first drive in that new-found heart throb. The rig checked out OK under your poking, probing and peeking, and there's apparently nothing seriously bent, broken or missing. Nothing's leaking, rubber-bushed connections are all intact, and there are no frame or crossmember cracks that you could find, nor any fresh welds.

The seller may volunteer to drive at first. This is fine, but don't let him turn on the air conditioning or crank up the radio. You want to *listen* to the sounds of the engine starting and idling, and whether there are any squawks or groans when shifts are made or, with a manual transmission, when the clutch is worked. Try and distinguish between tire hum and gear whine when your chauffeur gets up to speed. Your ride with someone else driving won't tell you much, but at least you'll have an idea of how the beast reacts when underway.

Then switch places with the seller. Of course, you'll need to find some soft soil to drive on, or at least a nice dirt road. Stop when you get there, shift into first gear and drive for a prolonged distance. Get a feel for engine response and listen for unusual sounds at higher rpm. Do this in each gear, all the way through high.

Now, shift into 4WD, high range first. Go through all the gear drives again. Are there howls emanating from underneath that indicate a suspect transfer case? Go through it all once again in low range. And, don't forget to lock the front hubs if they're the manual type.

Somewhere along the way, stop. Then start off hard in low gear. Can you tell if the front wheels are pulling? If not, shift

By all means, take a test drive. And be certain the seller lets you put the rig through some medium-duty dirt-road driving. Photo by John Lawlor.

back to 2WD and start off hard enough to spin the rear wheels. Put it back in 4WD and repeat. If rear wheel spin is less, or all four spin a little until they get a bite, then the hubs are working OK.

Make sharp left and right turns at moderate speed and slam on the brakes. If groans or ka-thunks come from the front suspension, the upper control-arm bushings (on independent front suspensions) or the forward spring and shackle bushings (on solid-axle rigs) need replacement. Drive hard over rough ground while veering right and left. If everything's quiet downstairs, then the suspension and chassis are probably in pretty good shape, especially if the vehicle is unmodified. Be awfully suspicious if the rig has multiple shocks, larger tires, or anything similar. Big rubber may rub on a chassis or sheet-metal part if the suspension is cycled through its limits, especially when the front wheels are

turned to full lock. So, walk away from the seller if you hear or feel anything untoward.

Even if you're happy so far, there are more checks to make. Go back to where you started. Now, try each of the electrical accessories in turn: audio system, air conditioning, heater/defroster, and so on. See if all the external lights are working: headlights and parking lights, turn indicators and warning flashers, backup lights and brake lights. Check the dome light and dash lights, too.

Be leery of any electrical aftermarket accessories: auxiliary driving lights, a winch—everything. Try each of these in turn and get the seller to unspool the winch. Deduct big points for any winch cable with broken wire strands, kinks or crushed spots. And listen carefully to the motor and gearcase when the cable is spooled back in.

Underhood—We've saved this chore for last simply because you'll want to peer into the engine compartment after the engine has been freshly run. Leaks wiped dry before you got there may have started up again. Follow along all the lines and hoses for possible dribbles, especially at fittings and connections.

Unscrew the radiator cap and look inside. Many engines, especially the imports, use aluminum components. If the antifreeze solution hasn't been changed in at least a year, the solution may turn caustic and will attack aluminum. As the aluminum deteriorates, deposits will find their way into the radiator core and plug the tiny passages. If the coolant looks old and muddy, ask to have some of it drained out until you can look down into the filler neck and see the top of the core. If there's any sort of deposit buildup, ask to have the radiator serviced before you get your wallet out.

Words to the Wise—All along, we've been assuming you know how to shop the used-vehicle market. Unless you were born yesterday, we think that you know enough to see if the driver's seat upholstery is worn out, that the clutch-pedal pad is worn down to the metal even if the odometer shows only a few thousand miles, that the seller is actually that, the seller, and the vehicle's identification number (VIN) matches that of the registration card.

If seller claims engine has been recently tuned or appears to have been cleaned up to impress buyer, pull off air-cleaner lid and check condition.

We can't help you worry about financing, about any warranties, or tell you what your recourses are if the transfer case falls out on your way home. These are things any used-vehicle buyer should know about and watch out for. No, our duty has only been to alert you to the special checks to be made of a four-wheel-drive vehicle. We've noted the most important and the illustrations reveal a few more.

But once you've made your decision, we fervently hope it is a happy one for you, your family, and your four-wheeling buddies. If this is your first four-wheeler, there's a world of fun and exploration ahead of you. If you've owned 4WDs before, then we hope you've made a wise upgrade in vehicle choice. Whatever your particular case, many of the things you'll want to see and do with your, uhh, previously owned 4X4 are dealt with on the following pages. So at this point, the very best thing we can do for you is let you get on with the rest of this book. Happy Off-Roading!

5

How It Works

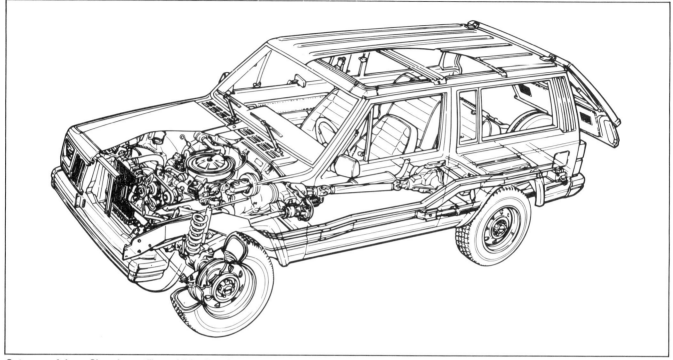

Cutaway of Jeep Cherokee utility vehicle. Drawing courtesy American Motors.

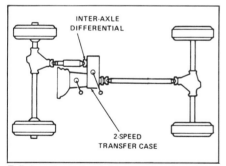

Full-time four-wheel-drive system has inter-axle differential in transfer case, permitting speed variations between front and rear axles. Most effective inter-axle differential is viscous drive which delivers limited-slip-type action.

This chapter explains the mechanical ins and outs of four-wheel drive. We discuss mostly about how it's different from the conventional two-wheel-drive vehicle you're probably more familiar with.

What we're not going to do is start with the invention of the wheel. We assume that you already know how a four-stroke engine works, what a transmission is, the purpose of the differential and other basic fundamentals of this ilk.

If you aren't familiar with these things, you can easily fill this void by obtaining one or more books on automotive fundamentals from your local bookstore or public library. You might also want to peruse the listing of other HPBooks inside the back cover of this book.

With these preliminaries out of the way, let's leap right into the subject of four-wheel drive.

4WD VS. 2WD

In a conventional two-wheel-drive car or truck, the engine is mounted at the front and after going through the transmission, drive shaft, differential and axles, the power generated by the engine drives the rear wheels. A conventional four-wheel-drive system does the same thing except that through another drive shaft, differential and axle shafts, the front wheels are driven as well.

Four-wheel drive is great. You've got all four wheels helping to pull/push the vehicle along instead of just two. This not only gives you the ability to continue in motion when the road surface provides marginal traction, it also offers greater stability when driving on any surface that is less than hard, clean and dry. Because the front wheels are also participating, the rear end is less likely to slide around. Try it and you're almost sure to like it.

Part-Time 4WD—In almost all four-wheel-drive systems in current production, you motor along in two-wheel drive under ordinary circumstances, then shift into four-wheel drive when you want the

Some Jeep vehicles are equipped with simple, finger-operated four-wheel-drive controls. To engage 4WD on this AMC Eagle, stop, pull out knob at bottom, then move thumb switch to position marked 4WD.

Transfer-case levers are always marked with the shift pattern. The gear positions differ between manufacturers.

High/low-range lever on senior Jeeps is small and placed to left of transmission tunnel under driver's right leg where it's out of the way and leaves an unobstructed floor.

extra tractive force. Because it is only used part of the time, this system is known as *part-time* four-wheel drive.

In the early 1970s, *full-time* four-wheel drive became popular. This was back when gasoline was cheap and nobody worried too much about gas mileage. With full-time, you didn't have to shift in and out of four-wheel drive. It worked all the time and that was great. Except that it increased fuel consumption by about 10 percent, which was sufficient to make it unpopular and caused it to rather quickly fade from the scene.

These days, all popular four-wheel-drive trucks and utility vehicles use a part-time system. Currently, American Motors still offers a full-time system on its Eagle and some Jeeps. And the VW Golf Syncro and Vanagon Syncro, as well as the exotic Audi Quattro are full-time, but all the other 4WDs are part-time. So what we're going to talk about mostly is the conventional part-time system.

Transfer Case—To shift into four-wheel drive, it's necessary to engage the front axle. This is usually done by moving a transfer-case, or range-selector, lever that sprouts from the transmission hump alongside the gearshift handle. Some other systems use a vacuum switch to actually move the gear from one posi-

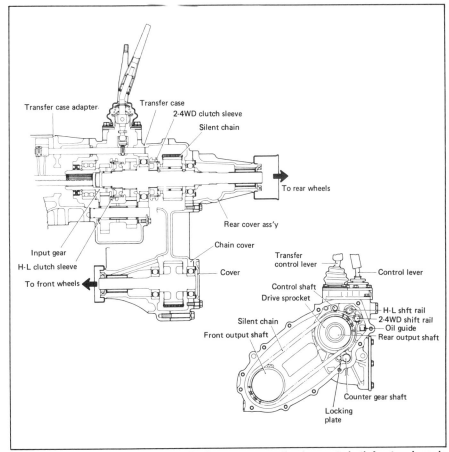

Typical transfer case has two ranges. For low-range operation, power to both front and rear is delivered through a low-range gear with a reduction factor of about 2:1 for additional torque. Drawing courtesy Mitsubishi.

TYPICAL TRANSFER-CASE RATIOS

Gear	High-Range Ratio	Low Range Ratio
1st	3.740:1	7.255:1
2nd	2.136:1	4.144:1
3rd	1.360:1	2.638:1
4th	1.001:1	1.940:1
5th (o.d.)	0.856:1	1.661:1

Example of transmission ratios between High Range and Low Range assuming a transfer-case ratio of 1:1 in High, 1.94:1 in Low.

tion to another so there's no real necessity for a shift handle. For instance, on some late-model Jeep Wagoneers, there's a simple range-selector switch on the dash panel. No matter whether it's by lever or switch, what happens is that the front-drive system is brought into action so both the front and rear drive shafts are driven.

In most four-wheel-drive vehicles so equipped, the transfer case bolts onto the side or rear of the transmission case and drives the transfer gear through a duplex-type flat chain. In other vehicles, the transfer case is integrated into the transmission housing.

Low-Range—Most current four-wheel-drive trucks and utilities use a two-speed transfer case. This means that in addition to a straight, direct transfer from the transmission, there's also a step-down gear that delivers a lower ratio to both the front and rear drive shafts.

This lower gear, which is called *low range,* usually has about a 2:1 ratio. This, in effect, doubles the torque that is delivered to the wheels. And this, in turn, gives you the ability to climb a steeper grade, providing you can get traction, by delivering greater low-end grunt. It also allows you to idle along at very slow speed, which is often the best way to approach some types of terrain.

Shift Pattern—To show you the different positions of the transfer case, the shift pattern is usually etched into the knob on the transfer case lever. On most vehicles, these read 2H, 4H, N and 4L.

The 2H position means two-wheel drive, high range; 4H stands for four-wheel drive, high range; N is for neutral and 4L is for four-wheel drive, low range. The specific instructions for the use of your particular range-selector lever will be found in the owner's manual.

If your four-wheel-drive vehicle is a Subaru, Honda Civic, Colt Vista Wagon or Toyota Tercel 4WD, the system is different. These are basically front-wheel-drive vehicles, and when you shift into four-wheel drive, you engage a gear which turns a drive shaft that goes to the rear wheels. As mentioned previously, not all 4WD cars derived from front-drive designs use a transfer case.

Also, some Subarus have no low-range gear in the transfer case. Likewise, in the 4WD Tercel, there's no low-range gearset, but there is a six-speed transmission in which first gear is an extra-low low. This stump-puller or granny gear is useful for those times when you need additional pulling power or the ability go super slow but keep engine rpm up in the mid-range.

FRONT-WHEEL HUBS

If nobody told you any differently, you might think that all you have to do to switch to four-wheel drive is move the transfer-case lever to the 4H or 4L slot and keep on truckin'. With today's four-wheel-drive vehicles, that may or may not be true.

In early four-wheel-drive machines, such as the sacred Jeep of World War II, it was true. When you wanted four-wheel drive, you jiggled the transfer-case lever until it finally engaged, then mushed ahead to the grinding of the straight-cut transfer gears.

The disadvantage of this system was that the whole front-drive system, even when not engaged via the transfer case, was still dragged through the motions. The front wheels turned the front axle shafts, which turned the front differential, and so on, right back to the transfer case. This was wasted motion and raised fuel consumption.

Free-Wheeling Hubs—So, free-running or free-wheeling hubs were born. A free-wheeling hub is one that can be disengaged from the axle. This allows the wheels to turn by themselves so they don't have to drag the whole front-drive system along as you motor down on a hard, dry road.

Engaging Manual Hubs—To engage and disengage a conventional, manually operated, free-wheeling hub, you rotate a slug that is usually inset into the end of the bolt-on hub mechanism.

So what are the two things you have to do to engage four-wheel drive? One is to move the transfer-case lever from 2H to 4H (or 4L) and, two, engage the front hubs. In off-roader talk, this is known as "locking the hubs" or "throwing the hubs."

Similarly, when you come to the place where you want to disengage four-wheel drive, you shift the transfer-case lever back to 2H and disengage the hubs. If you find that the locking mechanism doesn't want to disengage at this point, you back up a few feet to take the load off the splines and try again.

If it's raining, or muddy, or if you are simply feeling lazy, you can drive all the way home without disengaging the hubs, assuming you've moved the shift lever back to 2H, of course. You will be wasting fuel because the whole front-drive system is being whirled uselessly. But doing so won't damage the system.

Or, if you're traveling on a dirt road, come to a stretch of pavement but are going back onto the dirt again shortly, you don't have to disengage the hubs. Just shift out of 4H into 2H for the time you're on the hard road, then back to 4H again when you return to the dirt.

Shifting Without Stopping—If you have manually operated, free-running front hubs and these hubs are engaged, you can shift from 2H to 4H, or vice versa, without stopping. This is possible because the front drive shaft is being turned by the front wheels and as a result, the drive shaft and transfer-case output gear are turning at the same speed. So, they will engage and disengage without grinding, assuming you ease up on the throttle a little. If you're hard on the throttle, the gears may bind and make it impossible to do.

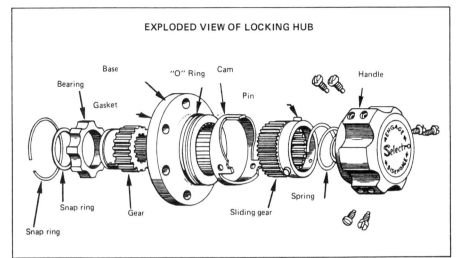

EXPLODED VIEW OF LOCKING HUB

Base
Bearing
Gasket
"O" Ring
Cam
Pin
Handle
Snap ring
Gear
Sliding gear
Spring
Snap ring

Selectro ENGAGE DISENGAGE

Exploded view of manual lock/unlock front hub: Twisting hub cover to "lock" drives clutch into free-wheeling hub body and engages inner hub on end of axle.

Some vehicles offer a simple selector switch that lets you choose driving mode at any speed.

You cannot shift from 4H to 4L without stopping, however. The speed of the front drive shaft and transfer-case output gear aren't synchronized. So, you have to come to a stop, engage low range, then proceed.

Incidentally, if you have manual hubs, always engage them before shifting into low range. Remember that low range doubles the torque delivered to the drive shafts. If you haven't engaged the front hubs, the additional torque could damage the drive shaft, universal joints, differential gears or axle shafts. When both the front and rear drive systems are engaged, torque is divided between the two.

You don't want to leave the front-drive system engaged if you're driving on a hard, paved surface. This causes everything to bind up and not only increases wear, it could also conceivably break something.

The four-wheel-drive Subarus and the 4WD Toyota Tercel, Colt Vista and Honda Civic are exceptions to this chatter about hubs. None of these is equipped with free-running hubs. To engage/disengage four-wheel drive with these, you simply move the engagement lever from the two-wheel-drive position to the one for four-wheel drive. Also, to avoid damage to the front-drive system of the 4WD Tercel, the extra-low first gear cannot be engaged unless you're already in four-wheel drive.

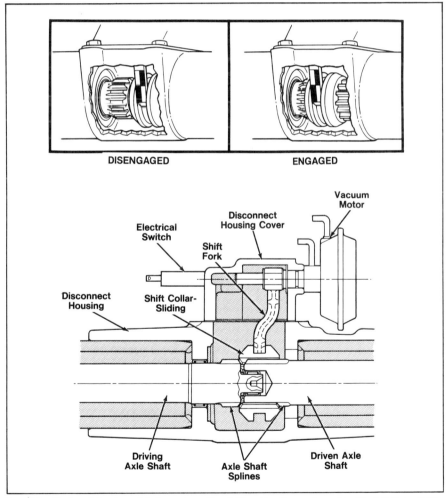

DISENGAGED   ENGAGED

Vacuum Motor
Disconnect Housing Cover
Electrical Switch
Shift Fork
Disconnect Housing
Shift Collar-Sliding
Driving Axle Shaft
Axle Shaft Splines
Driven Axle Shaft

For '85, Dodge introduced fully automatic shift-on-the-fly system for its full-size 4X4s. Vacuum-operated inter-axle disconnect is mounted between carrier and left spring seat. Drawing courtesy Chrysler Corp.

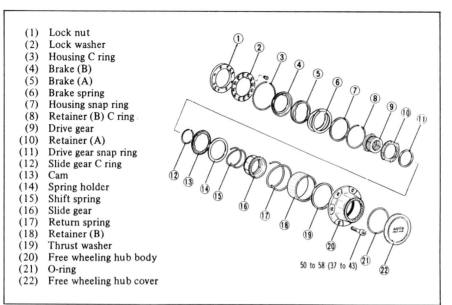

(1) Lock nut
(2) Lock washer
(3) Housing C ring
(4) Brake (B)
(5) Brake (A)
(6) Brake spring
(7) Housing snap ring
(8) Retainer (B) C ring
(9) Drive gear
(10) Retainer (A)
(11) Drive gear snap ring
(12) Slide gear C ring
(13) Cam
(14) Spring holder
(15) Shift spring
(16) Slide gear
(17) Return spring
(18) Retainer (B)
(19) Thrust washer
(20) Free wheeling hub body
(21) O-ring
(22) Free wheeling hub cover

50 to 58 (37 to 43)

Typical automatic lock/unlock front hub is more complex than manual type. When 4WD is engaged, front hub "senses" drive-shaft (axle) rotation and cam drives slide gear into hub body, locking component solid. When 4WD is disengaged and vehicle is backed up a few feet, hub is automatically disconnected.

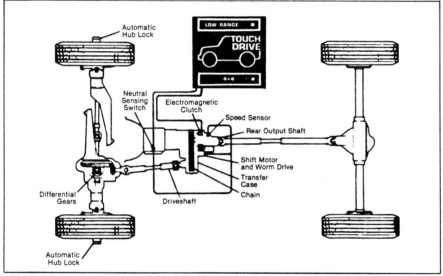

For '86, Ford introduced its electrically-activated "Touch-Drive" system. The touch of a finger selects two- or four-wheel drive, or high/low range. Drawing courtesy Ford.

AUTOMATIC HUBS

Automatic locking front hubs are either standard or offered as options on several conventional four-wheel-drive vehicles. With these hubs, the procedure for getting into four-wheel drive is simplified. You come to a halt, move the transfer-case lever to 4H or 4L and proceed. The hubs will lock automatically as you drive forward.

To get out of four-wheel drive with the automatic hubs, come to a stop, move the transfer-case lever back to 2H, then back up a few feet. You may hear or feel a click as the hubs unlock.

4WD Indicator Light—By the way, don't assume that your hubs are unlocked simply because the 4WD indicator light on the instrument panel goes out. Such lights are wired to the lever itself and don't really know if the hubs are locked. So, always go through the backing-up routine to be sure the hubs have unlocked themselves when you're switching back to two-wheel drive.

As with manually operated hubs, you can still shift to 2H for a short stretch of paved road if you don't want to bother backing up and unlocking the hubs before jumping back into the dirt again.

SHIFT ON THE FLY

In addition, some vehicles also have a "shift on the fly" four-wheel-drive system. This enables you to shift into or out of 2H and 4H at any time and at any reasonable speed. However, shifting from 4H to 4L still requires a complete stop.

If you have a choice, we'd suggest that the "shift on the fly" system is the easiest and most convenient to use. Then, in reverse order of convenience, comes automatic locking hubs and, finally, manual locking hubs.

SUSPENSION SYSTEMS

The suspension system of most four-wheel-drive vehicles is basically the same type as on a conventional two-wheel-drive car or truck. That is, there's independent suspension in the front and a live axle on leaf springs in the rear.

Independent Front Suspension—In the most common type of independent front suspension used on four-wheel-drive vehicles, the differential is solidly mounted to the frame and there are axle shafts with universal joints—U-joints—at each end of the shafts. The purpose of the U-joints is to allow the wheels to maintain a vertical attitude when moving up and down through full suspension travel. This contrasts with a solid-axle, swing-axle or Twin I-Beam design which allows *camber* changes—that is, allows the wheels to tilt in or out with suspension travel.

The wheels are located by wide-based upper and lower A-arms and instead of the coil springs you're likely to be more familiar with, torsion bars are generally used.

Torsion Bars—Think of a torsion bar as a coil spring that's been straightened out. Its major long suit is packaging. A torsion bar is located *longitudinally*—fore/

aft—and doesn't steal room required to run axle shafts and U-joints that a coil spring would. But don't think that torsion bars are used because of any inherent superiority over coil springs.

There is also a conventional telescopic shock absorber on each side. Some 4WDs also have an anti-sway, or stabilizer, bar to help control body roll.

As we said, this is the most common type of independent front suspension used on current four-wheel-drive vehicles. Ford four-wheel drives also have independent front suspension, but this design is considerably different. In the Ford system, the differential as well as the axle shafts are carried as part of the unsprung weight.

Twin I-Beam Design—The axle shafts are not articulated in the Ford design so the wheels change camber with suspension travel. The Ford 4X4 system is a variation on the classic swing-axle suspension, but because Ford's wheel travel is limited, the tuck-under bugaboo inherent in the swing-axle design is avoided. It works better than it sounds like it should, except that suspension travel is limited and this results in the front wheels being easier to get off the ground than other independent front-suspension systems.

The independent front suspension of the American Motors Eagle is also different than that described above. Upper and lower A-arms are used, but there are coil springs instead of torsion bars. In this design, however, the coil springs sit on top of the upper arms where they do not interfere with the axle shafts from the solidly mounted differential.

LIVE FRONT AXLE

In addition to the independent front-suspension systems used on four-wheel-drive vehicles, there are still a couple of vehicles being built around a live front-axle design.

It is called a "live" axle because it contains the drive mechanism—differential, axle shafts and attendant mechanisms. It is the same as the conventional driven or live rear axle except that it's mounted in front and the wheels are steerable rather than solidly fixed to the axle housing.

In case you're wondering, a "dead"

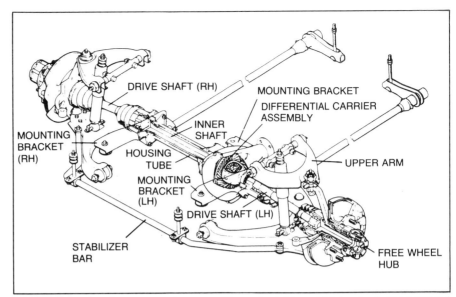

Typical independent front suspension on small four-wheel-drive vehicle has torsion bars instead of coil (or leaf) springs. Note that differential bolts solidly to vehicle frame. Drawing courtesy Mitsubishi.

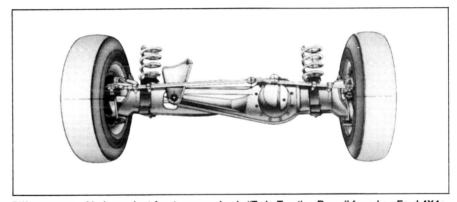

Different type of independent front suspension is "Twin-Traction Beam" found on Ford 4X4s. Note that differential is carried in long suspension arm and moves up and down with it. System is very rugged but suspension travel is limited. Drawing courtesy Ford.

axle is a simple beam that joins non-driven wheels. Before cars and pickup trucks had independent front suspension, they used beam front axles. Now dead-beam axles are found if at all, at the rear of some front-wheel-drive cars.

Which is better, independent or live-axle front suspension? It depends. The virtues of independent front suspension include a better ride, better handling and lower ride height. You also hear that, with independent front suspension, there's less unsprung weight. This is true for most designs, but it's a moot point because off-road wheels and tires are generally so heavy as to make the whole argument largely academic.

Some live-axle designs, such as the British Range Rover and the downsized Jeep Cherokee and Comanche, offer ride and handling nearly comparable to IFS designs, largely due to greater than normal suspension travel. Other solid-axle designs, like the pre-'86 Toyota 4X4 pickup, Toyota Land Cruiser, Jeep CJ, Jeep Wrangler or XJ, full-size Cherokee, Wagoneer and Jeep pickups also use leaf springs, have limited useful suspension travel and give up a lot in both ride and handling.

Tire Wear—A further disadvantage of the live-axle design is tire wear. The gyroscopic effects resulting from having a steered wheel on a solid axle result in cupping and other strange tire-wear patterns. This may also result in tires that won't stay in balance and a poor highway ride.

The great virtue of the live front axle is that it is more nearly indestructible than any other system. We don't mean to suggest by this that independent front suspension is inherently deficient in durability. By the nature of the design, such things as stamped suspension arms are less indestructible than a solid front axle perched on semi-elliptical leaf springs. However, the more tender parts of most independent front-suspension systems are well protected by skidplates. So, you don't need a live front axle to get durability.

DIFFERENTIALS

If you have a choice when you buy your four-wheel drive, get a limited-slip differential in the rear.

As you probably know, a differential is an arrangement of gears that makes it possible for the wheels on connected axle shafts to travel at different speeds. As a result, when you go around a corner, the inside wheel turns more slowly and covers a shorter distance than the outside wheel. And it does this without skidding or scuffing, the way it would if the two wheels were on a solid axle that had to turn at the same speed.

Loss of Traction—The problem with the conventional differential comes when one wheel loses traction. All tractive force is delivered to the wheel that has lost traction. It sits there and spins and no power is delivered to the other wheel. You're out of business until you can figure out some way of providing traction to the spinning wheel.

A limited-slip differential is designed to overcome this problem. So what happens when one wheel loses traction? Through a clutch pack or gears, the two halves of the axle are locked together so both rear wheels turn. The wheel that has traction will turn as well as the one that hasn't.

In this way, forward-going mobility may be maintained and you can slog, slosh or mush on through, scarcely even aware how close you were to being stuck. A limited-slip differential, commonly called a limited-slip rear end, can be useful wherever there's marginal traction whether it's mud, snow, ice, sand or whatever.

Glare Ice—The only problem we've ever experienced from having a limited-slip rear end came on glare ice. This was on the highway in the wilds of Idaho one winter. We were lightfooting it along in four-wheel drive when we noticed that the vehicle, a Jeep Wagoneer, wasn't tracking straight. We had to keep nudging the steering to keep it going in a straight line.

What was happening was that the rear wheels were hunting for traction and the differential was locking and unlocking, locking and unlocking as we traveled over this slippery surface. Ultimately, we drove under an underpass, got hit by a blast of wind when we came out and made a big gentle loop into a snow bank alongside the road.

Limited-Slip in Front—If you have a chance to get a limited-slip differential in the front of your four-wheel-drive vehicle, our advice is don't. We've also had that experience and don't recommend it for general, all-around use because of its tendency to steer you where you may not want to go.

The steering effect occurs whenever the front wheels have widely different degrees of traction. We had our bad experience in the wilds of Canyonlands National Park in Utah. We were traveling up a sandy wash and barely making headway when we got the left-front wheel onto clean rock and had the right wheel in loose sand just as we were sneaking past a rocky neck in the canyon. The left front wheel suddenly got a good bite on the bare rock and this caused the whole vehicle to veer to the right, right into this great, solid rock.

If you have limited-slip in the rear and it suddenly locks or unlocks, you can control the result with the steering. But when you have limited-slip in the front and it locks, you may get more steering from the sudden grab of traction than you can control.

Axle Ratios—It is obvious that in any four-wheel-drive system the front and rear differentials must always have identical ratios. Otherwise, the front and rear wheels would be trying to travel at different speeds, and on a hard surface, that would soon lead to disaster.

New vehicles are supplied with identical ring-and-pinion ratios front and rear. If the time ever comes when you want to change to a longer-legged ratio for better highway fuel economy or to a shorter one to increase off-road torque, you do have to install two gear sets.

There are rare exceptions to this general rule, however. For instance, a friend of ours whose favorite weekend activity was playing in the sand and climbing higher, steeper dunes than anyone else, used different ratios front and rear. He installed a slightly lower ratio in the front of his Chevrolet 4X4, something on the order of 4.10:1, where he had a 3.90:1 ratio in the rear.

As a result, on steep sand the rear tires provided most of the pushing power while the fronts spun faster to give him improved steering control. He was always king of the hill in the dunes but he couldn't use his 4WD system anyplace else unless he was in very soft, loose terrain where the front wheels could spin and not let the strain build up.

6

Engine Protection

This is what's known as silt with the consistency of cement dust or talcum powder. It can get into anything and everything, so it's wise to protect your engine. Photo by Spencer Murray V, courtesy CBS Publications.

Because you travel off-road, your vehicle's engine may need some additional protection to keep out dirt and water, or a combination of the two that adds up to muck and moisture. If you're going to be prepared for any eventuality, you'll need to be ready for these.

Specifically, you need to protect the ignition system and fuel system. In addition, after you've exposed your vehicle to extremes such as heavy dust or deep water, there are other things you should look after when you get home.

IGNITION-SYSTEM PROTECTION

To troubleproof your ignition, you must exclude contaminants from the system. First, make sure that all wiring is in as-new condition. Specifically, make sure there is no sign of abrasion or cracked insulation, no cracked or loose-fitting boots and no corroded terminals. There's no sense in doing all of this work if the wiring is no good.

Seal Distributor—To start ignition troubleproofing, you'll need a spray-on, no-residue solvent such as contact cleaner, clean, lint-free rags and silicone sealant. Depending on your approach, you may also need a spray can of ignition sealant, some extra chunks of 1/2-in. foam and your ever-faithful roll of racer's tape.

Remove the distributor cap and use the spray cleaner to remove any traces of dirt or oil on the sealing surfaces between the cap and distributor body. Then, lay a bead of sealant around the base of the cap, making sure that the bead doesn't have any gaps in it, and carefully put the cap back in place. If you want to be double-sure, run another bead of silicone around the joint between the cap and body.

Next, find the small-gage wire that runs from the coil to the distributor body. Using contact cleaner, spray the connection where it attaches to the distributor and let it dry. Then fit a blob of sealant over the connection, covering all exposed metal parts and sealing around the insulation of the wire, as well.

Now, check the sparkplug wires where they plug into the distributor cap. Work on the wires one at a time to minimize the chance of cross-wiring them. First, if there are rubber boots on these wires,

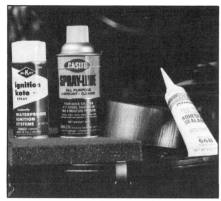

Engine-proofing can be an easy home-garage, do-it-yourself project. Start with a chunk of foam rubber, some racer's tape, silicone sealant, and spray cans of ignition waterproofing and an all-purpose no-residue cleaner.

You should guard against moisture as thoroughly as against dirt. These folks didn't think they'd get into water on an off-roading weekend. But they did and it was a long push home. Photo by James T. Crow.

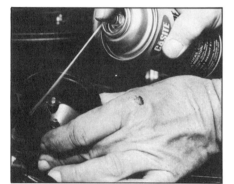

Remove distributor cap and spray some cleaner to remove any traces of dirt or oil, then wipe clean with a lint-free rag. Give edge of cap same treatment.

Run a bead of silicone sealer around edge of cap, then carefully replace it. Whenever cap is removed, peel away old silicone and re-apply a new bead.

slide them up the wire out of the way. Then, clean the plug-in cap on the end of the wire, and the wire itself for about an inch or so. Finally, dampen your cloth with cleaner and clean the socket into which the wire is inserted.

When you've done all the wires, lay a sealing bead around each wire where it enters the distributor and don't forget the center wire from the coil. Then, slide the boots into place down over the sockets in the distributor. If you believe in wearing both belt and suspenders, you can put silicone around the boots, as well.

If you do not wish to go to the trouble of using silicone sealant on all distributor and sparkplug connections, try a spray-on ignition sealant that works like lacquer to exclude water. We prefer silicone sealant because it is more durable, especially off-road where vibration may crack a less flexible material.

Before you leave the distributor, check to make sure there aren't any other places that need to be sealed. However, *don't* seal up the air vents in the base of the distributor. Sealing these holes will cause condensation inside the distributor body, leading to all sorts of dire results. For instance, the engine might die every time it's hit with cold water unless air can get in and out of those vents. Again, if you're a belt-and-suspenders man, put a piece of *open-cell foam* over each of these holes, then tape it in place, being

sure to leave an opening through which air can pass. Or, for a more permanent seal, cut a piece of open-cell foam to fit *inside* the base of the distributor after removing the distributor shaft and advance plate from the body.

Before leaving the distributor, there's one more task to accomplish. Cut a chunk of 1/2-in. foam, wrap it around the bottom part of the distributor cap so it overlaps down onto the base, then wrap everything with racer's tape. The foam will protect the fragile Bakelite cap from flying objects and the tape will hold it together if it does get cracked. This may not be necessary if your distributor is in an area that's well sheltered from flying rocks. On the other hand, it may be just what's needed to keep you from walking home due to a broken distributor cap.

Coil & Sparkplugs—The bare-metal connections on the coil get the same treatment as those on the distributor. That is, spray clean, then seal with a blob of silicone. The larger high-tension wire that goes to the center of the distributor gets the same clean-and-seal treatment as the sparkplug wires.

Depending on the type of connectors used, you may or may not need to go through your clean-and-seal routine at the sparkplugs. A tight-fitting rubber boot will probably do the job if you make sure the fit-together surfaces are clean and free of grease. If your sparkplug

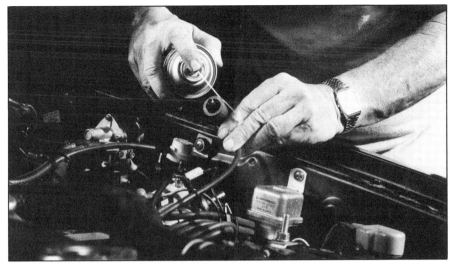

Use spray cleaner to remove any foreign material from coil wire ends. Use more silicone around rubber boot after it is replaced, unless push-on caps fit extremely tight. Do same for sparkplug-wire ends.

Simple clear-plastic inline fuel filter is added insurance against dirty fuel reaching engine. As on this VW buggy, mount filter between fuel pump and carburetor(s) or injector(s) and away from heat sources to minimize vapor-lock problems. Photo by Ron Sessions.

wires do not have tight-fitting boots, then you'll want to either add them, use small cable-ties around the existing boots, or do a clean-and-seal treatment.

Scal Alternator—The alternator is sealed at the factory with lubed-for-life bearings and its own built-in cooling fan that helps keep dirt out of the works. However, you will want to clean and seal the bare-metal electrical connections, and do the same for the external voltage regulator, if there is one.

While you're doing this, it's also a good time to check accessory-drive belt(s) and replace any that show signs of wear. Never leave the pavement without a spare belt or two.

Starter, Starter Relay & Battery—While it's unlikely they'll give you any problems, you should also clean and seal the electrical connections at the starter and starter relay. Likewise, don't overlook the battery connections. A good two-thirds of all the electrical problems we've ever encountered started with dirty battery connections. After removing any residual corrosion with a weak mixture of baking soda and water, and flushing it clean, scrape the battery posts and clamps clean. Then spray them with contact cleaner to remove any moisture. After the cables are installed on their posts, and *not before*, you can also seal them with silicone or petroleum jelly.

Replace Broken Sealant—Silicone sealant is one of the great inventions of our time, but do remember that it must be replaced whenever you break the seal created when you put it on. For example, when you remove and replace the distributor cap, you must then reseal it with fresh sealant. Fortunately, the old sealant easily peels off like soft rubber.

FUEL-SYSTEM PROTECTION

Your main concern in troubleproofing the fuel system is to keep the air and fuel entering your engine clean. This means keeping the air filter and fuel filter in top condition.

Fuel Filter—Pleated-paper, in-line fuel filters are inexpensive and do an effective job of trapping foreign particles, such as dirt and fuel-tank rust, in the fuel. Water traps, however, are another story. And see-through plastic filters provide the added dimension of allowing you to see when they've become clogged. We suggest carrying a spare in case you encounter a batch of dirty gas or other difficulty such as losing your gas cap and sucking in a load of silt before you notice its absence. Incidentally, if you do lose a gas cap, a wadded sock or a chunk of foam stuffed in the filler neck makes a pretty good dust filter, except when it rains, of course. In which circumstances you can make a satisfactory water-excluding cover from plastic or foil if you remember to poke a couple small holes in

it so the fuel-tank vent can breathe; otherwise, your fuel tank might collapse from negative pressure.

Always mount an in-line fuel filter between the fuel pump, whether it be electric or mechanical, and the carburetor or fuel injectors. *Do not* mount it between the tank and fuel pump, as this may lead to *vapor-lock*—fuel boiling into vapor—problems in hot weather. A fuel pump is much better at pushing fuel than it is pulling it out of the tank, and any restriction added there could cause problems. Fuel pumps can move liquid fuel, but once the fuel has boiled into vapor, your engine will be fuel-starved until the gas cools and returns to a liquid state.

A partially plugged fuel filter can be difficult to diagnose because it seldom shuts off fuel flow completely so the engine won't run anymore. Instead, there's more likely be an intermittent miss, especially under load or wider throttle openings. Ahah, you are likely to say to yourself, the ignition is breaking down. So you stop, check the ignition for good

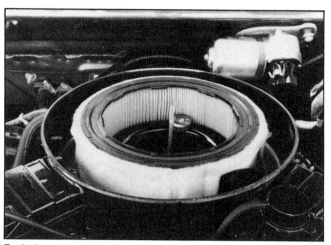

Basic dry-paper air filter that probably came with your vehicle is OK for recreational off-roading if there is no serious dust. Shown is dual-stage dry-paper/foam element used on late-model Dodge 4X4s. Photo by Ron Sessions.

Reusable wet-type filter is best way to go in heavy dust. This K&N unit has a much greater filtering surface area than the stock filter it replaces. When a visible amount of dirt accumulates, the filter can be washed in solvent, reoiled then reinstalled.

spark and find nothing wrong. The engine will sit there, idling perfectly and respond to the throttle without a hint that anything's wrong. So you start up again, thinking the problem has healed itself. But then, shortly after you're back up to speed and relaxed, there's the dreaded buck, stutter, wheeze again. What's likely happening is that fuel flow can't keep up with demand at wider throttle openings, and once the float bowl is drained dry, the engine sputters and dies—for a short while.

We've had this happen to us often enough that we have created a rule: It's never the ignition; it's always the fuel filter. And since we've adopted this rule, we've never been wrong. So don't assume it's a problem with the ignition. Check the fuel filter first.

Don't just check a see-through filter visually and assume it's OK if it looks clear. If you have a spare filter, it's a five-minute job to replace the old one. If you don't have a spare, remove the filter, hold your fingers over the ends to keep the fuel inside, then rapidly agitate the filter, tapping it against a tire while you let the fuel trickle out of the inlet side. By doing this, you'll at least shake loose

enough of the crud so you can reinstall it and travel on until you find a place where the filter can be replaced.

If you do have a chronic problem with plugged-up fuel filters—and you can, if you have the bad luck to get a tank load of rust from the bottom of a rusty storage tank—add an extra filter to the line. And carry *two* spares. Then, get your tank cleaned out or replaced!

Air Filter—You can buy reusable air filters that do a marvelous job and will last longer than the typical pleated-paper filter that probably came with your vehicle. However, we have never seen any evidence that these are actually necessary except in off-road racing or at dusty construction sites. What it boils down to is downtime. If a racer has to stop to change or clean a dirty filter, it may cost him the race. Similarly, big construction rigs sometimes have to run day and night to meet building schedules.

A typical pleated-paper air filter does a highly effective job for most *recreational* off-road vehicles. Yes, a filter of oil-wetted foam or cotton gauze, or one that combines oiled foam with paper, has greater filtering capacity and will continue to deliver clean air long after your

basic dry filter has plugged up. But we find it a lot less trouble to replace the standard-type filter than clean and reoil the reusable type. It's really a matter of personal choice.

There are those who will tell you that to use anything except a special off-road filter is to invite disaster. That's not true. If you do drive through so much heavy dust or silt that your standard pleated-paper filter is overloaded, what happens is that your engine begins to run rich and foul sparkplugs. If you continue, the engine may eventually refuse to run at all.

At this point, you haven't harmed the engine. The filter is simply plugged. It's not passing enough air to let the engine run, but it's not letting dirt through, either. The point is this: **DON'T REMOVE THE PLUGGED FILTER AND RUN WITHOUT IT!** Doing so will sandblast your engine from the inside out and destroy rings, cylinders and bearings in quick order.

If you do have a plugged filter, carefully remove the element to keep from getting dirt in the air-intake system. Tap the element around its periphery to shake off the loose dirt. Don't be brutal, or you may tear the paper or seal, or deform the

K&N also produces its own special air-filter cleaning solvent and oil solution so one filter can be used over and over for about as long as you own the vehicle.

To prevent rust and corrosion starting from damp pockets of mud on and under your vehicle, give it a good dousing as soon as you can after an off-road weekend. Photo by John Lawlor.

body and create a real problem—air leakage. And when you've tapped out everything you can, clean off the sealing surfaces of the filter cartridge and the housing it goes into. Then put everything back together, fire up the engine and motor on. That's all you have to do, and you're not going to destroy your engine.

DRIVING IN DEEP WATER

Besides fouling up your rig's ignition system, there are several ways water can damage your vehicle. If you can't figure out any other way and must drive through water as deep as the axles, read Chapter 15 and follow those recommendations.

After driving in deep water, you should change all drive-line lubricants as soon as possible. Besides the rust and corrosion that water contamination can cause drive-line bearings, gears and axles, water is also contaminated with dirt, grit and sand. So you need to change the engine lubricant and filter, repack the front wheel bearings, drain and refill the front and rear differentials and also lube the universal joints and drive-shaft splines.

Keep It Clean—In assuring dependability from your fine off-road vehicle, cleanliness is not only a virtue, it's essential. Dirt is bad stuff. Let a good layer of dirt build up on your engine and a heavy dew can turn everything to mud, creating shorts in places you never dreamed of. Further, mud tends to hold moisture in place, especially in cold weather, where it can accelerate corrosion and eat holes in sheet metal.

So, get in the habit of hosing your vehicle down after you've made a trip to the great nowhere, even if you aren't going to wipe and polish every square inch. Flush the mud out of the wheel wells and off the drive line. And when doing this, don't neglect hosing the engine down, too. Your engine will not only look better and be more inviting to tinker with as a result, it will thank you by being more dependable, keeping running when it otherwise might not and get you back some time when otherwise you might still be there when Christmas comes. Just make sure you Baggie the distributor and air cleaner so it starts after you hose it down.

Be sure to blast out accumulated mud from the wheel wells. Photo by John Lawlor.

Suspension & Lift Kits

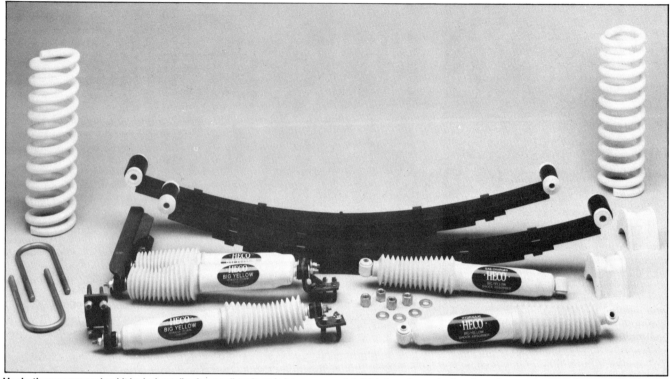

Heckethorn suspension kit includes taller front coil springs (where appropriate), high-arch rear leaf springs, heavy-duty shocks, long U-bolts and necessary hardware. Photo courtesy of Heckethorn Mfg. Co.

Off-road rigs come in various configurations with a variety of suspension setups. There are full-size and compact 2WD and 4WD pickup trucks and sport utilities, VW-based dune buggies and Baja Bugs, and all-wheel-drive passenger cars. Suspension setups vary from the most basic solid-axle, leaf-spring Jeep CJ or Toyota Land Cruiser, on through pickup-truck-derived independent-front-suspension Blazer, Bronco or '86 Toyota, VW-based independent-rear-suspension buggies, to the modified passenger-car four-wheel independent-suspension Subaru or Audi Quattro.

Throughout this wide array, however, a common denominator is woven. In order to withstand the rigors of off-road travel, whether it be just unpaved roads or 2-mph rock crawling, the vehicle must have greater-than-stock ground clearance and plenty of wheel travel. Usually, this means modified springs or torsion bars and shock absorbers.

SHOCK ABSORBERS & SUSPENSION TRAVEL

You can sure get a lot of differing opinions about shock absorbers. Most of these, unfortunately, are based on everything from bum information to pure ignorance. What we're going to do here is give you the straight scoop on shocks so you'll never have to be in doubt again.

How Shocks Work—A conventional shock, fitted between the suspension and the frame or body of a vehicle, damps the oscillations of the spring—be it a leaf, coil spring or torsion bar. A conventional shock does not *support* weight. Without a shock, a deflected spring, suddenly released, will rebound, deflect, rebound again and keep doing so until friction or other outside influence finally brings it to a stop. You've probably seen a car going down the road with worn-out shocks, bouncing up and down every time it hits a bump. Because these shocks are not effectively damping the oscillations of the springs, the car is unsafe and its roadability terrible.

In the old days, shock absorbers worked through friction like a bicycle coaster brake. There was a series of discs tightly squeezed together. Half of them, every other one, was linked to the suspension which bumped up and down as the wheel followed road undulations. The alternate discs were fixed to the chassis. Friction between the disc surfaces created the damping effect and, on some old cars, the shocks were adjustable so the friction could be increased or reduced depending upon the quality of ride desired or as they began to wear.

In essence, friction shocks are heat exchangers. The energy absorbed by a deflected spring is passed to the shock, turned into heat through friction, then dissipated to the air through the shock body.

Hydraulic Shocks—Today's conventional shocks do the same thing, but instead of friction they rely on hydraulic fluid to provide the damping action. Nevertheless, they are still heat exchangers. Most modern shocks are telescopic, with one tubular part sliding in and out of the other. One end of the shock is a cylinder and the other is a piston. As the wheel moves up and down, the piston forces hydraulic fluid through tiny orifices or valves inside the shock.

The size and number of valves and orifices dictates how much force is required to move the shock, or how much energy can be absorbed. Many shocks installed by vehicle manufacturers are valved in the 30/70 to 20/80 range. This means that it takes three or four times as much force to move them one way as the other. What you want is little on *jounce*—compression—and more resistance on rebound. This lets the suspension work. Friction shocks were 50/50, of course, and one of the advantages of the hydraulic shock is that it can be valved to give a better ride by letting the wheels be pushed upward easily on the compression stroke, yet provide the desired amount of damping on rebound.

Heat—Shock absorbers produce heat from the energy imposed on them by the movement of the springs, then dissipate it to the air through the shock body. The size and number of the valves and orifices through which the hydraulic fluid moves are matched the weight of the vehicle on which the shock is installed.

The harder a shock works, through the length of piston travel and the frequency of the strokes, the hotter it gets. As the heat of a conventional shock increases, the air in the cylinder gets churned into the oil, turning the fluid into foam. This

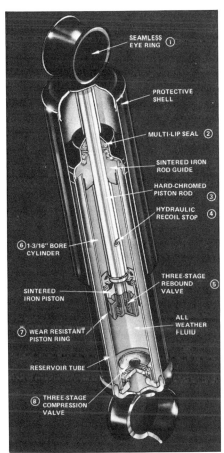

SEAMLESS EYE RING ①
PROTECTIVE SHELL
MULTI-LIP SEAL ②
SINTERED IRON ROD GUIDE
HARD-CHROMED PISTON ROD ③
HYDRAULIC RECOIL STOP ④
⑥ 1-3/16" BORE CYLINDER
SINTERED IRON PISTON
THREE-STAGE REBOUND VALVE ⑤
ALL WEATHER FLUID
⑦ WEAR RESISTANT PISTON RING
RESERVOIR TUBE
⑧ THREE-STAGE COMPRESSION VALVE

Typical shock absorber is nothing more than a cylinder and a piston which pumps hydraulic fluid through a series of orifices, or valves, as the shock is expanded and compressed. The smaller the orifices, the more pressure is required to move the fluid and a "stiff" shock is the result. Courtesy KYB of America.

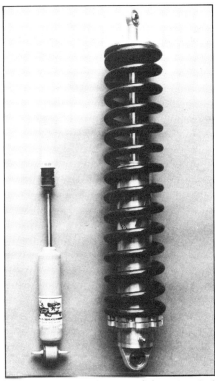

Shocks come in all shapes and sizes. A typical aftermarket shock (left) is compared here to a giant coil-wrapped, off-road racing shock that goes for about $1500!

Quality aftermarket shock (bottom) has larger cylinder than original equipment. Photo by James T. Crow.

Dual shocks reduce heat buildup because there is twice the heat-dissipating area. But shock damping is doubled and resulting ride is terrible unless shocks are valved to work as a pair.

On race-truck four-shock setup, one shock has been removed temporarily. Notice seatbelt-type fabric strap to limit downward travel of suspension.

That old adage, "If some's good, more's better." seems to apply here. With four shocks per wheel, this high-lifted 4X4 mini may have had some of its 16 shocks rendered ineffective to promote a more tolerable ride.

foamy substance provides less resistance as it passes through the valves, reducing the damping ability of the shock and leading to what's commonly called "shock fade."

If this continues until the shock gets hot enough—and it isn't unusual for a hard-worked shock to reach a temperature of 350—400F—the internal seals begin to go away. In other words, heat reduces shock effectiveness and, ultimately, can result in the hydraulic oil leaking out of the cylinder through burned-up seals. Or, if you work a gas-type shock (we'll get into these in a moment) hard enough, it will plain blow up. This actually happened to us during a hard and fast Baja run.

Some manufacturers of conventional shocks have overcome the tendency for hydraulic fluid to foam by adding a plastic pouch of freon gas to reduce the amount of free air inside the cylinder. Freon, commonly known in A/C systems as R-12, is highly compressible and can exclude free air from inside the cylinder, thereby reducing oil foaming and extending the shock's effectiveness.

Multiple Shocks—To reduce the heat generated by one shock, it is possible to use two or more at each wheel. Using two shocks with identical valving, for example, theoretically halves the heat each shock generates and dissipates, thus doubling effectiveness. But this is not entirely true, unfortunately, because the two shocks in our example double the resistance and neither piston will move as easily or as far as the single piston did before. Thus, more of the up-and-down motion of the wheels will be passed to the chassis, making for an uncomfortable, *overdamped* ride.

The solution, of course, is to use multiple shocks especially valved to work together so their full stroke and damping qualities are realized. Quality aftermarket shocks can be designed to work like this, tailored to vehicles of specific weights. These are readily available from specialty suppliers as are the special mounting brackets needed to install them.

The trouble is, many do-it-yourselfers replace the standard shock with a heavy-duty shock, and this is fine. But later, they add a second and even a third shock under the "if some's good, more's better" theory. This is the worst possible thing they can do and they wind up with a bone-jarring ride without realizing, or at least admitting, why.

It's too bad that so many 4WD enthusiasts—those who actually spend far more time on smooth paved roads than they do in the dirt—add multiple shocks only for appearance sake. Because shocks are often visible through the front wheel wells, especially on trucks with body- or suspension-lift kits, it's considered "macho" to install as many shocks at each wheel as possible. But these show-only vehicles ride like empty dump trucks lurching down the stairs of

An example of why maximum wheel travel is essential to successful off-roading. This four-wheel-drive Ramcharger has all four wheels on terra firma for traction. Less suspension travel here would have put two wheels in the air. Photo by John Lawlor.

Supple suspension with proper shock absorbers is more than just useful off-road. It will also soak up jolts of paved-road potholes.

the county court house. Some die-hards will drill the shock bodies and drain the fluid out of all but one shock per wheel. This way, they regain something at least close to their original ride and still preserve the illusion of having multiple-shock setups. Sensible off-roaders, of course, don't go in for such futility or wasted money.

Suspension Travel—As we've mentioned so often, the best off-road ride is a function of suspension travel. The more the better. Have you ever wondered why an off-road racing buggy with perhaps only 100 HP can go faster over rough terrain, and win more races, than a 500-HP truck or 4X4? It's suspension travel. A competitive buggy may have as much as 15-or-more in. of vertical wheel travel, while the 4X4s often have only 6—7 in. So, thanks to its ultra-supple suspension, a buggy can roll over higher obstacles at greater speed than a vehicle with a stiffer suspension.

Buying Shocks—When buying aftermarket shocks, make sure they have a stroke at least equal to the maximum travel of your rig's suspension. An inch or so longer is even better. If you plan to retain the stock suspension, ask the shock-absorber dealer to show you an application chart so you'll get the proper shocks for your rig. But if you have already modified, or plan to modify its suspension, you'll have to accurately measure suspension travel at the shock-mounting points to determine the length of stroke required. The point is, you don't want the shocks to bottom out against the upper or lower limit of piston travel, or they'll hammer themselves to death.

Look for a shock with the largest-diameter piston shaft for strength, and the greatest body diameter for its volume of hydraulic fluid and potential heat-dissipation capabilities.

Most original-equipment shocks and standard-replacement shocks have a metal sleeve covering the piston shaft to protect it from grit and damage by stones. But many aftermarket shocks are constructed differently and the shaft is exposed. Protective, bellows-like boots are supplied with some sets of shocks, or they may be purchased separately. Because they often come in bright colors, many four-wheelers will add them for no other reason than appearance sake.

There are three basic shock mounts: the bayonet-type, with threaded stud that fits through a hole in the chassis and secured with a pair of locknuts; the loop-type that's secured by a bolt; and the twin tab-type with two projecting ears fastened by a pair of bolts. Some shocks have similar mounts at either end; others have different mounts to make sure they are installed right-side up. Installing an aftermarket shock designed for a specific, unmodified vehicle is a foolproof operation. But you may run into installation problems when custom-fitting a special shock or adding one or two shocks beside the stock-mounted one.

When installing *any* type of shock, *always* replace the rubber bushings or biscuits at the shock mounts and make sure the shocks you buy include these necessities. High-speed photography of shocks being battered by shock dynos, and in action on off-road racing vehicles, shows that the very first suspension movement is absorbed or deflected by the bushings, *before* the shock itself begins to move. That's why the pro racers are turning to ultra-hard Teflon bushings, although the casual off-roader needn't go this far. When the bushing rubber begins to deteriorate, the shock absorber itself is doing nothing through the first 1/2-in. or so of suspension travel, and all the roughness comes through to the chassis.

For real ride improvement, Teflon bushings can be used with loop-type shock mounts. These deflect less than rubber when shock is expanded and compressed.

Coil-over front shocks on Manny Esquerra's Class-7 Ford Ranger have specially fabricated upper mounts that tie into chassis structure. Photo by Tom Monroe.

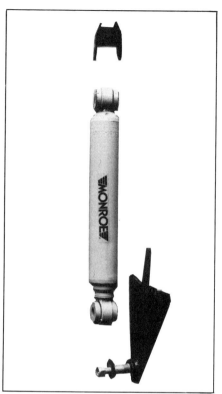

Shocks not designed for a specific vehicle can be installed by adding prefabricated mounts. Photo courtesy John Baker Performance Products.

Because very first movement of suspension is absorbed by rubber shock bushings, some off-road racers use shocks with spherical-bearing ends which forces every bit of motion to be damped by shock.

Ride Quality—We've all seen shock-absorber advertisements with oscilloscope images reproduced to compare Brand X shock against "the others." Shock specialists can, indeed, accurately monitor such things as temperature, piston speed and length of shaft travel, seal life and whether the hydraulic fluid is being churned to froth which will render a shock as ineffective as air in a brake line. These tests and comparisons are conducted on a machine called a "shock dyno," which can simulate all the conditions that a shock will ever meet.

But while such things are important, even more important is the quality of the ride a shock produces—and no machine can tell you this. The ride comfort a shock provides has to be *felt*. Unfortunately, there's no way to learn what sort of ride a given set of shocks will produce short of trying them out. And then it's too late to return them. *If* you can find someone with a truck like yours and shocks like you want to buy, then you can get a firsthand feel of what the ride will be like after you install yours. But this is a rare situation.

Even with all their resources, General Motors does not rely on computers or space-age equipment entirely to judge the ride a given shock will produce. When they design a new vehicle and the shocks to go with it, they can come pretty close to what they want in suspension quality before trying it out on a prototype. But then a whole series of shocks is made up with different valving and these are tried on the proving grounds, one set after another. It's up to the drivers and the riding engineers who do the dirty work to decide which shock gives the best ride and wheel control *according to their personal feelings*. This seat-of-the-pants "engineering" is the only way a shock's effectiveness can be judged.

Coil-Over Shocks—These are similar to conventional hydraulic shocks, but incorporate a small-diameter, low-rate coil spring around the shock body. The spring is far lighter than the coils used on front-suspension systems. Coil-overs are designed to add to its *rate*—make it stiffer.

Coil-overs may be useful on the rear of trucks and other vehicles that regularly haul weighty cargos, such as heavy trailers or slide-in campers. But on an unladen vehicle, they tend to be harsh and stiff, especially over rutted back-country trails. The effectively higher total spring rate means that it takes more force for the suspension to move the shocks, and a rough ride is the result.

Gas Shocks—Becoming increasingly popular are gas-filled, or pressurized, shocks. These are *single-tube* designs. Some new vehicles offer them as standard or optional equipment. Because the hydraulic fluid in the shock is under pressure, there is less tendency for it to mix with the fluid and aerate under hard usage.

One of the characteristics of the conventional hydraulic shock is that it does

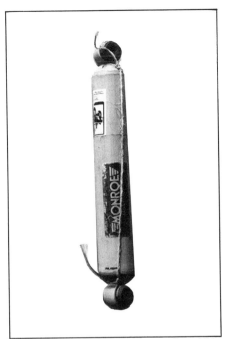

Gas-pressurized shocks are usually sold in compressed position to ease installation. Leave string intact until lower end of shock is bolted in place. Then, cut string and guide shock toward upper mount.

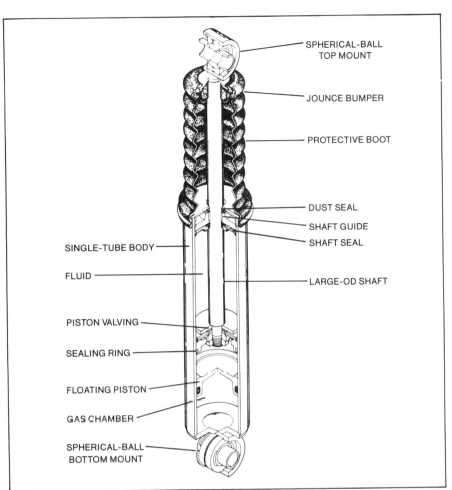

Cutaway of single-tube, high-pressure gas shock. Courtesy KYB of America.

almost no damping in the first part of its travel. In some conventional shocks, you can feel this as a lack of resistance when you start to stretch or compress the shock. With a gas-type shock, however, the gas that's under pressure keeps any such dead space from existing. So over bumps of very small amplitude, such as slightly rough pavement or an almost-smooth dirt road, a gas shock will soak up the irregularities and deliver a better ride. It helps keep the tires on the road instead of letting them bounce.

Some time ago, we conducted an interesting shock test using a standard Toyota 4X4 as the test vehicle. We tested nine different makes of shocks by timing the truck over a typical desert track. The course was 12.5 miles long and included everything from fast, hard-packed dirt to whoop-de-do's and deep sand. The results were decisively in favor of the gas-type shocks. In fact, the slowest of the gas-type shocks was quicker than the quickest of the conventional shocks. The shocks that let us go the fastest were also those that felt best, and this was undoubtedly due to the fact that they provided the best control. We also found that all nine sets of aftermarket shocks did a

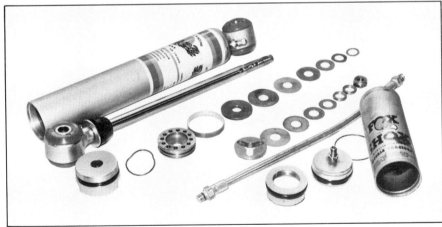

Racing-type Fox Shox gas shocks can be disassembled to change valving or repair seals. But they don't come cheap. Photo by Ron Sessions.

better job than the stock shocks that came from the manufacturer.

We also came to this general conclusion: If your rig has stiff suspension, it should be matched with soft—under-damped—shocks. And if you have soft suspension, use shocks with greater damping.

45

Extra weight of snowplow causes front-end sag. Fix is to install longer, and/or higher-rate springs, adjust torsion bars or add inflatable air bags inside front coils. Shown are Polyair Springs courtesy Air Lift Company.

You say there's nothing new under the sun? This "lift kit" was produced in the 1950s for launching boats across wide mud flats. Rocks on frame help lower center of gravity, tsk, tsk. Photo by Ralph Poole.

Replacing Shocks—Regardless of which type of shocks you use, they'll eventually wear out and need to be replaced. The question is, when?

One good rule of thumb is the time-honored oscillation test. If the old shocks require more than one oscillation to return the vehicle to its normal stance, they're probably worn out. Even over the biggest of bumps, what you want the vehicle to do is make one cycle, period. One stroke down, compressing the springs, then one rebound stroke back up to the proper position. That's it. If the shocks let the vehicle float up and down on the springs, replace them. In fact, replace them if they overshoot even once on the rebound stroke.

Also replace shocks if their function deteriorates after you've been off-road for a while. One of the characteristics of a shock that's overchallenged is that it loses its damping ability when it's worked hard. We'll discuss the reasons for this a little later.

In addition, there may be other times when you want to consider replacing your shocks. Obviously, if a visual inspection shows oil leaking from a shock or if it's broken at a weld from an encounter with a rock or whatever, replace it. Better yet, replace all shocks in pairs or *axle sets*.

If you own a full-size U.S. built 4X4 with independent front suspension (a la Ford), you will improve your ride and handling by replacing the original-equipment shocks before you ever go out into the dirt. Years ago, U.S. manufacturers got into the bad habit of saving money on shocks and never quite got over it on the full-size models. The new generation of small 4WDs are far better in this respect, undoubtedly because the cheapo OEM shocks aren't asked to handle as much unsprung weight as those on a full-size truck or utility vehicle.

If your 4X4, whether domestic or imported, has leaf-sprung front suspension, shocks are less critical due to damping supplied by *interleaf friction*. In fact, on a good, old-fashioned, hard-sprung Jeep, Land Cruiser or four-wheel-drive Toyota pickup, you can hardly tell the difference between good shocks and bad shocks. In general, it's the vehicles with willowy front suspension that respond best to good shocks—and worst to bad ones.

Summing Up—Quality aftermarket shock absorbers can make a terrific improvement in vehicle ride and handling. Factory shocks have to provide an acceptable ride over many kinds of surfaces for an enormously wide range of people and driving habits. Shocks designed spe-cifically for off-roading do a better job than those intended for a set of averages.

Also, we've found that the cheapest gas shocks are better than the most expensive conventional types. And, as with most other commodities, you get what you pay for: Those cheapie discount-store shocks probably won't perform as well as name-brand aftermarket shocks, conventional or gas-pressurized.

LIFT KITS

We neither praise nor censure lift kits. Their use is strictly up to the individual off-roader. There are benefits and disadvantages to each of the two popular types of lifts and it is only fair to consider the ramifications of each. What we will do is try to give a cursory description of both types, note their attributes, warn you of the pitfalls, explain some ins and outs of the installations and let you alone decide whether a lift kit is really what you want. Also, it is important for you to understand that a lift may affect your vehicle's warranty and it may actually be illegal in some states, where there are rigid bumper- and headlight-height laws, depending upon the amount of lift.

Types of Kits—To modify what we just said, there are actually three types of lifts. But one of them, the chassis lift, is outside the realm of the everyday off-roader because it involves procedures practiced chiefly by professional off-road racers. So, we're back to the two basic types of lift kits useful to the average four-wheeler who will use his vehicle in the outback some of the time but will do most of his driving on pavement.

The two types of lift kits, body lifts and suspension lifts, have one thing in common. Each will increase vertical wheel-well space to allow the addition of larger-than-stock wheels and tires—at least on most vehicles. There are a few models where tire/fender interference occurs at the *sides* of the front wheel openings and no amount of vertical lift will cure this, short of a 12-in. kit. And you certainly don't want one of these!

But the average kit on the average vehicle will increase wheel-well clearance for large tires and these, in turn, provide added ground clearance so the things that hang below the chassis won't be so easily snagged or hung-up by obstacles encountered in the back country. No kit by itself will increase ground clearance *per se* if you're worried about the distance between the terrain and the differential(s), which is usually the lowest point on a vehicle. This is provided only by tires with a greater diameter than those that came as standard equipment.

Most lift-kit manufacturers offer a choice of heights. Some are relatively inexpensive and can be installed in the home driveway given the proper tools and enough mechanical moxey to make sure the job is done properly and safely. Others can run into sizeable bucks, and may require additional hardware the kit doesn't include. Also, some may require the services of a specialized shop, so you can drop a lot of money into the project over and above the cost of the kit alone.

Body Lift—Imagine a stock truck with a conventional ladder frame. Remove the bolts, nuts and other fasteners that secure the front sheet metal, the cab, and the pickup bed to the frame. Then, put spacers between the mounting points and use longer bolts to screw everything back together again. Essentially, this is a body-lift kit. It raises the body sections above the frame by the added thickness of the spacers, usually 2—4 in. When you're finished, the chassis—frame, engine, drive line and suspension—is no

This off-roading Toyota uses both body lift and suspension lift to gain wheel-well clearance for those he-man tires.

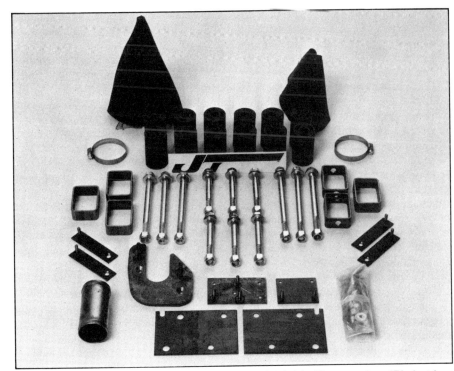
Proper body-lift kit contains all hardware necessary to do job right. Photo courtesy JT Industries.

Snow-country Toyota 4X4 uses suspension lift to fit 12.00-15 tires under sheet metal which, in turn, provide under-axle clearance owner Dale Black needs for slogging through really deep white stuff.

You have to get the axles up to clear obstacles, and only oversized tires can do this. Photo by Dennis Casebier.

higher off the ground than when you started. But the sheet metal stands higher, thereby increasing the vertical space in the wheel wells. This, in turn, *usually* lets you mount large aftermarket rubber which *does* increase ground clearance and which is, of course, the goal of the whole exercise.

Body-lift kits come with spacers, bolts and other fasteners where required and, of course, installation instructions. Each make and model of vehicle for which body lifts are available will differ in the steps and procedures involved, but most require "stretching" the fuel-filler connections, fuel and brake lines, and sometimes the wiring between the body and chassis. Some kits provide a pattern for notching the fire wall at the steering column and suggest a way to alter the cab's floorpan for shift-lever clearance, if that's required.

Understand that body-lift kits are not available for some vehicles when equipped with certain options. JT Industries, for example, the largest body-lift producer, does not have kits for imported trucks with automatic transmissions or air conditioning, nor for certain makes with tilt steering columns. Be sure there's a kit for your specific vehicle the way it's equipped before you begin dismantling anything.

What it takes to install a body lift depends greatly on the make and model you're dealing with. Obviously, it's more difficult to do a full-size truck or utility vehicle than a small pickup. But essentially, what's required is time, patience and a modicum of mechanical ability with some ingenuity thrown in for good measure. A strong and willing friend may be necessary, too. In addition to a set of sturdy jack stands, you'll find it convenient to have a couple of small hydraulic jacks and an assortment of odd-length wooden blocks that you can use to extend the lift of the jacks. Beyond these, you probably won't need anything more than common handtools, and perhaps a rotary file chucked into a drill motor to cut sheet metal.

Two mechanically inclined people should be able to install a body-lift kit in half a day, but the average do-it-yourselfer should allow a full day from startup to driveaway.

Body-lift kits are relatively inexpensive. But if you decide to have a professional shop do the installation for you, a good idea if you don't feel adept working with tools, they'll charge anywhere from three to five times as much as the kit itself. This will give you an idea of the work involved if you decide to tackle the job yourself.

Body-lift kits not only raise the body of the vehicle but also elevate its *center of gravity*—cg—which can adversely affect roadability and induce increased body lean when cornering. The degrees of either, obviously, depend on the amount of lift the kit gives. Also, in some cases, the steering angle to right and left may be reduced by the new relationship of the suspension and other chassis components with the front tires. As far as body lean goes, an anti-sway bar added to both the front and rear suspensions, or heavy-duty replacements for the stock bars you already have, will help reduce this unfortunate tendency.

Suspension Lift—This type of kit, as its name implies, utilizes replacement suspension parts to gain the extra lift. The hardware requirements for the various types of suspensions used under the many off-roading makes and models are extraordinarily varied. And there's a greater complexity of parts for a 5- or 6-in. lift than for one of only 2 in.

But basically, the typical leaf-spring suspension-lift kit consists of new leaf springs, with a greater amount of arch than the originals and often more individual leaves, longer spring U-bolts, and possibly new spring hangers or at least extended shackles. For coil-spring setups, the kit includes taller coil springs with an increased material diameter.

In the case of front torsion bars, some off-roaders will try and settle for a simple readjustment of the stock bars to gain an inch or so of added height. But this overstresses the bars and will eventually let the vehicle settle back to its original height and nothing will have been gained. There are stouter aftermarket torsion bars that remedy this. A good suspension-lift kit for a so-equipped vehicle will include these.

Suspension kits, obviously, can include a sizeable pile of hardware, but this usually requires only straightforward replacement of said parts. Good kits are on the expensive side, starting at about four times the cost of a body-lift kit. But as with the body-lift kits previously mentioned, additional costs may crop up before you're completely satisfied with the job. A suspension lift that increases ground clearance of everything but the differentials may also add to vertical wheel travel. But some kits may require taller shocks or new shock brackets. And if your vehicle didn't come with a steering stabilizer, you'll probably need one after adding the new suspension, so there go even more dollars.

Drive Shaft—There's also the possibility that you'll need to have the drive shaft(s) lengthened after adding a suspension-lift kit. We went through this with a Jeep Wagoneer. After the lift kit was installed, everything was fine in the flat-and-level drivealong mode. But every time the brakes were applied, the nose dipped and the rear end came up a little, the splines of the drive shaft pulled out far enough to make a hair-raising rump-rump-rump sound as the two parts of the drive shaft got too close to the end of their engagement. Turning the old drive shaft into a new, longer one was an expensive lesson in what can happen when you start fooling around with suspension-lift kits.

Good Kits—Luckily, there are quality suspension-lift kits on the market for the more popular off-road vehicles. When you're shopping for a kit, look for a name brand and don't try cutting corners by rooting through a dealer's shelves trying to piecemeal everything together yourself. A suspension system is a critical part of your car or truck and it affects everything from control to passenger comfort. Don't skimp on a so-called economy kit. They may provide the main components you need but leave a lot of other hardware up to you. And if your kit requires any welding, make sure you know what you're doing or let a qualified welder do the job for you.

Installation—While most suspension

kits can be installed by anyone with good mechanical ability, it's helpful to have at least watched a competent mechanic remove and replace a leaf spring or coil spring if you're going to attack this job. If you don't at least have this knowledge, you run the risk of serious injury because springs can be dangerous. While some coil springs can be removed and replaced by using a floor jack to lower and raise the control arm, some coils need to be compressed with a spring compressor to replace them. And it's always a good idea to safety-chain a coil spring so that it doesn't fly out and hit something or someone.

Torsion bars, on the other hand, are a reasonably straightforward replacement and you could jump into that with greater impunity.

If you do decide to install your own suspension kit on a vehicle with semi-elliptic leaf springs, you'll need the proper equipment. First, you not only need jack stands, you also need a tall bumper jack such as a High-Lift (two are better). You'll also want to have a pair of small hydraulic jacks to make fine tune adjustments that are necessary to support the weight of the axle, for example, so you can pull the bolt out of the spring eye without having everything fall on the ground or your hand. Otherwise, you don't need any special equipment beyond the usual handtools, a big screwdriver and a hammer. And you may not need the screwdriver and hammer.

Alignment—Whether or not you install a suspension-lift kit by yourself, have a friend help you, or have a pro handle the springs, it should be left to a professional shop to properly realign the front wheels. Wheel alignment is critical to proper handling and steering, to say nothing of tire wear. A wheel-alignment shop familiar with off-road equipment should have the necessary equipment and knowledge to reset caster, camber and toe-in to work with the suspension kit and larger tires you have probably added. These settings may differ from what the factory shop manual recommends.

Rough Ride—Most suspension-kit manufacturers put almost all of their effort into lifting and stiffening the springs, which is *not* what most off-roaders need. Yes, they do need more

Some front-suspension height can be gained by substituting a taller factory-available spring. Spring at right is for truck with air conditioning, while shorter spring is for non-air vehicle.

suspension travel and increased wheel-well height, but they don't necessarily need stiffer springs. By and large, they need springs that are more supple, and this requires a greater number of thinner leaves. But that direction is rarely taken by the kit suppliers.

If you're thinking about a suspension-lift kit, find someone with a vehicle like yours and a kit like the one you're thinking about. Ask him to take you for a ride—over some rough pavement as well as lumpy dirt trails. Also ask if he'd install the same kit if he had a chance to do it all over again. Consider his truck's ride and his comments carefully.

An example of the point we're trying to make is the all-too-true story of a Dodge Ramcharger belonging to the Bureau of Land Management. The big utility was regularly carrying hundreds of pounds of specialized equipment and rolling up 36,000 miles a year with an unreal 22,000 of these in the harshest sort of off-road environment.

In order to fit large, aggressive tires, a suspension-lift kit with multiple shocks was ordered from a well-known supplier and installed by a competent shop. The BLM personnel assigned to the truck immediately began complaining about the stiff, uncomfortable ride, especially after eight-hour stints behind the wheel. Within a few months, the shock mounts

The Bureau of Land Management does a lot of serious off-road work and some of their drivers can relate horror stories about overkill suspensions.

heat from welding may warp the housing, so if you choose this route, have the axle housing checked by a machine shop and straightened, if necessary.

The stumbling block to relocating the spring pads is that the resulting lift is often too great. To determine how much lift will result from relocating the springs, measure the diameter of the axle housing at the spring pads, then add the thickness of the leaf-spring pack. More often than not, it will come out to 7—8 in.; too much for a sensible lift and one that will raise cg to a dangerous level.

Helper Springs—It is possible to gain a little rear-end lift by bolting on a set of helper springs. These take several forms. Many of them are added to the spring pack between the bottom leaf and the spring pad on top of the axle housing. Some helper leaves are nearly straight and they come into play only when the stock springs are severely deflected by a bad bump or from vehicle overloading. Other helpers match the arch of the stock springs and are in contact with them all of the time. These are marginally helpful in preventing the vehicle from bottoming out when toting a heavy load such as a camper or when towing a trailer.

But helper springs were never intended to raise an empty vehicle to increase its ground clearance, other than in cases where the springs have sagged so far from continual overloading or other abuse that they can't hold the vehicle up where it belongs.

The bottom line is this: If the springs you've got aren't doing the job, face up to it and fix them right. And if this means buying new springs or taking your machine to a professional spring shop for re-arching, then so be it.

We both speak from bitter experience in this matter. Time after time we've both made the mistake of saying, "Well, this'll probably help," or "This should do it," and time after time we've regretted it.

Coil Springs—You may have seen advertisements for spacers or wedges you can force between the coils of a coil spring to raise the front end of a vehicle. "Restores original ride height," the ad might say. That may be true, but it's the only good thing it does. Don't even consider such gadgets, especially for off-road. What they do is reduce the working

broke, were welded, then broke again. Then, the frame began developing cracks.

Ultimately, the BLM removed the shock setup and replaced them with softer, single shocks. The high-arch springs were allowed to remain, however. The ride is improved enough now that breaks are no longer appearing in the chassis, but one of the authors spent a day patrolling the desert with a federal ranger, and the Dodge rode terribly.

This is just one case where a highly-touted and widely advertised set of suspension accessories was proven unworthy in a very practical sense. A harsh, jittery ride might do something for an off-roader's ego on an easy weekend cruise. But having to live with such discomfort as a steady diet is something that sensible four-wheelers should shun.

U-Bolts—Suspension-lift kits, and the helper springs we're going to tell you about in a moment, come with replacement U-bolts because the stock ones are too short for the increased thickness of the leaf-spring packs. These are almost always longer than necessary and, as a result, are excessively long after the nuts are tightened, and are susceptible to damage by rocks and other landscape. If they

aren't bent out of shape so later removal is impossible, the U-bolts are rapped out of position, which can break the spring center bolt or loosen the U-bolt nuts. The cure is to cut off the excess threaded stock after the nuts have been torqued.

Lift Blocks—The least expensive, easiest and *most dangerous* way to raise the rear of a vehicle with semi-elliptic leaf springs is to install spacer blocks between the spring mounting pad, when it is on top of the axle housing, and the spring itself. Our advice here is, *don't!* What happens is that increased leverage between the axle housing and the springs, caused by drive-shaft torque, will produce spring wrapup during acceleration and spring deformation during hard braking. This creates wheel hop, which can lead to early failure of drive-line parts. Having seen the damage these blocks can do and understanding the potential accidents they can cause, we have to categorically state that lift blocks should be outlawed.

Over & Under—Some vehicles, with leaf springs passing *under* the rear axle, can be lifted by relocating the spring pads from below to above the housing. This requires cutting off the original bottom pads and welding new ones on top. The

length of the spring which means you'll bottom out more easily and suffer a considerably harsher ride. It's possible that the coil spring will be bent permanently, or even break, at the point where one of the wedges is inserted. So just forget that you ever heard about them.

A little lift can be gained with a coil spring by inserting a thin spacer or shim in the bottom spring pocket. Due to front-end geometry, a 1/2-in. shim will produce about 1 in. of lift. But there are limits on the thickness of the spacers that can be safely used. See a wheel-alignment shop or chassis specialist about these.

If your rig has front-end coil springs and no air conditioning or other heavy options, you're in luck. In these high-tech days, manufacturers often use computers to determine the correct spring rate for each vehicle as it comes off the assembly line. A vehicle with no weight-producing options is lighter than one with all the bells and whistles, and the computer tells the assemblers which spring to install. So, if your vehicle isn't loaded down with factory-installed options check the dealership parts department for taller springs. We did this a few years ago to lift the front end of a lightweight sedan used for a 2WD off-roading project, and gained 2 in. of lift by merely substituting a station-wagon spring.

Expert Views—*Off-Road* magazine is one of several monthly publications that are experts about lift kits. Some of their observations are revealing:

John Baker, professional off-road race driver with dozens of wins during his career, including six in Baja California, said: "The more rubber between rim and road, the better for off-roading (up to a point) but the worse for highway driving. Any significant (not absurd) increase in tire size (which lift kits permit) must be matched by an increase in brake size, horsepower and axle ratio, or more will be lost than gained."

Chris Hawkins, of Hawk Independent Lift Kits, is a believer in professional lift-kit installations. "Lift kits are engineered to work properly only if they are properly installed. The do-it-yourselfer is more likely to circumvent a kit's quality because he doesn't have a proper tool, or is running short of time and the pa-

Professional off-road race driver John Baker does not advocate overly high body or suspension lifts or absurdly tall tires. John is holding one of the very special racing shocks he helped develop for his revolutionary one-shock-per-wheel BC-2 chassis.

tience of a pro."

Jim Conner, an off-road-racing pioneer with many major wins to his credit, and the builder of many successful racing Datsun/Nissan trucks, is categorically against any sort of suspension-lift kit for Nissan's independent front suspension, and only grudgingly approves body lifts: "Two inches is fine." Then he adds, "Steering, handling and braking performance can be seriously affected by merely raising the upper A-arm (of a Nissan) by 0.150-in. More radical manipulations of front-suspension components by home mechanics in order to obtain height increases that can be measured in inches, should not even be voiced out loud."

To Kit or Not to Kit—Whether or not to add a lift kit, be it a body lift or a suspension lift, is best left up to the individual. As noted at the outset, there are advantages in being able to add oversize wheels and tires, which is the primary reason for installing either type of lift kit, but there are shortcomings as well. We are undecided, really, whether a lift kit is absolutely the only way to go or something to be whispered about. It's your decision.

The Authors' Route—Sooner or later,

someone is going to ask what we have done to our suspensions. So we might as well tell you. Both of us own 4X4s, of course, and we drive them regularly. It was a pure coincidence that both rolled up 26,000 miles in the first year of ownership, though one saw more off-road duty than the other to the tune of 5000 miles. This is far above the use that the average off-roader will subject his 4X4 to, incidentally, according to market surveys.

The vehicle that sees the greater number of off-road miles wears tires and wheels larger than came on the truck originally. But rather than gain wheel-well space with a lift kit, the fenders have been modified for clearance, page 64. A lift kit was avoided in this instance, yet the bigger rubber has increased ground clearance.

The other author does much more pavement traveling, but still sees 2500 off-road miles annually. His rig carries a 1200-lb pop-top camper. So, to retain the unladen ride height of the truck, he had the rear leaf springs re-arched and an extra leaf added. Both of these methods are satisfactory for the use to which each truck is put.

Tires, Wheels & Wheelwells

If you had any doubt that off-road tires came in all shapes and sizes, here's a selection from Dick Cepek Co. that should dispel that notion.

TIRE LORE

Off-roaders tend to disagree about tires. If you can get two of them to agree that one type of tire is superior to another, they'll probably argue about inflation pressure or whether or not tires should be rotated. And they're almost certain to have different opinions about which brand is best.

Typically, we also have strong opinions on this subject. However, to prevent you from going too far astray, we're going to attempt to keep the more outlandish of our prejudices to ourselves. So, everything you read from here on is the absolute gospel unless it's labeled otherwise. Fair enough?

BEFORE YOU BUY

When you're making a heavy decision about which tires to buy, there are three main things to consider: size, construction and tread pattern. You may also want to put the manufacturer's name into the equation. Let's start with tire sizes.

Nothing dresses up an off-road 4X4 or 4X2 pickup faster than custom wheels and large off-road tires. Photo courtesy of Custom Fab Manufacturing Co.

Size Designations—It's unfortunate that most tire sizes molded into the sidewall of a tire are only marginally meaningful. Back in the early days, a tire size meant something. Before World War II, for instance, more than 75% of all passenger car tires were size 6.00-16. These numbers meant that the tire had a section width of approximately 6 in. and was fitted on a 16-in. wheel.

There are still a few tires with this type of straightforward size designation. For

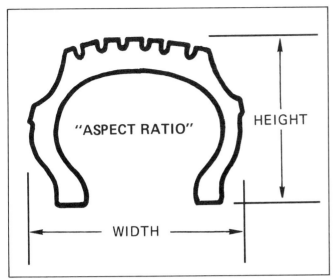

Aspect ratio of tire is section height divided by section width. So, the cross section of a tire with an aspect ratio of 78 is 78% as tall as it is wide.

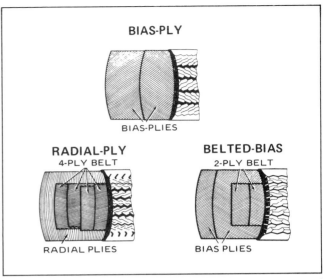

Three basic types of tire construction: Bias-ply tires with nylon-cord material offers utimate in durability. Radial design has less rugged sidewalls but delivers superior traction. Belted-bias is compromise design less commonly found these days.

example, you'll find off road vehicles with tires sizes like 10-15, 11-15, 12-15 and so on. As explained above, the first number is the nominal section width and the second, the size rim it fits on.

If it happens to be a radial tire, this fact is identified by the addition of an "R" after the first number. Like 10R-15, 11R-15, and so on. So far, so good.

Aspect Ratio—Chronologically, the next type of tire-size designation to come along was *alphanumeric*—combining a letter representing the size designation with a two-digit number denoting its aspect ratio. Take F78-15, for example, which was a popular size in the 1960s. The "F" is a comparative size, meaning that it's larger than an "E" but not as large as a "G." An "A" is the skinniest tire and, although the sizes go higher, an "L" is about the fattest you see in regular use.

The "78" is the *aspect ratio* of the tire, or percentage of section height to section width. In other words, a tire with an aspect ratio of 78 has a section height that's 78% of the section width. For example, if the section width is 10 in., the section height would be 7.8 in.

An aspect ratio of 78 was pretty much the standard for bread-and-butter passenger-car tires in the '60s, but as low-profile tires became popular, aspect ratios of 70, 60 and then 50 were widely used on zoomier models. By contrast, off-road tires remained tall to maintain ground clearance.

In the alphanumeric tire-size designation, a radial is identified by adding an "R" after the letter, such as HR78-15.

Metric Sizes—In Europe, tire sizes are given in metric units for both section size and diameter. However, when Euro-spec tires came to the U.S., the section size remained metric but the diameter was given in inches. So, we saw tires with sizes like 225-15, meaning that the section size was nominally 225mm—roughly nine in.—and it fit onto a 15-in. rim.

As if tire sizes weren't sufficiently complicated at this point, there came another set of sizes. This one combined a metric-type section size along with an aspect ratio. So the tire size might be given as 205/60R-15, or 195/80R-15.

On some tires, this was even further complicated by the addition of a "speed" rating to the size designation. So it might read 185/60VR-15, and in such a designation the "V" means the tire and wheel combination is rated for continuous operation at speeds over 130 mph.

P-Metrics—Then, just to show that there's no end to how ridiculous this can all be, there came what are called "P-metrics." For example, on a P185/60VR-15 tire, the "P" in front of the number designation indicates passenger-car use, as opposed to "LT"—light-truck use. Now you could tell it had the new P-metric section size instead of previously non-P section size and we won't bore you with the difference between the two.

Fortunately for the off-roader, not all tire manufacturers were heading down the path to greater obfuscation. For example, some specialized off-road tires began to show up with markings that told you more about the tire you were buying rather than less. What do you suppose it means when you see an off-road tire whose size is shown as 32/11.50-15? That's right. The "32" tells you the tire is 32-in. tall, the "11.50" indicates that it has a section width of 11.5 in. and the "15" still means that it goes on a 15-in. rim. Genuinely useful information in a marvelously simple and straightforward method. Terrific.

There could also be an "R" added to such a tire designation to identify it as a radial. So the size marked on the sidewall might look like 32/11R-15.

On an off-road tire, you may also find a letter behind the wheel size, such as 10R-15C. In this case, the "C" tells you the tire's load rating and we'll get into load ratings later on.

CONSTRUCTION TYPES

The two types of off-road tire construction you need to be familiar with are *bias-ply,* or *cross-ply,* and *radial.* There's also another type called *belted-bias,* popular on passenger cars before radials gained acceptance. Few are being made today, so you may never encounter one of these.

Bias-Ply Construction—As you can see by the drawing on page 53, a bias-ply tire is one in which the layers of fabric in the casing are placed at an angle—on the bias to each other. This is the oldest type of tire construction and basically the least expensive. This doesn't mean that it is not as strong as the other types. Heavy-truck tires are ordinarily of bias-ply construction, as are tires used on earth-moving equipment and the like. A bias tire is durable off-road, with strong sidewalls that are less vulnerable to damage than a radial tire. You can run a bias-ply tire at lower inflation pressure with fewer worries about ripping a sidewall.

What's the disadvantage of the bias design? Because the tread does a lot more squirming as it rolls along the road, the bias tire builds up more heat and rubs its tread rubber off faster than a radial. As a result, you can't expect to get as many miles of wear from a bias tire as a radial. Also, bias-tire traction is not as good as that of a radial. Finally, a bias-ply tire can't tolerate low inflation pressure at highway speeds. This builds up heat and can result in a blow out.

Long-range, if both types of tires survive until the tread is down to the replacement point, the radial will generally be less expensive on a cost-per-mile basis. In other words, buy premium-grade tires of each type and you'll get more miles per dollar with a radial. This assumes that you don't poke a hole in the sidewall, which you're less likely to with a bias tire.

Radial Tires—In a radial tire, the cords run across the tire from bead to bead rather than being arranged at an angle as in the bias-ply design. Around the cir-

cumference of a radial is a belt of material that strengthens and flattens the tread area. Belt material is usually woven steel, but fiberglass, aramid and polyester are also used. Woven steel is popular because it provides good tread support and gives superior puncture resistance over other belting materials.

Radial tires were originally developed by Michelin in Europe, then spread to the United States. They first began to appear on off-road vehicles in the early 1970s and, frankly, the early ones were not an unqualified success. But years of development and testing have greatly improved off-road radials to the point that they are standard equipment on virtually all current four-wheel-drive vehicles. Today's off-road radials are excellent tires with a good ride, excellent traction and good tread wear.

Compared to bias-ply, radials provide better traction and longer tread life. A radial tire delivers greater traction than a bias-ply tire because vehicle weight is more evenly distributed across the tread area. This means it better conforms to the surface it is traveling across and is less likely to lose its grip.

Any number of tests have been done that demonstrate that radials give better traction than bias-ply tires. In fact, we've seen it demonstrated that a radial of only modest width can provide better traction than a bias-ply tire with a considerably wider tread.

What is a radial tire's weak point? As noted earlier, the sidewalls don't have the same impact resistance as the sidewalls of a bias tire. Consequently, a radial tire will take less abuse than a bias tire when going off-road.

Belted-Bias—Belted-bias tires are a compromise design that combines features from both the bias-ply and the radial tire. The cord material is arranged as in a bias-type tire, but adds a reinforcing belt around the tire's circumference similar to a radial. This type of tire was devised by U.S. manufacturers to get a low-profile look at a time when European-built radials were becoming popular in the United States. This stop-gap measure enabled tire manufacturers to offer the low-profile look without having to invest in equipment required to switch over to radials. About the only good thing we can

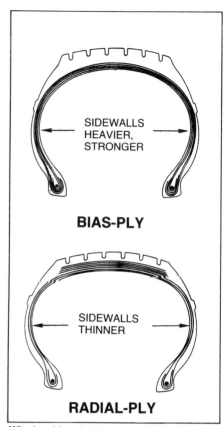

BIAS-PLY

SIDEWALLS HEAVIER, STRONGER

RADIAL-PLY

SIDEWALLS THINNER

Why is a bias-ply tire more durable than a radial? Bias-ply tire has stronger sidewalls than a radial. On other hand, radial's more flexible sidewalls, plus flattening effect of belting material, assures superior traction.

think of to say about them is that their bias-type sidewalls are more durable than radials and they're also less expensive than radials.

Passenger Car Vs. Light Truck—To avoid any possible confusion at this point, let's talk about the kind of tires you're likely to use on your vehicle. These will no doubt be either what are classified as passenger-car tires or ones that have a light-truck designation. It doesn't really matter which type you use because both can be the same type of construction (either bias or radial), are almost certain to be tubeless, and probably have the same size designation as well.

By looking at them, the only way to tell them apart is by the size designation molded into the sidewall. If it's a light-truck tire, the size will be followed by an "LT," such as 10-15LT. If it's not a light

If you load your rig as heavily as this, cancel our statement that most off-road vehicles are equipped with bigger, stronger tires than they really need.

Tall Yokohama Mud Digger radial flexes sidewall over rocks. Tread blocks are wide-spaced for good digging and self-cleaning, and rubber compound is comparatively soft for better traction. Assymetrical tread blocks help break up harmonic effects and assure a quieter-running tire.

truck tire, the size will be listed as a plain 10 15.

Another difference you'll find on the sidewall is that the light-truck tire doesn't have the notice about traction or wear rating that's required on passenger-car tires.

Incidentally, this is why many manufacturers prefer to call their products light-truck tires; then they don't have to go through the Department of Transportation—DOT—rigmarole to grade them as passenger-car tires. Nor are they required to have built-in tread-wear indicator bars that show when the tread is down to the point where the tire should be replaced.

You're not likely to use "truck tires" manufactured for large trucks. These are usually bigger, heavier and capable of carrying more weight. They're also mounted on split rims or compound wheels, and use tubes. You'll no doubt use tubeless tires.

Parts of a Tire—In the olden days, all tires had separate tubes. The tubeless variety came into common use shortly after World War II. If you take a slice through an ordinary tubeless tire, you'll see a smooth rubber liner on the inside. In effect, this is the tube. Its job is to keep air inside the tire. The tire beads fit tightly against the rim, making an airtight

seal. The base of the valve stem is also airtight. So, air is trapped inside and can't get out unless there's a leak.

Next, there are the layers or plies of fabric. This fabric is sort of like corduroy in that there are cords running in one direction but not the other. In the early days, cotton canvas was used for this purpose. But cotton has long since been superseded by more durable fibers such as rayon, nylon and polyester.

Nylon Toughest—Of the cord materials used in tire casings, nylon is the strongest and most durable. For this reason, nylon is used in off-road racing tires, tires used on heavy construction equipment and most other types where strength and durability are prime considerations. Nylon is not a popular cord material for passenger-car tires, however, because it tends to take a set when cold. As a result, you park the vehicle overnight and the tire develops a flat spot where it contacts the road. When you start out in the morning, you have a lumpy, bumpy ride that goes on until the nylon gets warmed up enough for the tire to regain its original roundness. This condition is sometimes called "morning sickness."

Nylon is also used as a belting material in some radials. But it's not commonly used in the sidewalls of radials because it does not take kindly to constant flexing.

Polyester Popular—Polyester is very popular among tire manufacturers as a cord material in both bias and radial tires. It is also used for radial tire belts. Polyester combines good flex strength and doesn't flat-spot. What it can't match is nylon's brute tensile strength.

Rayon Cord—Rayon-cord radials deliver excellent ride and traction and are popular for passenger-car use. Unfortunately, rayon is subject to deterioration if it gets wet, which is makes it less desirable in off-road tires. Passenger-car tires are less likely to be scuffed through the protective layer(s) of rubber and exposing the rayon to moisture.

Aramids Light, Strong—DuPont Kevlar is an aramid fiber that's the most recent "miracle" synthetic for tires. It's claimed to be five times stronger than steel, by weight, and is widely used as belting material in premium-grade radials. Aramid fiber does not have the puncture resistance of a woven-steel belt. But its lightweight construction makes it easy to work with during the manufacturing process.

Synthetic Rubber—Outside of the layers of fabric body plies and belting materials (assuming it's a radial) is the rubber that makes up the sidewalls and tread area. This is synthetic rubber, a petrochemical product rather than that derived from a tree. In fact, there's more than one rubber compound in a tire, each specifically compounded for its function. As a result, sidewall rubber is different than tread rubber, and so on.

To make a white-sidewall tire, a layer of white rubber is laid up in that area. To produce raised-white letters, there's a layer of white rubber with a thinner layer of black on top of it and the black is buffed away after the tire is finished to let the white show through. If you've ever run a set of raised-white-letter tires through a patch of nasty rock, you've no doubt been dismayed at how tacky the sidewalls become as the thin black layer gets torn off and exposes ragged patches of white.

Much Hand Work—Considering the automation that goes into the manufacture of virtually everything today, you might be surprised at how much hand work goes into making a tubeless tire. It starts with two coils of wire that make up the base of the tire beads. From then on, each individual part is laid up by hand, from the rubber liner that becomes the tube to the layer of rubber that eventually becomes the tread.

After the tire is assembled in its "green" form, it goes into a heated mold in which the rubber is cured. It is during this process that the heated rubber is forced into the matrix that puts the tread pattern into the tire as well as all information that appears on the sidewalls, such as the manufacturer's name, tire name, tire size, load rating, inflation pressure, and so on.

Ply Ratings & Load Ratings—The type of material used in the tire casing and the number of layers of fabric or plies determines the tire's ability to carry weight. The stronger the casing, the more weight it will carry and the higher its ply rating. We said "ply rating" because it may be different—in fact, probably is different—from the actual number of plies.

In fact, the term *ply rating* is not often used any more. What we talk about instead is *load rating*—the maximum load a tire is designed to carry. And this is almost certain to bear no resemblence to the actual number of plies.

As a result, what used to be known as a 2-ply tire is now designated as having a Load Rating A. A tire with what used to be known as a 4-ply rating is now called Load Rating B, a 6-ply-rated tire is Load Rating C, and so on. Most tires used on conventional off-road machines are in the Load Rating B or C category.

WHAT SIZE FOR YOU?

As we said earlier, the load rating tells

TIRE INFLATION/LOAD CAPACITY RELATIONSHIP
TIRES USED AS SINGLES

Tire Size	Load Range	MAXIMUM LOAD CAPACITIES PER TIRE (LB.) AT COLD TIRE INFLATION RATES (PSI)								
		20	25	30	35	40	45	50	55	60
L78-15	B	1520	1715	1900						
7.9-14	C	790	900	1000	1090	1180	1260			
8.25R-14	C	900	1000	1090	1180	1260	1340	1420		
27x9.50-14	B	1250	1325	1500						
9-15	B	1230	1400	1560						
10-15	B	1390	1580	1760						
10-15	C	1390	1580	1760	1930	2080	2230			
10R-15	C	1230	1390	1580	1760	1930	2080	2230		
31x10.50-15	B	1400	1595	1775						
31x10.50-15	C	1400	1595	1775	1945	2100	2250			
11-15	B	1500	1710	1900						
11-15	C	1500	1710	1900	2080	2250	2410			
32x11.50-15	B	1575	1795	1995						
32x11.50-15	C	1575	1795	1995	2185	2360	2530			
12-15	B	1780	2020	2250						
12-15	C	1780	2020	2250	2460	2660	2850			
12R-15	C	1575	1780	2020	2250	2460	2660	2850		
33x12.50-15	C	1755	2000	2225						
14-15	C	1780	2020	2250	2460	2660	2850			
17-15	C			2685						
8.00-16.5	D			1360	1490	1610	1730	1840	1945	2045
8.75-16.5	D			1570	1720	1850	1990	2110	2240	2350
9.50-16.5	D			1860	2030	2190	2350	2500	2650	2780
10-16.5	C			1840	2010	2170	2330			
10-16.5	D			1840	2010	2170	2330	2480	2620	2750
10R-16.5	C			1570	1840	2010	2170	2330		
12-16.5	B			2370						
12-16.5	D			2370	2590	2800	3000			
12-16.5	E			2370	2590	2800	3000	3190	3370	3550
12R-16.5	C			2170	2370					
14-16.5	C	1780	2020	2250	2460	2660	2850			
17-16.5	C			2685						
14-17.5	D			2820	3080	3210	3500	3790	4060	
14-17.5	E			2820	3080	3210	3500	3790	4060	4320

you the maximum amount of weight that tire is designed to carry. For example, let's say you have a four-wheel-drive utility with 15-in. tires and you want to know the minimum size tire you can use.

Weigh the Vehicle—The first thing to do is load your vehicle with all the stuff you're going to carry when loaded to the max. Then find a public scales in the *Yellow Pages* under Weighers, Public. Go there and weigh the front and rear of your machine. You do this by driving onto the scales until all of the vehicle ahead of the rear wheels is on the weighing platform. Record this number. Then, drive ahead until the front wheels are just off the platform and record this number.

What you've just done is figure out the total weight on the front wheels and total weight on the rear wheels. Divide these numbers by two and you have the nominal weight on each wheel.

Armed with this information, you're prepared to select tires that will safely carry the maximum weight you're likely to carry.

Check Load-Capacity Chart—The next step is to use a Tire Inflation/Load-Capacity Chart, either the one we have printed here or one from your tire dealer. In the section of the chart marked "Maximum Load Capacities per Tire," select the area that is close to the weight you're looking for. What you're interested in, mainly, is the minimum size tire you should use. Once you've determined this minimum, you can ponder how much bigger to go.

For example, let's say that the maximum weight on any one of your tires was 1225 lb. Using the chart, you find that for an inflation pressure of 20 psi, a 9.00-15 with a B load rating and a 10.00R-15 with a C load rating both have a maximum load capacity of 1230 lb. OK, those are the minimum sizes to consider—a 9.00-15B in a bias-ply design, or a 10.00R-15C in a radial.

You can see from the chart that you still have a lot of other choices to make. For instance, all of the following tires have sufficient load capacity for your truck—L78-15B, 10-15B or C, 31.5x10.50-15B or C, 11-15B or C, and so on.

When you do this, you'll probably discover that you don't have to worry about

Before off-roading as we know it today was "invented" this then-new 1941 Plymouth was driven from Detroit to the tip of South America. Before the days of lift kits and off-road suspensions, it got through with only oversized taxicab wheels and tires to increase ground clearance. Photo courtesy Chrysler Historical Collection.

your tires' load capacity. Hardly any off-roader uses tires so small that they're overloaded.

Be More Cautious—You *do* have to be more cautious of overloading the tires when towing a trailer or heavy boat, or if you've got a big camper on your pickup. But for the ordinary off-roader, you'll probably be well over-tired if you settle for the size that pleases your eye.

It's always better to be on the safe side of load capacity. Therefore, weigh your vehicle and check out tire size using the nearby chart just to be sure.

Sidewall Information—If you don't have access to a chart like this one, or if the tire size you're interested in isn't listed, look on the tire sidewall. The tire's maximum load rating is molded into the rubber and will read something like, "Max load 1620 lb at inflation pressure of 32 psi."

MAXIMUM TIRE SIZE

You probably want to know how big you can go on tire size on your particular vehicle. Maximum tire size is dependent upon the available space under the fenders and what size wheels you're going to use.

The "professional" way to determine the largest tire you can use is to mount the tire on the front and cycle the suspension

and steering through their complete ranges. This means moving the vehicle up and down to the limit of the suspension travel in both directions and at all steering angles. To do this, it's necessary to disconnect the springs or torsion bars and use bumper-type jacks to run the body/chassis up and down on the suspension. Not simple, but that's the way the big guys do it.

Check the Chart—If you're willing to settle for something that's less than absolute, maybe the first thing to do is take a serious look at the chart on page 58, "Vehicle & Tire Sizes." This may answer any questions.

If not, or if your vehicle isn't listed there, the basic rule is to use the largest tire that will go under the fender without modifying the sheet metal, outside of nipping off a sharp corner of an inner fender.

Even doing this, you have to be careful. A tire that goes under the fender without interference in the tire shop may not fit nearly so well when you get it off-pavement. What you have to account for is some relative movement between the body and chassis in real-world situations. One of us discovered this years ago when he blithely bolted a set of 9.00-15s onto his near-new 1966 Ford Bronco to replace its wimpy, stock G78-15s.

VEHICLE & TIRE SIZES

Full-Size Pickups	Without Modification	With Minor Modification*
Chevrolet K10 4WD	32/11.50-15	33/12.50-15
Chevrolet K20 4WD	10-16.5	33/12.50-16.5
Dodge W100 4WD	31/10.50-15	32/11.50-15
Dodge W200 4WD	10-16.5	33/12.50-16.5
Ford F150 4WD	32/11.50-15	33/12.50-15
Ford F250 4WD 1973-77	33/12.50-16	36/15-16.5
Ford F250 4WD 1978-up	33/12.50-16.5	34/13-16.5
Jeep J10	31/10.50-15	32/11.50-15
Jeep J20	10-16.5	10-16.5

Full Size Sport Utility	Without Modification	With Minor Modification*
Chevrolet Blazer	32/11.50-15	33/12.50-15
Dodge Ramcharger/ Plymouth Trailduster	31/10.50-15	32/11.50-15
Ford Bronco	31/10.50-15	32/11.50-15
Jeep Wagoneer/Cherokee	H78-15	L78-15
Jeep Cherokee Chief	31/10.50-15	32/11.50-15
Toyota Landcruiser Wagon	L78-15	31/10.50-15

Compact Pickup	Without Modification	With Minor Modification*
Chevrolet LUV 4WD	G78-14	27/9.50-15
Chevrolet S10 4WD	29/9.50-15	30/9.50-15
Dodge D50 4WD	G78-15	27/9.50-15
Ford Ranger 4WD	29/9.50-15	30/9.50-15
Izusu 4WD	215-14	27/9.50-14
Jeep Comanche	225-15	30/9.50-15
Mitsubishi 4WD	G78-15	27/9.50-15
Nissan (Datsun) 4WD	29/9.50-15	30/9.50-15
Toyota 4WD	31/10.50-15	32/11.50-15

Compact Sport Utility	Without Modification	With Minor Modification*
Chevrolet S10 Blazer	235/75-15	30/9.50-15
Ford Bronco II	205/75-15	32/11.50-15
Isuzu Trooper II	225-15	31/10.50-15
Jeep CJ-5	31/10.50-15	Same
Jeep CJ-7	31/10.50-15	Same
Jeep Wagoneer/Cherokee	225-15	31/10.50-15
Mitsubishi Montero	235-15	31/10.50-15
Toyota 4Runner	31/10.50-15	32/11.50-15
Toyota Land Cruiser	L78-15	31/10.50-15

*Minor modification consists of bending or trimming corners of front and/or rear inner fender lips. Does not include enlarging fender cutout or extensive under-fender work.

Note: This information is supplied for guidelines only. Because of variations in tire sizes between manufacturers and vehicle production tolerances, don't bet the farm that every size shown will bolt on without some sweat and strain. (Chart adapted from information supplied courtesy Dick Cepek Co. but blame the authors, not Cepek, for any misfits, please.)

Tire with typical passenger-car type tread does poorly in mud because spaces between tread elements quickly fill up and keep tire from digging into the surface for go-ahead traction.

Hacksaw May Help—The 9.00-15s looked fine sitting in the driveway but once he got the Bronco loaded and off into the dirt, the body was sitting lower and rocking back and forth with the uneven surface. And the rear tires were rubbing on every lurch. Fortunately, he hadn't forgotten his hacksaw, and what he ended up with were the ugliest rear fenders in the world. But they didn't rub anymore.

Later, he duplicated the contour of the front fender openings using a saber saw. Then, he covered the ragged edge with flexible plastic chrome trim. That looked much better. Later still, the first of the fiberglass fender flares became available for the early Bronco and that made it look better still.

So, think it over before you get a tire that's too big to go under the fender without chopping up the body. If there's a fiberglass or molded plastic fender flare available for your vehicle, that's one thing. But if you install tires that extend beyond the bodywork where they'll throw mud all over your end of the county, that's another. And illegal in most states, besides.

Yes, you can attach molded-rubber flares onto your fenders to satisfy legal requirements that the tires be covered. But it's our opinion that they look pretty tacky unless they're applied to a constant-radius opening. One sharp bend and rubber fender flares inevitably end up with a serious case of the uglies.

The best thing you can do is talk to other people with the same vehicle and find out what their experience has been.

TREAD PATTERN

There are three types of tread patterns to consider when picking out your next set of tires: street or highway, mud-and-snow, and special treads.

Highway Tread—A street or highway tread is the type of tread you find on the ordinary, everyday passenger car. These are usually smooth and quiet riding, provide good wear and work well for most ordinary purposes. This tread type may even be OK on off-pavement vehicles, especially with radial tires.

Mud-and-Snow Tread—A tire with a mud-and-snow tread is marked M+S on the sidewall. Its tread pattern is more open than the typical passenger-car tire. Most four-wheel-drive vehicles now come equipped with this type of tread. It offers a good compromise between the smooth, quiet-riding passenger-car tire and the open-block, sometimes noisy and often poor-riding, mud tire.

The M + S mark indicates that the tire is approved for use as a snow tire. One of the recent developments is a mud-and-snow radial designed for year-round use. These are called *all-season radials* and do a reasonably good job in all types of terrain, even off-road.

Specialized Treads—In addition to the dual-purpose mud-and-snow treads that most off-roaders find satisfactory, there are tires with more specialized treads.

A *mud tire* has large, widely spaced tread blocks or lugs. Wide-spaced blocks allow centrifugal force to throw mud off the tire, allowing the blocks to bite into the surface. Obviously, if the spaces between the tread blocks fill up with mud, the tire is unlikely to develop much traction. Some types of mud tires are noisy, hard-riding and treacherous on a hard, wet surface. Other, newer designs use a softer rubber that provides better smooth-surface traction. We suggest that you use a real mud tread only if you're a real mud runner.

Another characteristic of true mud tires is that they're of narrower section width than a typical dual-purpose tire with an M + S tread. In theory, you want an aggressive tread design that will claw the surface to get traction, throw the mud out of the tread and dig down into the mud to get a grip. A larger, flotation-type tire, even if it's self-cleaning, is much less effective in mud because it will "float" on the mud rather than dig down for traction.

There's mud and then there's mud, of course. Some is sloppy and wet, some is slimy but shallow, still other mud may be gummy and bottomless. So, see what tires the experts in your area have found to work best for your particular kind of mud.

Sand Tires—With the development of dual-purpose radials, there's less need for a highly specialized sand tire than before. With these radials, for instance, you can reduce tire pressure and convert them into perfectly acceptable sand tires.

Typical mud-and-snow radial is compromise between passenger tread and pure mud tread. M + S design has wider spaces between elements to provide greater digging power and help tire to be self-cleaning as it spins.

Find the right kind of mud and it will fill up any kind of tread design.

Specialized sand tires are designed with uni-directional "paddles" to help them dig into the soft surface.

There are specialized sand tires, though, and if you're a serious dune runner, you should know about them.

The most highly specialized and most effective sand tires are not approved for highway use. Most of these are designed to be used on dune buggies or other specialized sand travelers. Perhaps the most popular of these are *paddle* tires, with rubber lips running straight across the tread area. Another type is similar but the lips are set at an angle and meet in the middle to make shallow V's, or chevrons. Still another uses angled lips, but these are staggered instead of meeting at the head of the V.

A more all-around type of sand tire has grooves around the circumference but not across the tire face. This type of tire works very well on vehicles that spend a lot of time in the sand, such as off-road boat trailers that are used in sandy areas or in muddy shorelines. And it's also approved for highway use.

These are only some of the special sand tires made available through Dick Cepek, Inc. Photos by James T. Crow.

A dab of anything wet on a suspicious-looking tire blemish will tell you if you have a leak by its bubbles.

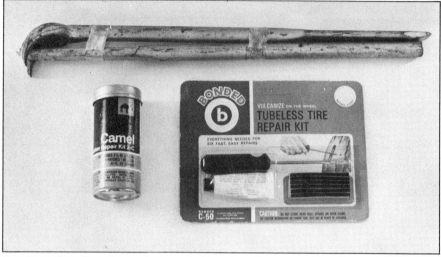

If you're really serious about going boondocking where there may not be a tire repair facility, take your own kit and some tire irons along. Photo by John Lawlor.

Racing Tires—If you're an off-road racer, you may want to use special racing tires. These have very strong casings to provide resistance to damage from rock and a fairly soft rubber compound for good traction. These characteristics add up to a hard ride and rapid tread wear but if you're a racer, you no doubt don't mind that. If you're not a racer, save your money.

Retreads—If you want to spend the minimum number of dollars, the cheapest tires you can put on your vehicle are retreads. If you calculate it, you'll find that retreads will give you more miles per dollar than any other type of tire, including radials.

You should also know that some hardcore owners of lightweight vehicles like Jeep CJs or dune buggies, prefer a retread on a nicely broken-in casing to a stiff new tire that has no give in the sidewalls.

Retreads with off-pavement type treads and in the popular off-road sizes are fairly rare, however. One source we can think of that has 10-15s with an off-road tread is Dick Cepek.

If you can't find a source for off-road retreads in your area, ask about snow-tire retreads. Although not as popular as they were before radials came into general use, many retreaders still offer a snow tire with a more open tread than a typical passenger-car tire. It's also unlikely that your local retreader will have anything larger than an L78-15, but that may be satisfactory for your needs.

If you can find a custom retreader who will put a new tread onto your own casings, all the better. You have at least some assurance that you're starting with a good carcass rather than a rotten one. On the other hand, maybe you'd rather not have new tread attached to those beat-up old tires of yours.

WORDS ABOUT WHEELS

Selecting wheels of the right size is also important. But first, you need to understand wheel nomenclature. Fortunately, wheel-size terminology isn't nearly so confusing as all those tire sizes. For example, a wheel size is usually given in diameter and bead-to-bead rim width. For example, a 15x5.5 wheel designation refers to a 15-in. wheel diameter with a rim that's 5.5-in. bead-to-bead. There may also be a letter designation added at the end like 15x5.5J or 15x5.5JJ. You can safely ignore these letters. They identify the cross-section design of the rim and don't mean anything to the typical off-road buyer.

A much more serious subject is, when do you need to put wider wheels on your off-road vehicle? The simple-minded answer is that you need to do it when the tires you've chosen are too wide for the wheels you already own. The question is, how do you figure this out?

The answer is to use another chart. This one's called "Recommended Wheel Size." For example, if your vehicle is equipped with 15x5.5 wheels and you replace your H78-15 tires with 10-15s, you're going to need wider wheels. If you look on the chart on page 61, you'll

RECOMMENDED WHEEL SIZE FOR VARIOUS TIRES

Tire Size	Wheel Width (in.)	Tire Size	Wheel Width (in.)
L or LR 78-15	6-8	12R-15	8-10
F or FR 60-14	6-8	33 x 12.50-15	8-10
G or GR 60-14	6-1/2-9	14-15	10
L or LR 60-15	7-10	17-15	10
7.9-14	6-7	8.00-16.5	6
8.5R-14	5-1/2-7	8.75-16.5	6.75
27x9.50-14-15	5-1/2-8	9.50-16.5	6.75-8.25
9-15	7-8	10-16.5	8.25
10-15	7-8	10R-16.5	6.75-8.25
10R-15	7-8	12-16.5	8.25-9.75
31x10.50-15	7-9	12R-16.5	8.25-9.75
11-15	8-10	14-16.5	9.75
32x11.50-15	8-10	17-16.5	9.75
12-15	10	14-17.5	10.50

see that the recommended rim width for a 10-15 is 7—8 in.

Rim Width is Important—It's important for tires to be mounted on rims of the correct width. If, for instance, you install a set of 10-15s on your stock 15x5.5 rims, you're asking for trouble. The wide tires installed on narrow rims don't have a wide-enough base and tend to roll under when you turn the steering wheel. This upsets handling, and can cause the front end to make an abrupt tuck-in. It can be very dangerous. The tuck-in problem can be alleviated somewhat by adding air to the tire, but the correct solution is wider rims.

In addition, a wide tire mounted on a narrow rim also tends to accelerate tread wear in the center of the tread because that's where the greatest amount of weight is riding.

Rapid Tread Wear—Conversely, you don't want too wide a rim, either. This can also result in quicker tread wear. Only this time, it will be along the shoulders of the tread, as if the tires were underinflated. But if the rim is much too wide, no amount of overinflation will cause the center of the tread to carry as much weight as the shoulders.

Use the Correct Wheel—When replacing your original wheels, it's important to get replacements that are designed to fit properly. Being practical about it, the simplest solution is to check the wheel manufacturer's application sheets to see what's available for your machine.

If you have an odd-ball vehicle or for some reason this kind of information isn't available, it's a lot more complicated. To start with, it isn't enough just to match up the bolt circle and number of holes. You've also got to worry about such things as *wheel offset* or, more properly, *back dimension*—the distance between the inner edge of the rim and mounting flange. Any attempt to install a wheel with different offset can cause interference problems with the brakes, steering, suspension, or all three. The best solution is to buy a wheel that's engineered to fit your vehicle.

Steel Vs. Alloy Wheels—For serious off-road use, we are inclined to recommend the use of steel wheels because steel will bend before it breaks. If you do something really dumb, like hit a boulder straight on, having a bent wheel is always better than having a broken one.

On the other hand, there's nothing wrong with high-quality cast-aluminum wheels. If you buy alloy wheels conforming to SEMA specs, you'll probably never have a problem. Another vote in favor of alloy wheels has been cast by U.S. vehicle manufacturers. You'll notice that all of them offer a cast-aluminum wheel for their utility vehicles. If they believed that cast-aluminum wheels would result in a single product-liability lawsuit that could be avoided by having steel wheels, believe us, those vehicles would have steel wheels.

In theory, alloy wheels should be bet-

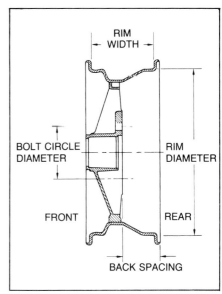

Cross-section of typical wheel for tubeless tire. Notice how rim has "gutter" in center. In dismounting, tire bead has to be forced into this gutter. Otherwise, you'd never get the bead over the rim.

ter because they are lighter than steel wheels and therefore help reduce unsprung weight. Unfortunately, the authors aren't in total accord as to whether this is worth worrying about in a typical four-wheel-drive vehicle. One says, "Phooey, as crude as the suspension is on most four-bys, the virtues to be gained by saving a few pounds by using alloy wheels is a snare and a delusion." The

Spun, stamped or forged aluminum wheels offer resilience of steel wheels without weight penalty. Modular two- or three-piece designs can be taken apart for repair or changing offsets. Photo by Ron Sessions.

Popular with off-roaders are flame-cut steel wheels, as on this Jimmy. Though heavy, thick-section spokes provide good strength for off-road use. Photo courtesy of GMC.

other says, "You're nuts, even a pound per wheel can make a difference!"

On further discussion, however, we came to a compromise that says if you have independent front suspension, using lightweight alloy wheels can make a difference. This is especially true if you can reduce the combined weight of the tire and wheel by at least 10%. This reduces the amount of inertia the suspension has to cope with and can make an appreciable improvement in the ride. But remember, it's the combined weight of the wheel and tire you want to reduce. It does no good to save 10 lb on an alloy wheel if you install a tire that weighs 15-lb more than the one you replace.

Tighten and Retighten—When you put on new wheels of any type, be sure to retighten the lug nuts after driving the vehicle a few miles. This is necessary to seat the lug nuts and assure that the wheels fit tightly against the wheel hub. The rule of thumb is to check them after one hour of operation, then retighten again after three more hours.

We once made the mistake of not retightening the lug nuts on a set of new wheels but were lucky. All that happened was that the left rear wheel worked loose, broke off one stud and buggered up the threads on two more. After retightening the remaining lug nuts, we light-footed it the rest of the way home, worrying whether three studs were enough to keep the wheel in place.

Cast-aluminum wheels reduce unsprung weight and are very rigid—good for off-road stadium racing. However, when a cast wheel hits a rock, it will crack rather than bend. Photo by Tom Monroe.

Another fellow we know wasn't so lucky. He lost a wheel and when he finally came to a halt he was in a ditch with the front wheel of his motorcycle in the cab of his pickup with him.

So tighten and retighten, *several times.* Do it until you're sure the lug nuts aren't going to loosen up any more. If

you have a torque wrench, lug-nut torque should be in the 100 ft-lb range.

TIRE ROTATION

There are several schools of thought about tire rotation. At one extreme are those that say you should rotate your tires every 1000, 2000, 2500, 3000 or

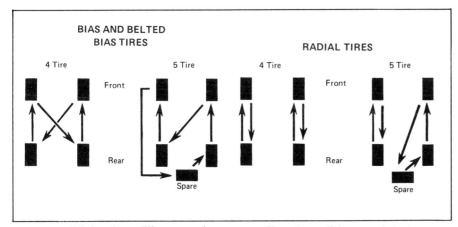

Bias and radial tires have different rotation patterns. Note that radials are switched so they always run in the same direction. Courtesy Rubber Manufacturer's Association.

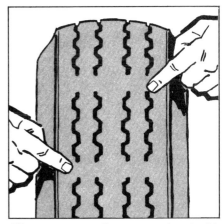

All passenger-car tires are equipped with "wear bars" that become visible when tread is worn to point where tires should be replaced. Courtesy Rubber Manufacturer's Association.

5000 miles. The distance depends on the expert you're talking to. At the other extreme are those who say, "why rotate 'em if you don't need to?"

Manufacturers recommend rotation. And there's a different rotation pattern for bias and belted-bias tires than there is for radials. The important difference is that radials are switched from front to rear on the *same* side so the tire always rolls in the same direction. Bias and belted-bias tires are rotated in an "X" pattern that moves the rear tires to the front but switches the left front to the right rear, and so on.

What's our recommendation? We're inclined to keep an eye on our treads and rotate them if uneven wear patterns show up. Otherwise, we leave them where they are. Also, we always keep them on the same side of the vehicle so they always roll the same direction. And we do this whether they're bias-ply or radials.

Admittedly, however, we'd be somewhat more regular in our rotation habits if we had a vehicle with a solid front axle. With steered wheels on a solid axle, there are gyroscopic effects that result in a tire-wear pattern commonly known as *cupping*. So more frequent rotation may help slow down the wear-out process on solid-front-axle trucks.

TIRE BALANCING

Balancing a big tire on a wide rim is tricky. Not every tire shop can do it. If you find one that can, be good to him. He may be your best friend.

Obviously, with big tires, balance is important for both a good ride and good tire wear. If you have a thumper, you're wearing your tires out unnecessarily.

So get as good a balance job as you can. That means dynamic balance as well as static—bubble—balance. It'll pay off in both ride comfort and longer tire life.

Tire Truing—If you have a tire that can't be balanced because it is out of round—and there are such tires, unfortunately—the problem can sometimes be solved by *truing*. This involves spinning the tire and shaving off the high spot(s) so the tire is perfectly round. This is another pretty specialized task when it involves large, wide tires and you may have to hunt around to find a specialist who can do the job.

If you become sufficiently desperate, you may decide to true the tire yourself. We know a fellow who did this by using a piece of chalk to locate the high spot, then ground it off using a belt sander. The job obviously wasn't perfect, but he at least got it close enough that the tire could be balanced.

Tread Depth—When should you replace your tires? That's easy. Replace them just before they wear out. How can you tell when they're worn out? When there isn't enough tread left on them to be safe. You can tell when this time arrives if you're using passenger-car rated tires

because these have tread-wear indicators built into them. When the tread is worn down to the point where the tire should be replaced, these wear indicators show up as a continuous bar across the tread.

However, light-truck tires aren't required to have built-in tread-wear indicators, so get out your rule. If minimum tread depth is less than 3/32-in., slip on another set.

Because we don't like to push our luck, we usually change tires before the old ones are that nearly worn out. When you're off-pavement, you often ask a lot of your tires. It's better not to start out on tires that are marginal.

LAST WORD ON TIRES

So what's the last word on tires? It's probably this: No matter how much you know about tires or how much you spend on them, it's the way you use them that makes the real difference. We know drivers who go everyplace and get along great even though they use battered old tires on which we'd never leave the driveway. We also know drivers who buy the most expensive skins in the store and have nothing but trouble with them. In other words, you be good to your tires and they'll usually be good to you. And vice versa.

Especially vice versa.

WHEEL WELLS

A wheel well is the housing that in-

Aesthetics play a small role in off-road racing. The front wheel openings of this Isuzu have been opened up to allow for the extreme vertical travel of oversize tires.

Most problems associated with larger-than-standard wheels and tires comes at the lower corners of the wheel openings. Steering angles result in interference between rubber and sheet metal.

Nissan offers removable plastic fender flares. Still fitted with factory rubber and boasting a body-lift kit, this truck has all the wheel-well space it can possibly use.

offered by a manufacturer, with a little extra space for tire chains.

Tire Problems—Of course, most off-roaders want to install larger-than-stock tires and wheels as soon as possible on their 4X4s, and this causes fitting problems. Small import and downsized domestic trucks and utilities are especially tight on wheel-well space due to smaller design parameters.

Original-equipment rubber isn't all that popular with serious off-roaders. Not that there's anything wrong with the really decent radials usually offered nowadays as standard or optional equipment. But oversize, aftermarket wheels and tires with increased diameters and wider section widths can cause interference problems that may require a trip to a body and paint shop. Not many do-it-yourselfers are brave enough to take tin snips to shiny new sheet metal.

Factory Solutions—The current Nissan 4X4s have a nice feature that no one else seems to have thought about. To keep their factory-supplied tires from looking lost in out-sized fender openings, they surround the front cutouts with bolt-on flexible flares. These are an option and if you order a new Nissan with the thought of adding bigger tires later, simply omit the flares from your order list. But if you already own one, you can remove them in a matter of minutes and find openings sufficiently large to house any tires within reason.

Fender Trimming—In this chapter, you've already read how to determine the largest (tallest and widest) tires that will fit your vehicle without making modifications. Beyond this, fender and possibly fire-wall (toeboard) trimming is in order unless you'd rather opt for a suspension or body-lift kit, either of which will elevate the body above the tires and provide additional wheel-well clearance. Or, for a limited number of 4X4 makes and models, you can buy a set of fiberglass fenders with ready-made oversize openings.

Some off-roaders, more interested in navigating the outback than in aesthetics, will simply cut away whatever parts of the fenders they need to and let it go at that. Others, with respect for appearance, will run narrow plastic edging around the trimmed fender opening to

trudes into the body of a vehicle to enclose the wheels, tires, and the brake and suspension components hidden behind them. The opening through which you see the tire and wheel is called, logically enough, the wheel cutout or fender opening. These combine to serve a purpose: to prevent mud, sand and water from spraying up from the tires and back along the sides of a vehicle and also, in front, to isolate the engine compartment from road muck. Openings in the front fenders

are usually larger than the diameter of the tires to allow them to steer to right or left. Rear fender openings generally conform more closely to the size of the tires or even partly conceal them, depending upon the whim of the stylist who shaped them in the first place.

The size of a wheel well depends upon the clearance allowed by the engineers for full suspension travel and, in front, full steering lock. They are sized to use the largest optionally available tires

But in regions of mild year-round weather, tire/fender clearance can be increased on some vehicles by removing the inner liner, snipping away some sheet metal, and adding fender lips.

Wheel-well liners guard against corrosion. Don't even think of removing them to help tire clearance if you live where roads are salted in winter.

hide the raw metal edge. The trouble here is that large tires on wide-base rims often extend outside the fender openings which will spray mud back along the vehicle. And most states have laws requiring that tires be kept within the confines of the body.

Fender Kits—The answer, of course, is to add what's known as a fender kit. Basically, there are three types of commercially available fender kits. *Fender flares* are molded from plastic and can be metal-screwed or pop-riveted in place. Some are stamped steel, which can also be screwed or riveted on. Appearance-conscious folks will weld on the flares then finish off the seams and repaint the fenders so the result looks factory-made. Available for most popular makes, fender flares are more of an appearance item than anything else. They do keep road junk off the body sides, but don't provide more tire clearance.

For extra tire clearance, you need *fender cutouts*. These are molded or stamped for specific vehicles after the fender openings have been enlarged from a supplied pattern or measurements. Like flares, cutouts are riveted or screwed in place after the fender opening has been trimmed. Cutouts also keep crud off the body.

Finally, there are *fender lips,* a flexible, molded plastic that conforms to any size fender cutout you need. Some can be painted to match the vehicle, but most are black so you can install them as-is regardless of the vehicle's paint scheme. Fender lips look best when the opening has no abrupt changes in radius. Many off-road vehicles have somewhat rectangular wheel openings. The problem encountered here is that, wherever it makes a sharper turn, the outer edge of the lip changes contour, sticks out more and gives a crude appearance.

An Example—Typical of wheel-opening problems with small 4X4 trucks is one faced by the owner of a Mitsubishi pickup. He wanted to fit 30-in. tall 9.50-15s in place of 28-in. G78-15s. The factory wheels had a 4-in. *offset*—the measurement between the inside face of the wheel center and the inner tire bead. His new ones had a 3-in. offset. With an additional rim width of 2.5 in. and 1-in. less offset, the outer edge of the new tires was 3-1/2-in. farther outboard. And the 2-in. greater diameter of the new tires caused them to rub on the front and rear lower corners of the front fenders at full lock. Suspension up-travel—jounce— was also limited by the new, taller tires.

He decided to add a set of fender lips after enlarging the wheel openings. Cycling the front suspension with a new wheel/tire in place and the torsion bar temporarily disconnected showed that the opening had to be increased 2 in. around the perimeter of most of the opening, tapering to 3 in. at the lower edges. As with many other trucks, this truck had a plastic inner fender liner which had to be removed to accommodate the taller tire. For corrosion protection, we recommend that you leave the liner in if at all possible. Mud and sand thrown up by the tires gets packed into every nook and cranny of the linerless inner fender and cowl, where it holds moisture and contributes to corrosion. The Mitsubishi owner lives in a warm, dry climate where the roads are *not* salted in winter, so he figured he could get by without the front liners.

A wide strip of masking tape was put around the wheel opening to serve two purposes: to use for drawing the new shape of the opening with a grease pencil, and to protect the paint from scratches by the saber saw used for cutting. The electric saw made quick work of the metal. The tape was peeled off and the fender lip was mounted after drilling screw holes. Pop-rivets would also have done the job, but the owner used screws in case the lips would have to be removed later on. Of course, the points of the screws were ground off so they wouldn't cut the tires.

And that was that. The job required a little more than an hour, no repainting

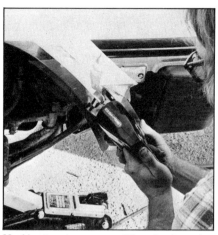

Masking tape is run around the wheel opening and the new shape of the opening is sketched on it. Tape also protects paint from scratches as saber saw is used to trim away metal.

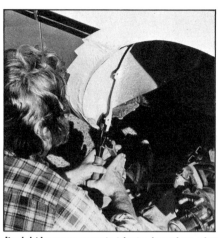

It might be necessary to trim toeboard area for clearance at full-lock steering.

Soft fender lips can be metal-screwed or pop-riveted around perimeter of opening.

Lip finishes off rough-cut edge of wheel opening and prevents mud and grime from oversize tires from streaking the body sides.

Screw-on fender flares from Bushwacker come with gloss-black or gloss-white finish. Photo courtesy of Bushwacker.

was necessary (the lips are black, against fenders of red and white) and the end effect is both pleasing and effective.

Rear Fenders—There is usually no problem with rear-fender openings because there is no steering to contend with. However, *really* big tires might rub on something. The same treatment given the front fenders will solve any problems with the rear ones. Many off-roaders use fender flares, cutouts or lips in the rear to match the front whether they need them there or not.

To the Point—Don't be intimidated by your wheel wells and fender openings if they interfere with the oversize rubber you want to install. None of the three fender kits absolutely require repainting the sheet metal—a possibly expensive proposition.

It doesn't take a pro to snip away a little metal and add one of the fender kits. Naturally, the *really big* rubber you see under (and outside of) the super-high-lift and "monster" trucks has required some heavy-duty metal surgery, among other things. But for the average off-roader who's only after ground-gripping traction and flotation from aftermarket tires, a fender kit is the way to go.

Jacks & Air Pumps

AIR PUMPS

One thing that the off-roader will eventually need is compressed air. And he'll usually discover this when far away from a service station. Tires partially deflated for driving through sand, for example, or a flat fixed beside the trail, need street inflation pressure when you head home. Low tires, remember, can suffer heat buildup and possible tread separation.

And there are always things in a weekender's kit of goodies that need air, like a raft or inflatable boat, air mattresses, various kinds of balls, and so forth. It's also easier to blow grit out of your distributor or clean an air filter with a source of compressed air instead of using your lungs. And on more than one occasion, a four-wheeler whose fuel-pump went belly up in downtown nowhere, jury-rigged a fuel line to bypass the pump. He went merrily on his way by pressurizing his gas tank from time to time with compressed air.

If you carry your own compressed air, life will be a whole lot easier. You'll also become the most popular off-roader in your group if you can supply air to friends who need it.

Ways & Means—There are several ways to have compressed air. One is to get an air-transfer hose, also known as a "borrower" or "thief," with valve-stem fittings on each end. With it, air can be piped from a fully inflated tire to another that's gone flat. Or the spare tire can be overinflated so you can bring the other four to at least near their recommended street pressures after they've been aired-down.

Another way is to carry a pressurized air tank. These should be made of heavy-walled steel, of course, to withstand high internal pressures. You can buy these new in auto-parts stores, usually with a 0-200-psi gage, or convert a large R-2 refrigerant canister. We've seen scuba diving tanks used, but this is not recommended. Dive shops often fill scuba

Air pumps for the off-roader vary from old-fashioned but practical bicycle pump (right) to sparkplug pump (lower left), which screws into a vacated sparkplug hole. The rest are electric pumps which plug into a cigarette-lighter receptacle.

tanks up to 2500 psi, the sudden release of which would turn a tank into a rocket. These are dangerous in the rough stuff, especially if a tank were to get loose and lose a valve. And you don't want a fully inflated tank sitting out in the sun in the heat of summer.

The trouble with all of these methods is that, first, you have to visit a service station or garage to get air. Many places are charging for this service now. Then there's the limited air supply and when it's gone, or when the pressure in your spare falls to the same level as the tire you're trying to reinflate, there ain't no more.

So an air pump is the best solution and there are several types. There are electric pumps that plug into a cigarette lighter socket or clip to the battery terminals. Some small industrial pumps can be adapted to run off your engine's crankshaft through a pulley and belt arrangement. And there's one ingenious device

that, when threaded into a sparkplug hole, uses the pumping ability of that cylinder to deliver compressed air while the engine idles. Finally, there are mechanical pumps, like the old-fashioned bicycle pump, or foot-operated bellows used for inflating fabric boats and rafts. However, mechanical pumps require physical exercise—perhaps more exercise than you bargained for.

Electric Pumps—There is a wide choice of electric air pumps available. Prices may vary widely. Most off-road or recreational equipment shops carry one or more brands, and some larger auto-parts stores also sell them. Often, the choice is more a matter of what brands are available in your area, but here's a rundown on some of them anyway.

Coleman Co., Wichita, KS 67214, has two models. Their 175 has an in-line pressure gage, a carrying case, a one-year warranty and includes, besides a

67

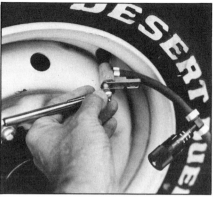

Pump has in-line pressure pre-selector to tell you when desired psi has been reached. Also note clip-on air chuck.

Maximum pressure a pump can achieve is not as important as volume of air it can produce.

Electric pump is chugging its little heart out and pressure has climbed to 40 psi on gage. Pumps have notoriously short air hoses but cords are sufficiently long to let pump be carried from tire to tire.

valve-stem chuck, a fitting for sports balls and other inflatables. Then there's the 150 model with its own on-off switch, an in-line gage, an air chuck for tires and other fittings.

Interdynamics, Brooklyn, NY 11232 offers its Model GEC-17 in a self-contained carrying case and has a novel, adjustable pop-up to tell you when a pre-selected pressure has been reached. It includes a tire chuck and other fittings for various "toys" including rafts. Their Model 105 has a gage tap for checking pressure without removing the air hose, a tire chuck and other fittings. It, too, comes in a carrying case.

Intercompressor, Inc., Culver City, CA 90230, gives a five-year warranty with their Model TI-8. It has a built-in pressure gage, a 15-ft power cord, a 3-ft air hose and several air chucks.

Universal Security Instruments, Inc., Owing Mills, MD 21117, sells its ingeniously designed Model AA 10-33 with a sports needle and other chucks. It's low-priced, but probably designed more for an occasional flat tire repair than the repeated airing-up of off-road tires.

Dick Cepek, Inc., Carson, CA 90746, sells the Auto-Flator with a 15-ft cord, an in-line on-off switch, a short air hose, a built-in pressure gage, a clip-on air chuck and other end fittings.

What to Watch For—Prices for electric compressors vary from about $15 to $40 and, as with so many other things, you usually get what you pay for. If a store offers alternate models, it might be safest to opt for the more expensive one.

Electric pumps are driven by small 12-volt motors that can overheat with extended use. But there's no way to judge how the one you choose will act until you buy and try it. However, you might ask for a clue from a friend. Pump makers like to boast about the maximum pressures their units will produce, some ranging as high as 200 psi, but averaging closer to 150 psi. Be advised that not many will reach their advertised pressures even after an hour's running, if at all.

But pressure is not really the major concern, and most electric pumps can handle the demands of a tire. What's more important is the *volume* of air a pump will deliver. Volume translates to how long you have to sit there while a pump chuffs its little heart out trying to air-up all four of your 10.50-15s.

Pumping Test—Not long ago, we devised a test of several electric air pumps for a magazine article. Of the brands checked, the Intercompressor Model TI-8 pumped the greatest volume, a little over one cubic foot per minute (cfm). A

completely flat GR78-15 tire was inflated to 24 psi in a shade over four minutes, and a 10-15LT in exactly eight minutes. The other pumps used in the comparison did the same thing with the smaller tire in up to 10 minutes, and with the larger tire in up to 15-1/2 minutes.

As far as pressure went, only the Coleman 175 reached the 175 psi claimed for it, but it took 1-1/2 hours to get there. One with a claimed pressure maximum of 105 psi made it to only 46 psi before its motor overheated. Another reached 75 psi, though it was rated to 150 psi. The Inter TI-8 mentioned above managed 180 psi after an hour, then rose slowly toward 185 psi until we grew tired listening to it struggle.

So when you shop for a pump, look for a unit with a high volume rating or take the advice of a friend.

Missing from that test was an electric pump introduced later. It is the Dick Cepek, Inc., Auto-Flator, Model DC-227. We timed it as it inflated a completely flat G78-15 to 30 psi, a process which required seven minutes, though its label said it should have taken eight.

Power—Electric pumps of the kind we've been discussing require quite a bit of electrical power and can deflate a battery as quickly as they can inflate your rubber ducky. When using a pump, let the engine idle so the alternator will help keep pace with demand. Also, there should be a fuse in the wiring system, should the pump motor go haywire (most pumps don't have their own fuse but the

Auto-Flator from Dick Cepek, Inc., was adapted to permanent mounting with addition of self-coiling hose, fittings and switches.

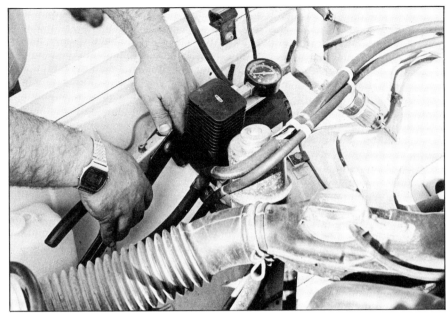

Pump was mounted on top of the right front fender well and secured with pop-rivets.

cigarette-lighter circuit does). But be sure the fuse is rated for at least 10 amps—15 amps is better.

Permanent Installation—Electric air pumps are small enough to hold in one hand and are easy to stow in a vehicle, especially pumps with their own carrying cases. But they do have a habit of working their way under your camping equipment and often require considerable digging to find—usually when you want it in a hurry.

So you might want to consider mounting one permanently. A friend of ours did just this using a Cepek Auto-Flator for his imported pickup. We happened to be standing by when he did this and here's how it went:

Mounting—Small pickups offer very limited space for mounting anything. Installing the pump in the bed seemed likely to encourage pilferage, so it was decided to mount it on top of the right front fender well, under the hood and away from the exhaust system. Electric pumps and compressed air generate enough heat of their own. Because the hood had to be open to use the pump in this location, fresh air could waft over it while it was doing its thing.

The Auto-Flator was not designed to be permanently mounted, and while it stands on little feet, it was deemed too awkward to drill through them and use hold-down screws. So, four small U-shaped brackets were fabricated from aluminum scrap to go around the feet. Holes were drilled through the brackets and into the fender sheet metal for 1/8-in. pop-rivets. Air pumps vibrate when running and it seemed better to rivet it in place than use sheet-metal screws that might loosen.

That part of the installation took only 20 minutes. More time-consuming was plumbing a new air hose and wiring the pump into the truck's electrical system.

The power cord from the pump was snipped off close to the pump and the air hose, connected with a crimped-on fitting that couldn't be unscrewed, and was cut to leave a 6-in. stub. A quick-disconnect coupler was fitted to the stubby hose and secured with a screw-type clamp. This seemed better than having a single air hose long enough to reach all of the truck's tires, and having to coil it up and store it under the hood. Our friend used a 25-ft, self-coiling air hose purchased at an auto-parts store, fitted it with the other half of the coupler, and put a lock-on air chuck on the other end of the hose. He carries it around under the front seat.

Wire of the same gage as the original power cord was spliced onto the pump wires, one leading to ground under a nearby fender bolt. The other wire was fed through a grommeted hole in the fire wall and lead to an on-off rocker switch mounted under the dash near the steering column. The other side of the switch was connected to a hot terminal on the fuse panel through an in-line fuse. And that's all there was to it.

The Auto-Flator had cost $29.95 but the self-coiling air hose, wire and various other fittings added another $26. Our friend feels that the convenience is worth the price. The pump will not tempt vandals as long as the hood is shut.

The Chuffer—The G.H. Meiser & Co., Posen, IL 60469, is the manufacturer of the Imperial sparkplug pump. During the authors' pump comparison already noted, the "chuffer," as this little gem is known, was not compared head-to-head against the electric pumps because its operation is different and some labor is involved in using it. It was, though, second fastest at inflating the flat GR78-15 tire to 24 psi (in slightly more than five minutes) and was the champ in blowing up the 10-15LT in under seven minutes.

The unit comes with assorted adapters that screw into a sparkplug hole. If you

An on-board compressor is also a good way to win friends and influence young ladies.

In utility vehicle, pump can be permanently mounted in out of the way place, such as in front of rear wheel well on this Jeep CJ.

get one, be sure one of the supplied adapters fits your engine or buy the correct one separately before you head for the great beyond. There is some inconvenience connecting a chuffer due to the maze of plumbing, wires and other impediments to sparkplug access on many engines. And if the engine was recently running, it will be hot enough to burn you if you aren't careful.

Once the pump is secured to a plug hole, start the engine but *don't run it above an idle*. The engine is operating on one less cylinder and high rpm can cause damage.

Engine compression works a diaphragm in the pump body which, in turn, pumps *fresh* air through the hose, *not* unfired fuel vapor as you might suspect. The supply hose will reach any of the vehicle's tires and it has an in-line pressure gage you can watch as the pump chugs along. The unit has a two-year warranty and is generally less expensive than good electric pumps.

While most off-roaders we know who use chuffers swear by them, there is one ham-fisted acquaintance who, not once but several times, crossthreaded a sparkplug and its hole. He now carries a spare plug and a thread-chaser in his toolbox.

JACKS

We have this theory that most vehicle manufacturers employ one special engineer to do nothing but design jacks. He works long and hard, saving the company as much money as possible by designing jacks that are so light-duty that they can be used only four or five times before they fail. The jacks are designed to lift a vehicle just high enough to change a flat—providing it's done in the home driveway or on a paved road. The engineer is likely so wrapped up in his job that he's never taken the time to go off-roading where jacks are a way of life. And he's probably never had to change a flat or been stuck in the back country.

Market researchers report that the first aftermarket equipment the typical buyer of an off-road vehicle purchases is a set of oversize wheels and tires. As soon as they're installed, it's a sure bet he or she will go looking for the worst dirt road or the softest sand just to see how much better the new tires work. Few of these eager beavers check if the standard jack that came with their vehicle will lift the rig high enough to remove a flat, let alone check if the fully inflated spare will go back on.

Have you ever had this happen to you?

We have and it's mighty annoying. A solution that will sometimes work is to dig a hole to provide clearance for the tire. Or, you can lower the vehicle back onto the flat tire, put a block under the jack base, then jack it up again. The permanent solution is to buy a real jack, of course, one with sufficient lift to do the job.

Standard Jacks—These are found held in place by bracketry under the hood, behind or under a seat, or fastened in place with a wingnut which may also secure the spare tire, jack handle and lug wrench. Original-equipment jacks come in many types and sizes, nearly all of them mechanical. A proper hydraulic jack is simply too expensive for most manufacturers to install in every car and truck.

Scissors jacks work with a long threaded bar that draws the ends of pivoted arms together, thereby creating the lift. To work one, insert the hooked end of a spindly, jointed cranking handle to the threaded bar and turn, and turn, and turn it until the jack pad is up against the axle or suspension part. Then you have to turn it more to raise the wheel off the ground. You have to get down on your knees to do this and the jack will often tip

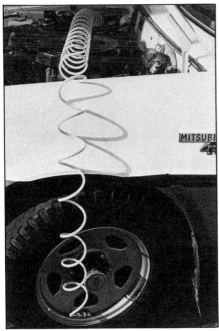

With quick-disconnect fitting to store self-coiling air hose remotely, it's a cinch to air-up the tires without having to dig the pump out from under the camping equipment.

There are jacks for all occasions, of many types, and there are good ones and bad ones. One of the best to take off-roading is the High-Lift jack which can lift to a full 38 in.

over a few times until you get it high enough to do any good.

Vertical worm-screw jacks also work with a wiggly long handle. Typically, one goes under the axle and you must crank, and crank, and crank it to raise the jack head. It's even more prone to falling on its side than the scissors jack. And it's likely that the cranking handle will become disconnected forcing you to fish the jack out and start over. Once it's finally up to where it belongs, it'll raise a tire an inch or so above the surface and that's all.

Most other factory jacks are also mechanical, including the old-fashioned (and rarely seen any more) ratchet-type bumper jack. Because these must lift a vehicle beyond the droop of its suspension in order to raise a wheel off the surface, they are a good step toward a proper off-road jack. Unfortunately, though, they will seldom rise quite high enough to be of value if the vehicle is sporting big off-road tires.

VW-Type Jacks—Incidentally, some vehicles (like Volkswagens, among others) are equipped with reinforced sockets on the body into which goes a specially designed jack head. These usually work pretty well, on Volkswagens that is, as long as you don't leave the pavement or use oversize tires. If your off-roader has this type of jacking system, you'll need to devise an alternate jacking system with increased lift. Also, the special sockets welded onto the body tend to get themselves bent out of shape on rocks and other obstacles. And when that happens, you're out of business if you don't have some other way of jacking up the sucker.

Good Jacks—But we're not here to complain so much about poor jacks, but to tell you about good jacks. There are many uses for a quality accessory jack off-road, and changing a tire is only one of them. While most stock jacks are intended to survive only a handful of tire changes during their lifetimes, an off-roader might have to use his jack a dozen times or more just to get out of a single situation. Or, he might have to elevate his vehicle extremely high to work it free of an offending boulder or something

else on which it has become high-centered.

There may also be an occasional off-road need for a specialized piece of equipment, such as a really strong spreading device or a huge clamp. A proper jack can do things of this nature and more. Other uses might be jacking a bent fender away from a tire, using it as a come-along when you're stuck, convincing a heavy fallen log off the trail, even stretching barbed wire or chain-link fencing for repairs. Where a lot of pulling or pushing force is needed, a good jack is the best way to get it.

There are a number of suitable off-road jacks on the market. While we won't try to describe or even list them all, there is one mechanical and one hydraulic jack that seem to be especially outstanding for off-road use.

High-Lift Jack—This is a mechanical bumper jack produced by the High-Lift Jack Company of Bloomfield, Indiana 47424. It's just the opposite of a wimpy stock jack. It's massive, heavy and even a little unwieldy. But, oh boy, does it work! Referred to also as a sheepherder's or railroad jack, it was probably designed more for farm or industrial use than for automotive applications. In fact, we had occasion to shop for one in a small midwestern town and while the local off-road shop had never heard of such a thing, we found one at a farm-implement outlet on the next block.

The High-Lift stands 48-in. tall and provides 38 in. of lift. It weighs approximately 30 lb, has a 29-in. handle for good leverage and it will raise a whopping 7000 lb. It will start its lift only 4.5-in. off the ground, which is great if you're deeply mired in mud or sand. (Obviously, the standard under-axle jack wouldn't be useful here at all.) Although if you're not axle-deep in something soft or caught in a hole, you might have to use up 15—20 in. of the High-Lift's lifting potential to get the hook up to the bumper. But there's plenty of lift left to get the vehicle above the droop of the suspension and a tire well off the ground.

The current price of a High-Lift is about $50, but one will last a lifetime. Our own High-Lift has survived hundreds of uses during the 12 years we've owned it and it has paid for itself many

One of the many attributes of the High-Lift is that it can go to work only 4.5 in. off the ground.

This has nothing to do with jacking. It's a cross-bed toolbox usually seen in commercial trucks.

In this case, though, the toolbox houses a High-Lift jack, secured by a stud and wingnut, among other off-roading necessities.

times over. Another good feature is that, unlike most accessories you'll eventually buy for your rig, this one can be transferred from any make or type of vehicle to any other.

The High-Lift can also be put to use as a come-along, for forcing things apart or squeezing them back together. Instructions with the jack show you how to rig it to do these things and many more. The jack is also useful for lifting either end of a high-centered truck, then pushing the jack sideways so the vehicle falls off a foot or more to either side of where it was stuck. This can be repeated if you want to shift your rig a long distance because of disagreeable terrain.

The High-Lift does have a few drawbacks, however, and which are mentioned just so you won't be disappointed. It is heavy, long and awkward when it comes time to stow one in a vehicle. The pad the jack stands on is too small to be used in soft ground. It's hard to pack so it doesn't rattle, get in the way, bang dents in the sheet metal, or eat holes in the upholstery.

Solutions—Quite a few suggestions have been advanced to answer the storage problems presented by toting a High-Lift. Wrapping its ends in burlap or scraps of carpeting will protect whatever the jack comes in contact with. This way, it's safe to store one under or behind a seat. Or you can clamp or bolt it down in a pickup bed, the cargo compartment of a utility vehicle, or somewhere out of the way in a trunk. Dick Cepek, Inc., sells a protective sleeve to encase the High-Lift, and they also have a special Loc-Rack which can be bolted to any flat surface

and the jack secured to it. We've seen them retained to flooring or other paneling with light U-bolts, J-hooks or threaded rod and secured with wingnuts. Bungee cords will also hold one down. Mounts can be made to carry one above or behind a bumper. One inventive friend has his bolted directly to the frame under the driver's door.

Finally, a slab of plywood or piece of planking carried wherever you go can be put under the base of the jack so it won't disappear from sight when you use it on soft ground.

The High-Lift works through a pair of locking pins that progress along a series of holes in the upright leg as the handle is pumped up and down. When sand or other grit gets into these exposed works, the jack may not function. Periodic cleaning, especially after use, and liberal doses of WD-40 or other spray lubricant are advised. Take care of this jack and it will serve you well. You'll wonder how in the world you ever got along without it.

Hydraulic Jacks—Another rugged bumper jack that we've come to love is a hydraulic unit produced by the Walker Company of Racine, Wisconsin 53402. It has a lifting capacity of 3000 lb, less than half that of the High-Lift, but it will raise one corner of just about any off-road vehicle. And we specify *one corner* because any type of bumper jack should only be used as near as possible to the brackets that tie the bumper onto the frame. **Don't ever try raising a vehicle by the center of the bumper** because it's not designed to handle that kind of a load.

The Walker jack is only 21-in. tall when compressed but goes up to 41 in. when fully raised. The useful lifting capacity, therefore, seems to be 20 in., but it will do more than this.

The jack's lift comes from a vertical ram that moves upward as you work the handle up and down. It glides downward by opening a valve in the jack's base. The hook that catches onto the bumper is one end of a flexible roller-type chain resembling a sturdy motorcycle chain. It's about 16-in. long and the other end is pinned near the top of the ram. The pin doesn't hold the vehicle's weight, however. Three of the chain's links lock into recesses atop the ram and these take all the strain. You can drop any three adjoining links into the holes; therefore, the length of the chain and height of the bumper hook are adjustable. This lets the hook down to within 5 in. of the ground to begin a lift, or start it as high as 19-in. up. In either case, the Walker jack will provide a useful 20 in. of lift because the hook can be attached to the bumper before any of the lifting potential is used up.

Another advantage of the Walker jack is that it can be used in two stages, providing you can securely and safely prop up the vehicle when it's lifted half-way up. If the vehicle is mired down, you can hook onto the bumper 5 in. from the ground. Jack it up until you've reached the 20 in. of upward travel. Prop the vehicle there, relax the jack, rearrange the chain links and start over. Now you can go up another 20 in. for a total lift of 40 in., nearly twice the height of the jack itself.

The Walker jack is not cheap, but will probably outlast even you. It retails in the neighborhood of $100, but if you find yourself in a situation where only the Walker jack will get you out, it's worth every penny.

Bumper Cautions—Unfortunately, the bumpers on a good many of the current off-road vehicles aren't designed for use with a bumper-type jack. With such bumpers, a jack may work if suitably

Walker hydraulic-jack bumper-hook's height can be easily adjusted without losing lifting capacity. Chain links drop into recesses and hook can start to lift anywhere from five to 19-in. above ground.

Hydraulic under-axle bottle jack only takes a few inches of lift to raise a wheel and does not pose the falling-over problem of a bumper jack.

padded with a chunk of heavy plywood or a 2x4 between the jack's hook and the lower edge of the bumper. Otherwise, the jack may leave a nasty crimp in the flimsy piece of stamped sheet metal that passes for today's bumpers. Or, it can put a permanent and unsightly twist into the whole thing.

With thin-gage original-equipment bumpers like these, you *might* be better off with an under-axle jack, even though they aren't as convenient to use as bumper jacks and, in fact, may be downright difficult to use. This is especially true if you're already down to the axle in gumbo, which is why properly equipped off-roaders always carry a shovel.

Under-Axle Jacks—Though we've managed to pretty well discredit the standard under-axle jack, it's only because of its ill-devised and skimpy construction rather than its true usefulness in certain situations. A heavy-duty under-axle jack can be a boon if you want to lift a wheel or one corner of a vehicle without letting the suspension sag to full rebound. There's still the matter of working down on your hands and knees, but if

it gets you unstuck....

A hydraulic axle jack is best for under-axle work, but don't rush out and buy a floor jack. These have steel wheels that refuse to work in dirt and sand. Good ones are expensive and most are extremely heavy and awkward to carry.

Get a vertical or "bottle" jack instead. One with a capacity of 1500 lb is adequate for light use, though anything up to 3000 lb would be a better choice. Find one that collapses to 7—8-in. of height and rises to 12—15 in. Prices vary considerably for good hydraulic jacks. Starting at around $30, you can buy a bottle jack that will not leak internally when laid on its side and render itself useless when it comes time to use it. Any type of jack is most easily carried and stored horizontally. Check with the salesperson or look for a label stating the jack is to be stored in a laid-down position.

Jack Safety—As with any piece of automotive equipment, safety should always be observed when using a jack. **Do not reach, crawl or work under a vehicle that is supported only by a jack.** To do any under-vehicle maintenance or repair, *always* use sturdy jack stands under the axles, frame or secure parts of the suspension. And always stand them on concrete or another paved surface when available. Use thick planking or heavy plywood under jack stands if you're forced to work in dirt.

Mechanical or hydraulic, bumper or axle jacks used alone can tip, fail or otherwise let a vehicle down with a crash. You don't want to be underneath when it falls. When using jack stands, raise the vehicle to the desired height, place two jack stands under solid parts of the chassis, then relax the jack until the strain is off of it. Only now is it safe to crawl under.

If an older hydraulic jack tends to creep downward instead of staying up where you want it, the internal valves or seals are leaking. Take the jack back where you bought it for service, or find a specialty shop listed in the *Yellow Pages* that repairs hydraulic equipment.

Finally, after you've procured the off-roader's jack of your dreams and devised a way to carry it, don't simply throw that much-maligned, stock jack away. Keep it aboard. It may someday prove itself useful as a backup.

Wood—We've mentioned carrying wood along when you go off-roading. You can use it as a base under a bumper jack and to prevent bending a bumper. Get a piece of plywood 1/2—3/4-in. thick and about 12-in. square or a foot-long length of 1x12. These will provide a firm base for any type of jack—none we've ever seen has a base that won't tend to disappear under sand or other soft terrain when the vehicle's weight is put on it—whether it's mechanical or hydraulic, a bumper-type or under-axle.

Also, a couple of 2x4s may be handy for when you need some extra lift or want to block a wheel to keep the vehicle from rolling. If you're mired to the axles, you might need the extra height from a piece of wood to enable your jack to reach the frame.

Lug Wrenches—Almost as wimpy as stock jacks are the lug wrenches that accompany them. These often double as a

This bottle jack is only 7-in. high when depressed, but raises to 15 in. through its two-stage ram. Any jack, mechanical or hydraulic, should be placed on a wide, firm base, regardless of the ground underneath. Always carry a chunk of wood when off-roading.

Cross-bed toolbox carries more than that High-Lift jack. A four-way, or star, wrench beats stock lug wrench by a mile, and this one is held by clips to keep it from rattling or sliding around. Ever-necessary shovel is held by a stud and wingnut.

jack handle, usually a bent metal bar with a hex-shaped socket formed at one end and sharpened like a chisel at the other for prying off hubcaps. Few are sufficiently long to provide good leverage for removing a lug nut that may have been installed with an air wrench. And, aftermarket wheels often have special lug nuts that the standard tool doesn't fit.

Every off-roader should carry a fully outfitted toolbox. In it should be a thin-wall deep socket to fit your particular lug nuts and a breaker bar to remove and replace the nuts. But far more versatile is the *four-way,* or *star,* wrench with four arms, each ending in a socket of a different size. You won't have four sizes of lug nuts on your truck, of course, so mark the appropriate one with paint or, better yet, a wrap of tape so you can feel it in the dark. This will eliminate having to try several ends of the wrench before coming up with the right one. The other three socket ends may come in handy someday

if you need to apply real force to a stubborn bolt somewhere on your vehicle. Possibly, you'll be able to help out a fellow off-roader who didn't have the foresight to equip himself with a star wrench like you did.

Even with a proper star-type or other form of lug wrench, you may still come out on the short end when it comes to leverage. This is especially true if the lugs were run down with an air wrench as already mentioned or if they were cross-threaded by the same ham-fisted tire buster. It'll simplify your life and probably save your back if you have a 2-ft length of metal pipe to slide over your lug wrench handle and break the nut loose. Or, lacking that, if you have a lug nut that won't budge, use the handle off your High-Lift jack to give the extra leverage you need.

There's another use for a star wrench worth mentioning. Use it to put under the base of your jack if you forgot to bring along a piece of wood. Laid flat on the ground, it will keep the jack base from sinking out of sight. Don't forget, though, to loosen the lug nuts before putting the wrench under the jack, and make sure to firmly hand-tighten the nuts before you let the jack down to free the wrench for the final tightening. Four-way wheel wrenches are available at auto-parts stores and tool outlets. Look for one with the longest arms so you'll have the leverage when you need it.

Winches & Winchery

A winch can add that last bit of go-anywhere ability and get you back from *anywhere* as well. If you've drowned the engine, are all alone and the creek is rising, no problem. Just hook onto a tree or rock and winch yourself out. Photo courtesy of Warn Industries.

The first question you must answer for yourself is if you really need a winch. True, if you only use it once and it saves you from having to make that long walk, it'll be worth it. It's also fairly easy to convince yourself that you'll get a lot more use out of it than you really will.

However, like driving lights and high-rise suspension systems, we're of the opinion that the primary function of 94.3% of all winches is cosmetic. The owner of the vehicle likes that go-anywhere, do-anything look. There's a lot of ego satisfaction in that.

Another basic truth about winches is that they're inevitably used more to help get some other poor fool out of trouble than of value in extricating the winch owner from some predicament.

Admittedly, the authors have different opinions on this subject. One has a winch on his 4WD, takes great pride in it, uses it often, wouldn't be without it and eagerly looks forward to having somebody get stuck so he can unreel his cable and charge to the rescue.

The other author admits to having had a winch at one time, but that was three vehicles ago and he used it exactly twice in three years—each time to pull somebody else out of trouble. After that experience, he came to the conclusion that he'd much rather have a friend with a winch than have one himself.

Nevertheless, the realistic way to think of a winch is as a labor-saving device. When you get yourself good and stuck and you don't have a winch, you're in for

some hard labor. Getting unstuck gives you the opportunity of spending quite a bit of time in close contact with Mother Earth as you jack and fill, move a little, then jack and fill some more. With a winch, life is easier. You stretch out your cable, hook on and within minutes you're on your way. Admittedly, digging out builds character. But frankly, a winch makes life much easier.

TYPES OF WINCHES

Historically, winches were shaft-driven by a power take-off—PTO—fitting on the transmission or transfer case. This setup tended to clank and clatter a lot. No more, at least not for our kinds of vehicles. What today's off-roader is interested in is an electric

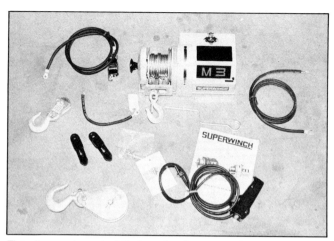

There's more to a winch that an electric motor and a drum with cable wrapped around it. This 3500-lb Superwinch includes hand controller, electrical cable, two sizes of snatch blocks and installation guide.

Warn unit has 8000-lb rated capacity, but is compact enough to fit most small and intermediate-size pickups or utility vehicles.

winch. This is a simple, reasonably fool-proof device consisting of a heavy-duty electric motor that drives a drum or spool through a series of reduction gears. On the drum, there's a wire cable that is drawn in through a roller-type guide called a *roller fairlead,* or a smoothed-off hole in a plate called a *hawse fairlead.*

Most electric winches are also equipped with a free-spooling device, usually a lever or handle to disengage the gears. This handy feature lets you walk the cable out rather than having to play the cable out at the leisurely pace at which most winches operate. You then re-engage the gears and you're ready to get on with the job.

There's also a way of reversing the direction the drum is driven, usually by reversing the polarity of the motor. This provides both power-in and power-out capability. *Power-in*—pulling the cable in—is the usual mode of operation. But being able to power-out also gives you the capability of using the winch to lower a load as well as pull it toward you. Good examples are letting your vehicle down a slope that's too steep to drive down, or lowering a boat trailer down a ramp that's impossible to back down.

You might also think you could use such a winch to lower the engine back into your car or other such work. The answer is, *don't!* Electric winches of this variety have fairly imprecise braking systems. It's next to impossible to make fine

adjustments required for that type of deli-cate adjustment. Better you should obtain a proper chain fall from your local U-Rent-Um. Or get a winch that's de-signed for that specific purpose.

In addition, there's a control cable that's usually fitted with a spring-loaded switch so the winch only operates when you hold the switch in the "on" position. Most of these have two switch positions, one for power-out, the other for power-in. This is not an ideal arrangement, be-cause an excited operator might push the switch in the wrong direction. To avoid a dangerous situation, always check which direction the winch is going to go when you press the switch. Take a little nibble, just to be sure, before you take the whole bite.

Given a choice, we'd suggest getting a controller that has a second switch, usually of the rocker variety. Use the rocker to select cable-in or cable-out, and add a thumb button to actually run the motor.

Big Winch vs. Small Winch—There used to be two sizes of winches: big and small. Today, it's not quite so simple because winches are available with capacities that range from 2000—8000 lb and more. The number of choices is greatly expanded.

Before selecting a winch, decide what you want it to do. If you're going to equip yourself to the max, then you want a big winch with a lot of load capacity. This

provides more sheer pulling power with less chance of overloading or damaging the motor or gears. This type of winch will also have a longer cable, which is sometimes useful. In addition, it will be heavier and more expensive. And it will look tougher.

Also, be aware that the winch adaptor or mounting kit can add a sizeable chunk to your investment. This is because, for some vehicles, you may need a new front bumper as well as all the other bracketry and supports required to firmly anchor that sucker in place.

Opting for a small winch gives away some of the capability available in a big one. On the other hand, how much winching power do you really need? Small doesn't mean puny, necessarily, and load capacities of 3500 lb are avail-able in highly compact winches. What are you going to use your winch for? Do you plan on using it to lower your vehicle down a cliff face or are you going to use it in case you or a buddy happen to get stuck? In 99.9% of simple stuck situa-tions, a small winch will get the job done. Also, being smaller and lighter, the in-stallation is usually simpler and less costly.

Incidentally, there are some small winches that are designed to be carried inside the vehicle and then hooked onto a hitch ball whenever they're needed. This way, by putting a hitch ball in front as well as in the rear, you can use the winch

Trim-looking but heavy bumper/winch combination from Pro-Zap is well protected. Cable spool remains visible so you can see how much cable had been played out. Cable opening is hawse-fairlead type.

Accessory cover to protect winch when not in use would keep grit and grime from working into cable strands and fraying them.

on the end that's in the best position to get the job done.

Then there are hand-operated winches often called *come-alongs*. One of these tucked under your seat may provide all the winching power you'll ever actually require. This type of winch is widely used on boat trailers. But there are models suitable for use on vehicles that are light, compact and have sufficient capacity to be of practical value to the off-roader. Slow, yes. More work, yes. But lots less expensive, too.

WINCH ACCESSORIES

When you buy a winch, you also need to make some decisions about some accessories to go with it. For the winch itself, you'll probably pay extra if you want a roller fairlead. This is generally a good investment because it is much easier on the cable for anything except a straight-ahead pull. A roller also looks better.

With most winches, a remote hand controller is included in the purchase price. If not, don't go away without it. This is something you need to operate the winch while you retreat to a safe position behind a tree or boulder.

Other accessories you'll want to consider include:

Snatch Block—This is a pulley arrangement that lets you multiply the pulling ability of your winch. If you've chosen a small winch, you may want to have a snatch block just to have additional capability when needed. Using a single snatch block doubles the pulling capacity of a winch. By using two, you quadruple capacity, and so on. The other side of the coin is that the capacity increase is directly proportional to a speed decrease. Each snatch block you use slows down overall winching speed by a factor of two, and the reach of your cable is diminished as well. Unless you go in for a lot of overkill—or have a seriously enfeebled winch—you probably won't get sufficient use from a second snatch block to make the investment worthwhile.

Anchor—If you go four-wheeling where there's always an abundance of trees or sturdy stumps to attach a cable to, you probably won't worry about carrying an anchor. On the other hand, if your off-roading is done in other types of terrain where there's a scarcity of natural features to hook up to, carrying an anchor is a very good idea indeed.

The best soft-terrain anchor we've ever used is a genuine marine anchor of the Danforth type. Shown on page 78, it's self-burying and the harder you pull on it, the deeper it tends to dig itself in.

Before discovering the Danforth solution, we once tried burying a spare tire and using that as an anchor. Old desert rats tell you that this is the way to do it. The proper procedure, they say, is to dig a hole deep enough to bury the tire standing vertically. Then, you place a four-

Snatchblock doubles effective pull of a winch though line speed is necessarily cut in half.

way lug wrench on the back side of the wheel to distribute the load and hook your cable to it through the center wheel opening.

This might work, given sufficiently hard ground. But what our author discovered was that digging a hole deep enough to do any good in sand or soft ground required more physical exertion than he was capable of expending, especially in the middle of summer. His only possible alternative was to winch himself and his vehicle into and through several mesquite trees. He found that preferable to the excavation work that would otherwise have been required.

In this particular adventure, he scuffed

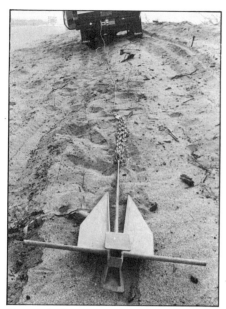

Buried anchor was quickly retrieved by simply pulling straight up on chain where it was secured to anchor stock.

Some winch manufacturers offer sand anchors but most of these are ineffective in loose soil. So we tried a marine-quality Danforth sand anchor, laid flat as it would have landed on the ocean floor when pitched off a boat.

At first, winch reeled anchor toward truck. But as anchor flukes got a good bite, Danforth buried itself out of sight. When it stopped moving, winch pulled truck up to it. Danforth anchor weighs only 12 lb, but can withstand a pull of 6000 lb.

the paint, scraped several sizeable patches of skin off his body and generally had a dickens of a time getting to firm ground again. Since then, he's carried the 12-lb Danforth sand anchor with him most of the time. Yes, it's a bit awkward to carry, but after you've winched yourself through a mesquite tree or two, you're willing to figure out a way of making space for your Danforth.

Basic Hookup—For attaching your winch to another object, it's sometimes possible to make a nice, clean direct hookup, such as attaching the hook on the end of your cable to a tow hook on the other vehicle. In most instances, however, it's handier if you have a short length of tow or logging chain with a hook on each end that you can wrap around a tree stump, rock or whatever to attach your cable to. This will help avoid brutalizing the cable, especially where the hookup angle is awkward.

Things Not to Hook Up to—There are several don'ts that should be observed when hooking your cable to another vehicle. Don't attach your hook or chain to a hitch ball. You may overpower the ball shank or through-bolt and slingshot the ball in an undesired direction.

Likewise, don't attach your winch to a suspension part, a component of the steering system or to an axle or axle shaft. All of these can be damaged by pulling on them with a winch. Also, don't take a turn around something sharp and hook the cable to itself. That will put a strain—and a permanent kink—in the cable.

Tree Pad—Another recommended accessory, especially for the ecology-conscious, is a tree pad or tree saver. This is a wide band of heavy belting material that you wrap around the tree to keep the chain or cable from damaging it. Or you can save yourself some money and use a nylon tow strap to protect the aforementioned tree.

Sloppy Leather Gloves—Gloves are virtually essential if you're going to do any winching without ripping your hands to shreds. In operation, the winch cable inevitably gets kinked and what started out as a nice, smooth cable develops skin-ripping broken and twisted wire strands that can do serious damage to your epidermis. So plan on using gloves, but not just any gloves. Don't use cloth gloves, for instance, because they won't provide sufficient protection. Make sure

they're heavy leather, like horsehide.

Also be sure that your gloves are a sloppy fit so you can slip your hand out if you need to. One of the horror stories told about winches is the guy whose glove got hooked by a broken strand and strained his hand through the fairlead opening and wrapped around the drum before he could get the glove off or the winch stopped. Don't let that happen to you.

INSTALLING YOUR WINCH

If your winch-seller offers the service, we'd suggest letting an experienced expert install your winch, especially if it's a full-size winch. The installation usually isn't an intricate engineering task, but it often requires more blacksmithery than the typical shade-tree wrench-bender is prepared to undertake. Manufacturers' adaptor kits are generally quite good, in our experience. But even so, there may be some modifications required to make everything fit like it should, such as cutting angle iron, drilling holes in 1/4-in. plate and the occasional use of a welding torch.

Installing a small winch may or may not require an expert installer. Obviously, bolting a small winch between the frame rails of a Jeep CJ is a reasonably simple task. But there's no such easy access if it's a small Blazer or one of the other more modern designs.

Rear Mount—As you can see in the photos that accompany this chapter,

Roller fairlead allows angular pulls without undue strain on the cable. However, massive adapter adds considerably to front-end weight, affecting ride and handling.

Bob Martin's 2500-lb Superwinch is mounted to a fixture that slides into the hitch receiver of his Bronco II, allowing it to be stowed inside when not needed. It also fits front towbar bracket.

Neater installation with 3500-lb M3 Superwinch mounted under bed of author's Mitsubishi pickup: No sheet-metal modifications were necessary, though license plate was moved.

Spencer's M3 Superwinch is attached to the rear of his Mitsubishi pickup rather than in the more conventional front position. He points out that backward is almost always the direction he desires to winch himself when he gets into trouble. The rear mount also makes sense when he's either rescuing a dumb friend (such as his winchless co-author) or using it to launch or retrieve a boat.

Admittedly, the Mitsubishi truck and the M3 Superwinch are an unusually fine matchup. The installation did require welding in some supports for the winch, but it's sufficiently compact that there's still space for the spare tire under the bed. The license plate had to be moved, but that was no problem at all.

Putting a full-size winch in the rear isn't as simple, even on a full-size truck, as you can see in the photo at far right. This type of stand-up winch, an 10,000-lb Warn, is too tall to go under the bed without stealing too much ground clearance, so the owner bolted it into the truck bed and cut a hole through the tailgate. He also relocated the battery to reduce line drop when the winch is in use. This is a practical and neat installation, provided you don't need to put anything large or heavy in the bed.

Warn does have an underbed rear mount, however, for a couple of their smaller 5000-lb and 6000-lb models. Also, the Sidewinder from Advance Adapters, which is ordinarily hidden be-

Author's winch is mounted to a steel plate welded to rear step bumper. Under-bed installation required length of square tubing for strength under base plate and chrome-moly tubes braced to bumper brackets.

hind the front bumper, is also available with rear mounting kits.

Weight Considerations—Being made of iron and steel, winches are heavy dudes. Even a small winch is likely to weigh near 50 lb, and some of the full-size models will add about 200 lb to the vehicle before the installation is complete. And hanging a full-size winch onto the front of just about any vehicle will upset weight distribution and handling. You'll quickly discover how much more easily the front end will hit its bottom stops than before.

Massive 10,000-lb winch is mounted at rear to pull off-road race truck onto a trailer. Unit didn't fit under bed so owner bolted it to bed with an opening cut through tailgate. Separate battery cuts down on power loss from extended battery connections.

Perhaps a cart-sprung Jeep CJ or Toyota Land Cruiser will handle this additional weight with more aplomb. But put it on a machine with somewhat softer and more sophisticated suspension and you're going to end up looking for heavier torsion bars or front coils. Or, you'll try to compensate for the additional weight with air shocks or air bags, both of which are crutches rather than ideal solutions.

You won't be faced with the same problem if you mount your winch in the rear. The rear suspension is designed to

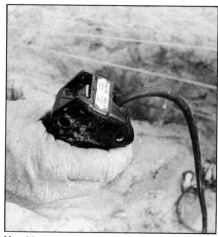

Hand-held cable control is trigger-operated. Another switch must be turned to either "cable out" or "cable in." Be sure which way winch is going before using it.

Tasteful winch installation on a full-size Chevy Blazer: Cable hook is held from dangling loose by one of two tie-downs.

carry varying amounts of weight and the additional weight back there may make your vehicle ride better than when it's empty.

Battery Considerations—As with driving lights, a winch uses a lot of current. If you're going to be more than a very occasional winch user, remember that it doesn't take very long for a working winch to suck up half, three-quarters or all the amps stored in the battery. Of course, you'll have the engine running while you're winching. But even at full output, your alternator can't keep up.

After you've quit winching, the alternator then has the opportunity to recharge the battery. Aye, there's the rub. A typical maintenance-free battery isn't designed to be discharged and recharged more than a limited number of times. In fact, after your winch has drained a lot of current out of such a battery, it never fully recovers its original storage capacity. And each time it is discharged, the storage capacity diminishes.

The point we're making is that if you're going to use your winch more than on rare occasions, install a heavy-duty, *deep-discharge* battery. Also called marine-type batteries, these are designed to handle this kind of treatment, and

aren't nearly as likely to go belly up just when the winching gets serious.

USING YOUR WINCH

Winching can be hazardous to your health. A winch is a piece of machinery with exposed moving parts and as such can do a lot of harm to you. If Ralph Nader ever sees one, we're all in trouble, because there are any number of ways a careless operator can do harm to himself—and others.

We've already mentioned the danger of getting your hand sucked through the fairlead. Another hazard is getting loose clothing caught up with the cable or drum. Still another is not having the hook firmly attached and having it come loose just when the cable is at full strain. And there's also the possibility that the cable will break and whip around with lethal potential.

Being deliberate and careful whenever you winch is the best assurance of safe operation. As noted earlier, wear sloppy-fit heavy leather gloves whenever you're working around the winch. The heavy leather will save your hands from damage by rough cable and the loose fit makes it possible for you to slip your hand out if your glove does get caught.

Also be careful that your clothing can't get caught up. Take off your tie. Tuck in that shirt tail. Zip up that jacket. Button that raincoat.

When hooking up, always be sure that you've got a solid anchor to which you can apply the hook; one where it can't slip off or pull free. If there's any doubt, use a short length of chain to make a wrap or two around something solid, then attach your hook to the chain.

If you're doing some heavy pulling and applying a strain to the cable, the standard safety measure is to throw a coat or blanket over the cable. This is surprisingly effective in minimizing the snakewhip effect of a broken cable end.

You should also be conscious that you're dealing with electricity and take whatever precautions are necessary to keep from dealing yourself a nasty shock or burn. Don't stand in a puddle of water while plugging in the remote control cable, for instance. And don't tolerate any cracks, frayed spots or other damage to the cable or controller unit.

Making the Pull—After you're hooked up and have taken the slack out of the cable, the best, safest place to stand is at full control-cable length over to the side. This gives you a good perspective on

Hitch adapter pivots on ball to align winch, cable and load for angle pull. Photo courtesy of Superwinch.

Most winches require additional expense of a mounting kit tailored for a specific vehicle. This is Warn kit (with winch) for installation on a Jeep CJ. Photo courtesy CBS Publications.

what's going on and is much safer than standing over the cable. If you have a helper, put him inside the cab with instructions to keep the engine running at fast idle (1500—2000 rpm) to keep alternator output high. Also, if you're planning to pull another vehicle toward yours, instruct your helper to keep his foot firmly planted on the brakes. This applies all four brakes and is more effective than setting the parking brake that acts on two wheels only. If you're on a smooth surface, it's also a good idea to chock the wheels.

Straight Pull—The simple, straight pull is what you'll use most often. This is usually done by driving or backing up to the poor fool who has gotten stuck. Stop far enough away to stay on solid ground and leave enough space to pull the stuck vehicle out of trouble. Although it's more trouble, gets more cable dirty and will take longer to reel in when you're finished, a long cable is generally considered better than a short cable, especially with a difficult pull. This is because a winch develops the least amount of pulling power when the drum is near full and the max when the drum is near empty. Don't run *all* of the cable out, however. Always leave at least one layer of cable

on the drum to avoid putting undue strain on the cable anchor. A good way to provide yourself a visual warning about the last wrap is to paint that much of your cable red.

When winching another vehicle, put a driver in the other vehicle to steer but tell him not to try to help under his own power. You and your winch will snake him out of there. Otherwise, your cable and winch may be subjected to shock loading, particularly if the vehicle being pulled grabs traction, then loses it and so on. If your winch doesn't have the capacity for the job, it's time to get out that snatch block.

Too often, you'll see a winch owner using a winch cable to tow another vehicle. This can be a bum idea since it can lead to shock loading that may result in damage to the cable or to the winch mechanism itself. It's better to draw the vehicle toward you and then, if the other machine isn't clear yet, back up and reel out another length of cable.

Angle Pull—Even if your winch is equipped with a roller fairlead, pulling at an angle is hard on the cable. For that reason, it's always better to do a straight pull whenever possible. Sometimes, even if both vehicles aren't perfectly

lined up, you can get your vehicle into a more advantageous position by applying your parking brakes and letting the winch pull the front end around. Then you can have a helper mash down on the brake pedal while you get on with the winching. This, of course, assumes that all four brakes will anchor the vehicle when the two rears applied by the parking brake wouldn't.

Inevitably, however, there will be times when an angle pull is all you can manage. One such occurrence was when Spencer's pickup broke through a layer of silt and he was instantly down to the door sills. This required a winching angle of nearly 90°, because that's where the only possible hookup was. Fortunately, he had a good, stout winch that was able to turn the whole dead weight of the truck around, then haul it out of the silt and onto firm ground.

When it's necessary to make a sharp-angle pull and you've scraped your cable around a sharp angle through your non-roller fairlead, you may end up with curly cable. That's a pain because it will have a tendency to kink and twist whenever there isn't a load on it. This condition can sometimes be minimized by anchoring your cable, putting a load on it and leaving it overnight. You can also help straighten it by winding it in under a real load, such as winching yourself toward it while braking lightly to put more tension on the cable. But if you end up with seriously kinked cable, the only satisfactory solution is to replace it.

TAKE CARE OF IT

Because it represents a sizeable investment, you'll want to give your winch the kind of care it deserves. Many manufacturers offer a winch cover and that's not a bad idea. But there are other precautions you should observe, as well. Winch cable is woven from galvanized steel strands and as such is pretty durable. Still, you should keep the cable clean. A dirty cable will fray more easily than a clean one because the cable "works" when it is stretched by a load and the grains of dirt can chafe and cut the strands. The easiest way to clean a cable is to stretch it out in the driveway and hose off the the dirt and grime.

Oiling or greasing the cable *is not* recommended, however. A lubed cable is nasty to work with, and tends to hold onto any dirt and grime it comes into contact with. Cleaner is better.

The geartrain in most winches is in a sealed, lubed-for-life package and you don't have to worry about it. But check your instructions to be sure.

The other part of the winch you need to take good care of is the remote-control cable and switch. Too often, these get thrown into the spare-tire well along with a lug wrench and other metal gadgets that can damage the cable or switch. It's better to find or make a stout flat box of the appropriate size that will slide under the seat. There, it will be kept clean, dry and out of harm's way. We've seen vehicles where the winch control is neatly coiled and held by clips under the hood. But we don't recommend this because engine heat will dry-rot the rubber insulation.

As your winch gets older, keep an eye on the electrical cables, connectors and boots between the winch and the battery, and from the winch to the remote control box, assuming it's separate from the winch. These items are relatively easy to replace when you're in your driveway, but can create problems you don't need when the fog has closed in, rain is beginning to fall and the vehicle lurches into a bottomless pit.

THE LAST WORD

In spite of our tendency to tease winch owners about being prepared for disasters that never take place, we agree that a winch can make life a lot easier for the serious off-roader. It may spend most of its life looking underutilized but when you really need a winch, nothing else works nearly so well.

A SAMPLING OF WINCHES										
Manufacturer	Model	Rated Pull, (lb)	Cable Dia. (in.)	Cable Capacity, (ft)	Power Out?	Free-spool?	No-load Line Speed, (ft/min)	Type of Mounting Kit		Weight w/cable, (lb)
Advance Adapters	Mini Sidewinder	7500	5/16	90	Yes	Yes	27	Bolts to frame, front or rear		76
	Sidewinder III	9000	5/16	120	Yes	Yes	17	Bolts to frame, front or rear		120
Desert Dynamics	1106	9000	5/16	150	Yes	Yes	23	Frame, front or rear		116
	1106-11	9000	5/16	200	Yes	Yes	23	Frame, front or rear		116
	1206	9000	5/16	150	Yes	Yes	23	Frame, front or rear		116
Haulamatic	FCW, LCW, IOW, PMW	3000	3/16	25	Yes	Yes	12	Trailer hitch ball		35-45
Koenig	EL-8	8000	5/16	150	Yes	Yes	10	Bolts to frame, front		130
Powerwinch	VR-182	2000	3/16	50	No	Yes	18	Trailer hitch ball		36
	VR-192	3500	7/32	50	No	Yes	16	Trailer hitch ball		42
	VR-202	6000	7/32	75	Yes	Yes	15	Buyer fabricates own mount		97
Ramsey	Rep 6000H	6000	1/4	100	Yes	Yes	17	Brush guard or bolt to frame		48
	2000/2001	8000	5/16	150	Yes	Yes	15	New bumper or bolt to frame		99
Rule	33S	2300	3/16	35	Yes	No	8.5	Brush guard		25
	33	2300	3/16	50	Yes	Yes	8.5	Brush guard		25
	42	3200	7/32	50	Yes	Yes	15	Brush guard		27
Superwinch	X1	1500	3/16	25	Yes	No	25	Trailer hitch ball or flat surface		17
	X2	2500	7/32	40	Yes	No	27	Trailer hitch ball or flat surface		21
	X3	3500	7/32	50	Yes	No	30	Trailer hitch ball or flat surface		34
	OX	8000	5/16	150	Yes	Yes	41	Brush guard		150
Tensen 2-speed	TX2	10000	5/16	150	Yes	Yes	15/65	Brush guard		110
Warn	3000	2000	3/16	40	Yes	No	47	Brush guard		30
	3500	3500	7/32	100	Yes	Yes	35	Brush guard		50
	5000	5000	1/4	100	Yes	Yes	25	Brush guard front, underbed rear		55
	6000	6000	1/4	100	Yes	Yes	22	Brush guard front, underbed rear		82
	8000	8000	5/16	150	Yes	Yes	65	Platform or brush guard		110

Driving Lights

Good driving lights are effective off-road partly because they put you into a tunnel of light. When you're driving in this tunnel, you're less likely to be distracted by the yeti, rhinoceri or wood nymphs that are cavorting in the fields along the road. At the same time, the lights help you pick out those things you need to know about. For example, with good lights, the edges of the road are fully lit, not just vague shadows, which gives you confidence.

In addition, your lights create shadows behind every hump and in every hollow. This helps spell out exactly what the road surface is like and makes it easier to read the road. In fact, on a long, arduous trail one of the authors drove one night using good auxiliary lights, he discovered that the shadows actually exaggerated the rough appearance of the ground. This caused him to be even more cautious than when he covered the same route in the daylight, making it easier on the vehicle and on himself.

Does somebody have a light? For serious nighttime off-road driving, auxiliary lights unleash a flurry of photons. Photo by Jon Jay.

LIGHTING NEEDS

We're pretty much convinced that for most off-road drivers, auxiliary lights are mostly cosmetic. They aren't installed because the driver has any genuine need for them, but because the driver thinks they look good.

If this is the real truth about your desire for driving lights, fine. Driving lights do give an off-road vehicle the right look and we've never yet seen an off-road vehicle that didn't look better for being festooned with a full array of auxiliary lights.

If you are buying lights for their cosmetic value, we'd suggest that you purchase the largest lights you can afford. Then mount them in the most prominent location imaginable. Which is on the roof or the rollbar or sportbar, assuming you have one. (We'll talk about the legalities of roof-mounted lights later.) If you want to go even further, put another pair on the front bumper. Then add one on each *A-pillar*—windshield pillar. And to be really complete, you should have a rear-facing light in case you need to do any serious, high-speed backing up.

With such an assortment of lights, you're prepared to illuminate the whole countryside and there may be times when you're glad you are able to do that.

Admittedly, however, this is overkill. It may also kill your alternator, your battery, or both. You need to think about this, too.

For most off-roaders, the most practical approach is to buy one pair of lights and put them where they'll do the most good. As you may know, there are different types of lights designed to do different tasks. This means you need to decide which tasks you want to accomplish. Then you can make intelligent decisions about the lights you buy.

Quality vs. Price—As you shop for lights, you'll discover that prices vary widely. You can find inexpensive lights at discount auto-parts outlets and mass merchandisers, ones that aren't much different from lights that cost a lot more.

So, the question is whether the more expensive lights are worth the difference in price. As always, the answer depends on what you want from your lights. There's no doubt that you get what you pay for. If it's image you're after, a big "Z" for Zelmot on the plastic cover of your driving lights is worth a lot more than a blank cover or one that announces a brand name that nobody ever heard of before.

Some of the prestige names in the driving light business include Cibie (pronounced "C-B-A") and SEV Marchal from France, Hella and Bosch from Germany and the aforementioned Zelmot lights from Poland. The biggest U.S. name in off-road lights is KC HiLites,

Sign of quality auxiliary light separate adjustments for up/down and right/left aiming.

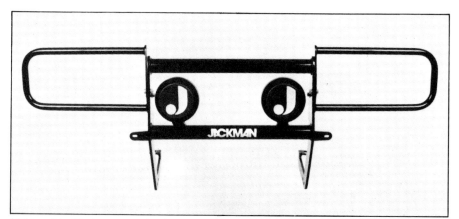

Lights subject to damage are best protected by pushbar/grilleguard. Also be sure to get padded covers that are usually sold separately. Some states even require covers for extra lights when not being used. Photo courtesy of Jackman Wheels.

Single adjustment for both vertical and horizontal aiming is hard to get "zeroed" and to hold there.

whose attractive padded covers have no doubt influenced more buyers to choose KC than anything else.

How to Recognize Good Lights— Some of the characteristics of the best driving lights include lenses with cut grooves and angles instead of molded, cases that are made of stainless steel or triple-chromed instead of single-chromed, and mounting brackets that have separate side-to-side and up-and-down adjustments. Good lights don't have to have metal cases these days as some of the best now are in super-strong plastic.

Good driving lights also work better on your vehicle. Because of their superior mounting brackets, good lights are easier to adjust and more likely to stay where you point them. Another characteristic is that they're less likely to dance on their mounts and produce a jiggly light that can both give you a headache and drive you crazy. The light pattern itself is also likely to be superior. A good driving light will have an even, well-distributed beam of light that has neither dark shadows or hot spots. Put the beam of a cheap, inferior light beside a top-line light and there's likely to be a world of difference in the quality of the light produced.

LIGHTING FUNDAMENTALS

In case you've never thought of it, light is not simply the absence of darkness. Light is finite. It has substance. It is a form of physical energy.

If you have trouble believing this, go to a night off-road race. Find a place where the lights from an oncoming car will land on you all of a sudden, perhaps over the top of a hill. You can feel the light when it hits your face. Even if you put pads over your eyes so you can't possibly see the light, you can still feel it. Maybe it's heat, maybe it's pressure, but whatever it is, you know it when it hits you.

Light is real, in other words.

Like a Garden Hose— With this in mind, think of a driving light as being like the nozzle on a garden hose. The water flows through the hose and is then sprayed into the air. By changing the shape of the nozzle on the end of the hose, you can change the shape of the jet of water. It can be a long, thin jet that reaches all the way across the yard or you can have a nozzle with a wide, fan-shaped spray that covers a wider area but doesn't reach out as far.

So it is with a driving light. Electrons "flow" to the filament and resistance of the tungsten molecules causes white heat—incandescence—thereby converting electrical energy to heat energy and light energy. The light that's created is shaped by the shiny reflector behind it and the angles cut into the glass lens in front of it. From there, the light "sprays" out into the air, very much like the jet of water coming from a hose. And you can tailor the spray of light coming through the lens to do any of several different tasks. Long and slim, short and fat, a compromise combination of the two, or most anything else.

You can also think of the wattage of the bulb as being like the amount of water pressure in the hose. With a 55-watt bulb, you have a certain amount of "pressure." With a 100-watt bulb, you have a greater amount of "pressure" to "squirt" the light even farther.

SEALED BEAM VS. HALOGEN LIGHTS

Aside from beam patterns, there are three basic types of driving lights: sealed beam, halogen and a combination of the two that's called sealed-beam halogen.

Sealed-Beam— On a sealed-beam light, the lens and reflector are one piece of

Filament of a quartz-halogen light is inside its own small bulb. Bulb can be replaced separately, not entire lamp unit as with sealed beams. Long fingernails are optional.

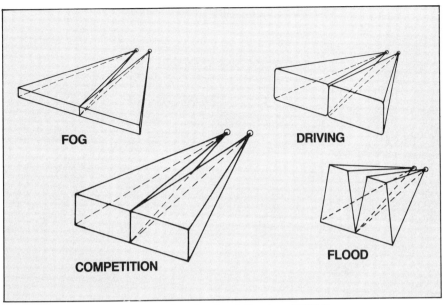
Driving-light beam patterns vary with task at hand. Courtesy KC HiLites.

molded glass, sealed from the atmosphere like a conventional incandescent light bulb. The filament, which is the little curly tungsten wire that glows when electrical current is sent through it, is inside this sealed package. If oxygen were allowed inside the sealed bulb, the filament would quickly burn itself out. So instead of air, there's an inert gas, usually argon, inside the bulb. Nevertheless, a little tungsten gets vaporized every time the bulb is on, and gets deposited on the sealed-beam reflector and lens as it cools. Eventually, these black deposits build up and the light loses some of its brightness.

Quartz-Halogen—The halogen or quartz-halogen light has a tungsten filament too, but it operates at much higher temperatures. Usually, the bulb is made from quartz to withstand the higher temperatures, and is separate from the reflector and lens.

The halogen-light filament is surrounded by halogen gas, either iodine or bromine. Halogen gas has the unique ability to keep the vaporized tungsten off the inner walls of the bulb and redeposit solidified tungsten back onto the filament as the lamp is shut off and cools. This regenerative cycle is the major reason that a quartz-halogen light retains the same degree of brightness rather than gradually getting dimmer.

Also, for the same amount of current, the halogen light is much brighter and therefore superior to the conventional sealed-beam driving light. It has the further advantage of having a replaceable bulb where the sealed-beam light does not. When a sealed-beam light burns out, you replace the whole light unit.

Incidentally, you should never touch the quartz-halogen bulb with your bare fingers. Oil deposits on your fingers can cause a concentration of heat and result in the bulb breaking. If you do accidentally touch a halogen bulb, clean it with a soft cloth dampened with naptha or similar oil-free solvent.

Halogen Sealed Beam—The third type of light, which combines characteristics of the other two, is the halogen sealed beam. The only excuse for its development was to get around a stupid law. The uniform lighting code agreed upon by all U.S. states in the late '30s requires that automobile headlights be of sealed-beam construction. Back in the '30s, sealed-beam lights were state-of-the-art replacements for composite lights with separate bulb, reflector and lens. But when the much superior halogen-type lights came along decades later, they couldn't be used in U.S. cars because they were not sealed beam, and that law still remained on the books.

Eventually, because it was obviously impossible to get all states to change their lighting requirements, lighting manufacturers began to build sealed-beam lights of halogen construction. So now, at last, we can use the superior halogen light, but legally for *on-road* use, it still has to be a sealed-beam halogen.

Dumb, sure, but there it is.

TYPES OF DRIVING LIGHTS

Now, to get back to our analogy of the nozzle on the garden hose being like a driving light. As we mentioned, the shape of the light beam that is "squirted" out from a light can be altered by changing the shape of the reflector and the angles cut into the lens. Basically, there are four different types of driving lights: short-range, mid-range, long-range and special-purpose lights.

Short-Range Lights—A short-range light puts a wide, flat beam out in front of the vehicle. Most manufacturers list this as a fog light. Fog lights may have an amber lens or clear lens. Because the beam is low and wide, it is very effective for off-road use. Pointed straight ahead or slightly out, this type of light helps you see what's along the edges of the road, especially helpful when you're batting down an unpaved trail. At the same time, because the light is low and close to the ground, its beam throws shadows into the holes, making it easier to read the con-

A pair of short-range driving lights sensibly mounted down low where they belong and protected by a pushbar.

Light bars that clamp to driprails are available for most off-road vehicles. Most are pre-drilled for five or even six lights, although four is legal limit in many states.

tours of the road. Also, if there's dust, the low-mounted light is more likely to shine under the dust and less likely to reflect the light back into your eyes.

Because the beam is wide and low, this type of beam is also effective in fog. As with dust, this makes it less likely for the light to be reflected back into your eyes. Incidentally, this is why a headlight's low beams are more effective in fog or dust than high beams.

As noted earlier, fog lights are available with either clear or amber lenses. In snow, heavy rain and some types of heavy, wet fog, an amber lens seems to be more effective than a clear lens. We don't know if there's a scientific reason for this or whether it's because the amber lens absorbs up to 20% of the total light so there's simply less light to reflect back and blind you. One thing is for sure: Fog lights with amber lenses can be seen more easily by oncoming motorists.

However, for off-road use, we'd suggest the use of a clear-lens fog light because it puts out more light than an amber-lens light.

Mount Them Low—For maximum effectiveness, mount short-range lights as low as practical. For an off-road vehicle, mount them no higher than on top of the bumper. Mounting them below the bumper makes the lights unnecessarily vulnerable.

The higher you mount this type of light, the less effective it becomes; the roof is the worst place of all. A short-range light is designed to light the area that's immediately in front of you. If you put a set of them above headlight level, you have to point them downward to be effective. From that angle, their light collides with that coming from the headlights. As with two streams of water from two garden hoses, you can't shine one beam of light through another without scattering the beams and making both less effective. Also, a high fog-light mounting position doesn't create the shadows and reveal road-surface irregularities as well as the lower mounting position does.

So keep fog lights low to help you read the road and get under the dust, and point them slightly to the sides for good road-edge definition.

Mid-Range Lights—The mid-range light is generally called a passing light. This has a longer, thinner beam than the short-range, or fog, light and is designed to increase the range beyond standard low-beam headlights. For off-road use, it is ineffective unless you're planning to illuminate the entire countryside.

Long-Range Lights—The long-range, or driving, light is designed to spread out beyond the headlights. It reaches farther to the sides as well as way out ahead. If you're intent on covering a lot of ground in a hurry, you may need long-range lights. What was an indistinct shadow can now be seen as a tree. What was simply a lump is now visible as a big rock. And that flicker of movement you weren't sure you really saw is now clearly revealed to be another abominable snowman crossing the road.

And when you combine the use of both short-range and long-range lights, man, you can SEE! The improvement is dramatic.

If you've never used these types of lights, you'll no doubt be amazed at how confident you feel about plunging into the darkness. We were once involved in a 24-hour speed run around a 15-mile desert loop. Unfortunately, the sponsor of the event didn't want his vehicles equipped with anything that wasn't dead stock, which meant no add-on driving lights. So we drove with ordinary headlights and through the long hours of the night this became very tiring. There was one long stretch of dry lake bed on the course and there, with those feeble headlights, you had the feeling you were about to drive off the edge of the earth. If we had had good lights, we could have sat back and relaxed on this long, straight stretch. As it was, it was always a relief to get off the lake bed and back into the brush where we were going a lot slower and couldn't drive fast enough to overdrive the range of our lights.

If you have both short-range and long-range lights, the long-rangers should be mounted higher than the short-range lights; higher, in fact, than the headlights, if practical. A good location on an off-road vehicle is atop the brush guard or thereabouts.

Roof-mounted lights on this off-road racing truck retract into a well in roof when not in use. This protects lenses from flying rocks and cuts down on high-speed wind resistance.

Roof-mounted spotlight (arrow) helps illuminate campsite or objects you're looking for off to the side. Photo by Jon Jay.

Personally, we don't like lights mounted on roof-top or rollbar because the light reflects off the hood. You can minimize this distraction by painting the hood flat black. Also available are glare shields that extend out from the bottom of the light. But we still prefer to have all lights ahead of our eyes rather than behind them. Also, in some states, a forward-facing auxiliary light cannot be mounted more than a few inches behind the driver. This makes lights on a sportbar or rollbar (or even to the rear of an extended cab) illegal in some states. The only way around this is to use a roof mount that places the lights no more than the legal distance behind the driver.

However, if you're going to use just one pair of long-range lights and no short-range lights, mount them lower, perhaps at brush-guard level. This lets the lights create shadows and helps you read the road.

Killer-type, 100-watt long-range driving lights make very effective light and many professional rallyists find that a pair of them mounted on the bumper is all they need. For everyday off-road use, we prefer the short-range lights, but then we're not driving at the speeds those pros are.

Special-Purpose Lights—In addition to short-range and long-range driving lights to supplement the low beams and high beams of your headlights, there are also special-purpose lights. The most common of these are super-long-range lights that are sometimes called *pencil beams*.

A pencil beam reaches way out and gives a clue about what awaits you out there in the darkness. For off-road use, these are of doubtful practicality because the very narrow beam never stays on any one object long enough to let you figure out what it is. If you're driving fast enough off-road to need a super-long-range light, you're probably bouncing around enough that your pencil beam is darting all over the earth and sky rather than lighting up the course.

Ideal Setup—A pair of short-range, or fog, lights and one pair of long-range driving lights is probably the ideal off-road combination. By using your headlights to fill in between the two types of lights, you've got your lighting needs covered.

If you're only going to buy one set of lights, however, get the short-range type. The long-range lights are great, but it's essential to see what's right in front of you. If you're a pro who drives fast and needs more light farther down the road, opt for a pair of 100-watt, long-range driving lights.

Another effective setup we've seen consists of a pair of short-range lights plus a single long-range light. Several super-lights are now available.

Other special-purpose lights you should be aware of are called "work lights." These are narrow-beam *spotlights* that you can adjust by hand to look around for that road you think you may have missed. Still another special-purpose light you may find useful is a *cargo light*. This type of light may be useful when you're trying to set up camp after dark or help some poor fool out of a bottomless pit he's driven into because he didn't have good off-road lights.

HALOGEN HEADLIGHTS

Up to now, we have discussed auxiliary driving lights to augment your vehicle's stock headlights. But if you're simply interested in improving the quality of your existing headlights, consider replacing them with sealed-beam halogen headlights. These are not as effective as three-piece halogen headlights, but are much better than the accursed old-fashioned sealed beam.

If your vehicle is new, or reasonably recent, it may *already* be equipped with sealed-beam halogen headlights. Check that before you make your purchase.

STATE REGULATIONS

As noted earlier, the uniform lighting code has settled on sealed-beam headlamps, either conventional or halogen, as the only legal fare *on-road*. But when it comes to auxiliary driving lights, almost no two states have the same regulations.

LIGHT-MOUNTING RECOMMENDATIONS

This chart indicates the mounting specifications preferred by the AAMVA (American Association of Motor Vehicle Administrators) and should be consulted prior to mounting auxiliary lights.

State	SPOT LIGHTS Max. No.	FOG LIGHTS Max. No.	FOG LIGHTS Mtg. Hgt. (in.)	AUX. PASSING LIGHTS Max. No.	AUX. PASSING LIGHTS Mtg. Hgt. (in.)	AUX. DRIVING LIGHTS Max. No.	AUX. DRIVING LIGHTS Mtg. Hgt. (in.)
Alabama	1	2	12-30	1	24-42	1	16-42
Alaska	2	2	12-30	2	24-42	2	16-42
Arizona	1	2	12-30	2	24-42	2	16-42
Arkansas	2	2	12-30	2	24-42	2	16-42
California	2(1)	2	12-30	2	24-42	2	16-42
Colorado	2	2	12-30	2	20-42	2	16-42
Connecticut	2	2	12-30	2	24-42	2	16-42
Delaware	2	2	12-30	1	24-42	1	16-42
D.C.	2	2	12-30	2	24-42	2	16-42
Florida	1	2	12-30	2	24-42	3	12-42
Georgia	1	2	12-30	1	24-42	1	16-42
Hawaii	—	—	—	—	—	3	12-42
Idaho	2	2	12-30	2	24-42	2	16-42
Illinois	1	—	—	—	—	3	12-42
Indiana	2	2	12-30	1	24-42	1	16-42
Iowa	1	—	—	—	—	3	12-42
Kansas	2	2	12-30	2	24-42	2	16-42
Kentucky	—	—	—	—	—	—	—
Louisiana	Prohibited	2	12-30	2	24-42	2	16-42
Maine	1	2(2)	—	2(2)	—	2(2)	—
Maryland	1	2	12-30	—	—	2	16-42
Massachusetts	1	—	—	—	—	—	—
Michigan	2(5)	2	12-30	—	—	2	24 Min.
Minnesota	2	2	12-30	2	24-42	2	16-42
Mississippi	1	—	—	—	—	2	24 Min.
Missouri	1	—	—	—	—	3	12-42
Montana	2	2	12-30	2	24-42	2	16-42
Nebraska	1	—	12-42	—	—	2	24 Min.
Nevada	2	—	—	—	—	2	16-42
New Hampshire	2	—	—	—	—	3	12-42
New Jersey	1	—	—	—	—	2	12-42
New Mexico	2	2	12-30	1	24-42	1	16-42
New York	—	—	(6)	—	—	—	—
North Carolina	2	—	—	—	—	2	—
North Dakota	2	2	12-30	2	24-42	2	16-42
Ohio	1	2	12-30	2	24-42	2	16-42
Oklahoma	2(3)	2	(4a)	—	—	—	—
Oregon	1	—	—	—	—	3	12-42
Pennsylvania	1	—	—	—	—	(4a)	12-42
Rhode Island	2	—	—	—	—	2	(4)
South Carolina	1	2	12-30	1	24-42	1	16-42
South Dakota	1	—	—	—	—	3	12-42
Tennessee	—	—	—	—	—	—	—
Texas	2	2	12-30	2	24-42	2	16-42
Utah	2	2	12-30	—	—	—	—
Vermont	—	—	—	—	—	—	—
Virginia	2	2	—	1	—	1	—
Washington	2	2	12-30	2	24-42	2	16-42
West Virginia	1	2	12-30	1	24-42	1	16-42
Wisconsin	2(3)	2	12 Min. (4ab)	—	—	—	12 Min. (4ab)
Wyoming	2	2	12-30	1	24-42	1	16-42

(1) Cannot exceed 32Kcp or 30 watts
(2) Total of two fog or aux. lights permitted
(3) Must be mounted at height between 30- and 72-in.
(4a) Below headlight centers
(4b) Not to exceed 75Kcp
(5) Emit white or amber light only
(6) Affix amber lights below headlights and avoid glare or dazzle

Chart courtesy KC HiLites.

To provide you with the basic details about driving-light regulations in the various states, we've included a chart provided by KC HiLites. It should be of help if you're thinking of adding anything beyond the most simple-minded fog lights.

As you can see in the chart, fog lights and passing lights are acceptable in almost all states and won't get you into trouble with the law, assuming they're mounted and adjusted properly. If you put a set of killer long-range lights on your roof and blaze down the highway with them on, you're almost certain to feel the hot breath of the highway patrol.

In almost all states, roof- or rollbar-mounted driving lights are plain *illegal*. You can be cited just for having them on the vehicle, not just because they're on the roof but because they're well above the legal height allowed in most states. In some states, even though long-range lights aren't really legal, you won't get any static if you keep them covered on the highway. In California, for instance, roof-mounted driving lights are not legal, but they are usually tolerated, provided they're covered and cannot be turned on. The generally accepted way of fixing them so they can't be turned on is to remove the fuse or fuses from the circuit.

We asked our local police department about their views on auxiliary lights. The officers we talked to explained that because the laws themselves are couched in legal jargon and are not easily understood by the layman, it is the interpretation by the officer that will determine whether you'll be cited or not. Fortunately, there's usually a "policy for enforcement" in most police departments to promote uniform enforcement. This still doesn't mean that you won't get cited if the officer you happen to encounter is feeling grouchy that day.

Because of the state-to-state variation in laws covering auxiliary lighting, many vehicle manufacturers don't offer auxiliary lights as a standard option or accessory. Some, like Jeep, offer only passing/fog lights that are legal in all states. Others, like Mitsubishi and Toyota, provide auxiliary-light options only in those states where that particular type of lighting is legally acceptable. If you buy such lights and install them where they are legal in Arkansas, however, it doesn't assure that you won't get stopped in Texas or some other state where they aren't legal. The best advice we can give you is to check with your local highway-patrol office before traveling to another state.

INSTALLING LIGHTS

Light installation is a relatively simple task, but some basic precautions are in order. First, determine whether your vehicle's electrical system is capable of handling the extra load imposed by adding auxiliary lights. The basic rule of thumb is that the rating of your alternator should be 50% greater than the total of amount of current required by all electrical accessories. In other words, if you add up the current used by the stereo, air conditioning, headlights and driving lights, the alternator should be rated at half again as much current as total system demand.

Quartz-halogen fog or passing lights with 55-watt bulbs present no problem because a pair of these draw just over 9 amps. But adding a set of 100-watt driving lights to those 55-watters would take an additional 17 amps out of the system. This combination would be drawing 25 amps out of a system that would have to operate all other accessories and keep your battery alive at the same time. And if you have four killer 100-watters on the roof plus another pair on the front bumper, you're almost certainly going to end up in darkness if you don't have a high-output alternator.

Wiring Kit—When buying lights, it's best to purchase a wiring kit at the same time. Such a kit includes all required wire, connectors, fuse holders, switches, and so forth. One word of caution, though. If you're wiring 100-watt lights, you'll want 14-gage wire and you won't need a relay in the circuit. If you've selected 55-watt lights, you can use lighter wire, a lighter switch and a light relay.

Headlight Switch—When wiring lights for use on the highway, tie them into the headlight circuit so they will only go on when the headlights are on the appropriate beam. For example, mid-range or fog lights should work only when the low beams are on and go out when the headlights are switched to high beam. If you live in a state where driving lights are

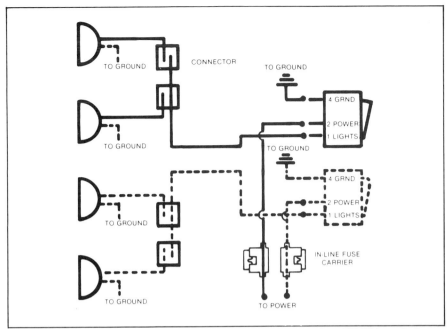

Most driving-light kits provide simple wiring instructions. This one from KC HiLites eliminates need for remote relay. Courtesy KC HiLites.

If auxiliary lights you're interested in don't come with an on/off switch, wiring and other pieces for installation, kits can be purchased separately. Make sure there's enough wire of right gage to do the job.

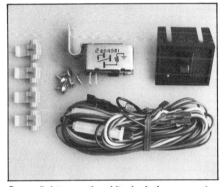

Some light-mounting kits include a remote-mounted relay which allows use of smaller-gage wire and low-capacity switch.

legal, however, these should be wired into the high-beam circuit so they go off when the headlights are switched to low beam.

This is most conveniently accomplished by taking power from the fuse block because high and low beams are usually on separate circuits. If it isn't possible to tap into the fuse block, use the appropriate terminal at the back of the headlight. Headlights are wired so the top terminal is the low beam, the black wire is the ground and the other wire goes to the high-beam filament.

For off-road use, you need *individual* switches that allow you to turn on any combination of lights at a given time. So don't wire off-road lights into the headlight switch; rather put each pair of auxiliary lights on a different switch.

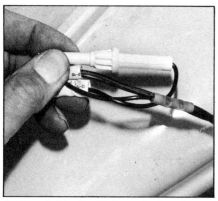

Auxiliary lights should always be fused separately from other electrical accessories.

Individual switches, such as these illuminated ones from KC HiLites, allow you to turn on any combination of lights at a given time, and find them at night as well. Photo by Jon Jay.

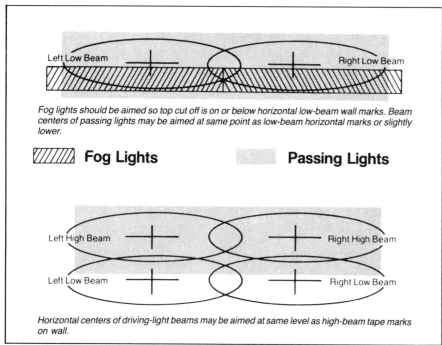

Fog lights should be aimed so top cut off is on or below horizontal low-beam wall marks. Beam centers of passing lights may be aimed at same point as low-beam horizontal marks or slightly lower.

Horizontal centers of driving-light beams may be aimed at same level as high-beam tape marks on wall.

Auxiliary driving lights are only effective when adjusted correctly. Courtesy KC HiLites.

ADJUSTING YOUR LIGHTS

After the lights are installed, the final step is to adjust them. Too many drivers skip this step, thinking they'll do that when they need them out in the bush. It's always better to adjust them properly before starting out. It takes a little time, but it's always worth the trouble.

To adjust the lights, you need a vertical surface to shine the lights on and a flat, level surface 25 ft away to park your vehicle. A garage door or wall can serve as the vertical surface, and a driveway, if it's flat and level, is a practical place to park your machine. You'll also need several lengths of black electrician's tape and a tape measure.

Before starting, be sure that the fuel tank is full, that the vehicle is parked 25 ft from the vertical wall and that somebody is sitting in the driver's seat while the adjustments are made. It's also a good idea to rock the vehicle from side to side

to settle the suspension after you've jockeyed it into position.

Next, mark the vertical center line of the truck on the wall with a length of tape. Measure the height from the ground to the center of the auxiliary lights and put a length of tape on the wall at this height. Now you have a cross on the wall.

Now, measure the distance between the centers of the lights. Divide this distance by two and put a shorter vertical length of tape on each side of the vertical center line. You need this so you can fine-tune the location of the beams. Loosen the light mounts enough that the lights can be adjusted.

Adjust fog lights so the center of the beam is just below the horizontal center line and the beams from the two lights just overlap in the center. This should provide a wide, flat beam that extends well to the sides of the vehicle. With the headlights on, the center of your short-range beams should be just below the center of the beam of your low-beam headlights. That is, they should fill in below the low beams.

Before adjusting driving lights, turn on the headlight high beams. Then, adjust your driving lights so the center of their beams are just above the center of the high beams. High-quality lights should provide a well-defined and uniformly lit pattern of light without dark spots or irregularities.

These instructions work best when the auxiliary lights and headlights are mounted near the same level. With rooftop-mounted lights, it may be necessary to aim them a little higher so their beams don't collide with the headlights' high beams. In fact, you may want to fine-tune the adjustments once you have tried them off-pavement. Remember, you want to supplement your headlights, not overpower or waste the lighting power your headlights already offer.

SUMMARY

As you can tell from all this, we like driving off-road at night, especially with good lights. In fact, we find this kind of driving so much fun that we welcome the opportunity, or the excuse, to make a good night drive. Get yourself some good lights and we think you will, too.

12

Fuel Tanks

Five 5-gal fuel cans strapped to roof of GMC Suburban would be dangerous in a rollover, but no doubt gave Garry Sowerby and Ken Langley the extra range they needed for 12,500 mile, 29-day trek. Among other things, pair survived rebel attack in Kenya and military action in Iran. Bully! Photo courtesy GMC.

Increasing the number of miles you can travel between fuel stops gives you a measure of security and convenience that you can't get any other way. Even more fun, when everybody else has to bail out to find gas, you get bonus points in the game of off-road one-upmanship play because you're able to stay on the trail.

Gas Cans—Although carrying one or more 5-gal gas cans may seem to be the simplest way of adding miles between fill-ups, there are several disadvantages that you should be aware of, and hazards to avoid.

First, where do you carry these aforementioned cans? Because of the danger of rupturing a can in a collision and setting fire to everything in sight, carrying extra gas on the rear of your vehicle as you motor along the highway isn't a good idea. The solution, if you use cans, is to leave them empty while you're on the highway, then fill them only when you leave the pavement, or as soon before this as possible. Because the chances of getting rear-ended out in the boonies are pretty remote, the hazards are thereby greatly reduced.

Carrying cans on the inside of your vehicle is even more hazardous. Something you don't need in a collision or a simple-minded rollover, is a gas can or two ricocheting around the interior. A full gas can can do serious damage to

In some states, it's illegal to carry a filled GI-type fuel can on an exterior rack on the highway. It's vulnerable to damage in an accident and constitutes a real fire hazard.

However, a gas can may be safely carried in a pickup bed if clamped or bungeed securely to prevent shifting. If your rig runs unleaded gas, make sure filler spout fits or you'll have to carry a funnel.

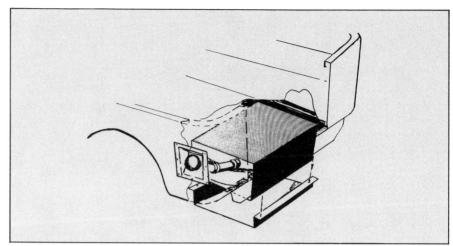

Typical auxiliary-tank installation under pickup bed with fuel filler recessed into body. Drawing courtesy Con-Ferr, Inc.

European-type "jerrican" from East/West Creations is available with quick-disconnect outlet and threaded coupler to allow can to double as emergency fuel tank when connected to fuel-pump line. Photo courtesy East/West Creations.

your body even if it doesn't split open and spray gas over everything. And if it does split, you become an instant torch just waiting for a spark.

So where should you carry gas cans? The safest place from an impact and occupant-protection standpoint, assuming you have a pickup truck with an open bed, is to mount the can or cans in the bed itself.

However, this raises the question of using cans in general, regardless of

mounting location. You have to remember to always carry a long, thin funnel to go into the unleaded-fuel filler-neck restriction of late-model vehicles or, better still, a length of hose or tubing you can use as a siphon to get it out of the can and into the tank.

Fortunately, there's a better way. That's to add fuel capacity by installing either an oversize main tank or putting in a second one.

Legal & Other Details—Most bolt-in auxiliary fuel tanks from commercial suppliers are made of 14- or 16-gage steel. But others are made from aluminum or molded polyethylene. A plastic fuel tank, you ask, raising your eyebrows? Actually, there are several advantages to plastic as a fuel-tank material. First, a plastic tank weighs about one-third as much as a 14-gage steel tank of the same capacity. Also, a plastic tank isn't subject to rust, and its useful life should be at least as long as a steel tank. If you're still doubtful about a plastic tank, you should know that Dodge trucks have been using them with excellent results for several years now.

Baffles—Regardless of the fuel-tank material, be sure your new tank is fully baffled. *Baffles* are partitions that prevent uncontrolled weight shifts and the damage that this sloshing can do to the tank. All professionally manufactured tanks are equipped with baffles, but it's something you may need to consider if you're having a custom tank built for

your vehicle by the local blacksmith or welding shop.

Speaking of blacksmiths, whenever you install a fuel tank, consider whether it needs skidplate protection. Some tank manufacturers are sensitive to this and use double-thickness metal on the bottom side, while others offer skidplates as an option. Still others are happy to provide you with a simple diagram of the skidplate that's needed.

Other Legalities—If you buy your tank from a reputable manufacturer, you can be reasonably sure that it meets all appropriate requirements of Federal Motor Vehicle Standard 301. This isn't a complicated regulation. It merely specifies that the tank's basic integrity be retained after impact and that it meets certain other common-sense precautions.

All tank manufacturers offer their tanks with filler systems designed for use with leaded or unleaded fuel. So you specify which type you need and that's the type of filler neck you'll get.

Do you have to install a second charcoal canister and complete bypass plumbing when you increase fuel capacity or add another tank? Usually not. It's like this: If your total tankage is over 50 gal, the law says you must have a second canister. Otherwise, don't worry about it.

TWO TYPES OF TANKS

There are basically two kinds of tanks to be considered for extending your

Flange-type stock Toyota pickup tank has been removed and stripped of all reusable hardware, such as gage sender, float, filler tube, and vents. Photo by Jon Jay.

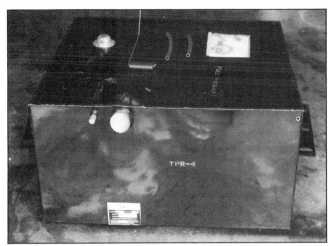

Steel 22-gal replacement tank from Northwest Metal Products fits in place of stock Toyota tank and reuses most of original hardware. Photo by Jon Jay.

range. One is the replacement-type tank with a larger capacity than the stock model. The other, which we're going to refer to as an auxiliary tank, is completely separate from the standard tank but is spliced into the vehicle's main fuel system upstream of the fuel pump.

The oversize or replacement fuel tank, assuming there's one available for your vehicle, is generally the simplest solution. Are you wondering how an oversize tank can fit into the space provided for the factory tank? Factory fuel tanks are stamped from sheet metal in two halves, then welded together like a clam shell. As a result, they have rounded corners and a lip around the circumference. Custom metal tanks are welded up with square corners, and their slightly enlarged dimensions hold a greater volume of fuel. And, on some vehicles, there's extra space into which a longer, or wider, or deeper (or longer, and wider, and deeper) tank can be fitted.

Fitting a replacement tank into your vehicle may not be as simple as unbolting the carriers of the stock tank and slipping the replacement tank into its place. We once had an oversize tank installed in a small pickup truck and it required removing the drive shaft and rigging in special hangers, as well as removing and replacing numerous hoses and fittings. The operation took the better part of a day and it was done by an experienced installer. So don't assume it's going be a casual Satur-

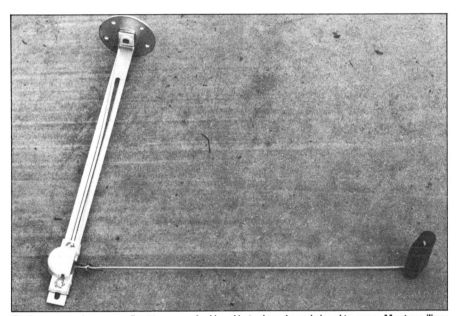

Fuel-gage sender uses a float to sense fuel level in tank and send signal to gage. Most auxiliary tanks need their own level-measuring system which can complicate installation.

day morning's worth of effort to install your replacement tank.

On some replacement tanks, specifically those in which the new tank is the same depth as the factory model, the factory fuel-gage sender can be reused. If the replacement tank's a different depth, it's a general industry practice to include a new fuel sender. This conveniently hooks directly up to the same wiring as the stock tank's sender and uses the stock gage as well.

What's a fuel-gage sender, you ask? That's the gadget with a float on it that goes into your tank and sends a variable voltage signal to the fuel gage based on the level of fuel in the tank.

If a replacement tank doesn't include a sender unit with the price of the tank, and you can't use the sender from the original tank, pay the extra amount to get one. Otherwise, your fuel gage may not work properly. Get the sender *before* you do the installation because the sender enters the tank from the top and access is restricted once the tank is strapped into place.

Limitations of Oversize Tanks—An oversize replacement tank may be the simplest solution, but adding a second tank will net the largest fuel-capacity increase. With an auxiliary tank, you can often double your fuel-carrying capacity. A replacement tank, however, rarely adds that much.

For example, one aftermarket supplier offers a 40-gal replacement tank for the full-size Chevy Blazer, where the stock tank holds 25 gal and an oversize factory-option tank holds 31 gal. With a single auxiliary tank, you can add up to 20 gal, and there are pairs of auxiliary tanks available that let you bolt in twice that much.

Of course, there's a third way to go: Buy an oversize replacement tank and then add one or more auxiliary tanks, as well.

Auxiliary Tanks—As mentioned earlier, an auxiliary tank is separate from the stock tank. A few vehicles are offered by the manufacturer with an optional auxiliary tank. But for most off-road machines, it's up to you to obtain the tank and either install it yourself or hire somebody else to do it.

If you add an aftermarket auxiliary tank, it has to be plumbed separately and joined to the main fuel line via a *crossover valve*. The valve may be either manual or electric. The electric switching device is easier to use, once installed, but it isn't as simple to bolt into place and is also less foolproof than the manual type.

For example, one of the authors proudly installed a pair of 10-gal auxiliary tanks to the rear of the fender wells in the bed of a small pickup, and eagerly took off for the boonies to try them out. Unfortunately, in the interest of simplicity, the manufacturer designed these tanks to drain into the main tank. This meant that you had to empty the main tank first, then hit the electrical switch for whichever auxiliary tank you wanted to dump into the main tank.

Beware of Switch Trouble—So, he drove until the engine sputtered, hit the electric switch and instead of catching and running, there was a sputter-cough-gasp and his faithful pickup coasted to a

halt. Hmmmm, no gas. So he tried the switch to the other auxiliary tank, listened at the filler neck for the sound of gas running from the auxiliary into the main tank and heard nothing but a meaningful silence.

After double-checking the wiring and everything else, he finally concluded that the switch wasn't working. Terrific. There he was, 20 gal in two auxiliary tanks but unable to deliver any of it to the engine.

Ultimately, applying his native genius, he loosened a hose clamp, disconnected the appropriate plastic tube and drained gas from the auxiliary for transfer to the main tank. This makes it sound far easier and quicker than it was, because the only container he had was a soft-drink can. The process involved filling the can, plugging the line with a pencil, then crawling out from under the truck, emptying the can into the main tank (using a piece of wire to hold the no-lead filler flap open) and repeating the process until approximately 2 gal had been transferred. This got him to the nearest gas station where he filled the main tank and drove home, ready to kill.

After returning to the tank manufacturer's establishment and relating the problem, he was told, "Oh, yeah, we've had some trouble with that switch. Here's another one…" After the new switch was installed, the system worked fine.

Mechanical Valve Installation—The experience with the electrical switch isn't a blanket condemnation of all such devices. For instance, on his next vehicle, he even screwed-up the installation of a mechanical valve. With this installation, the tank was at the rear of the vehicle in the location where the spare tire formerly lived. Unfortunately, when he decided on the location for the switchover valve, he decided it would be more out of the way if he put it on the floor just under the front edge of the driver's seat. And when he tried it while standing in the doorway and reaching in to twist the handle, it worked fine. What he'd forgotten was that when he was occupying the driver's seat, he couldn't reach the handle quite so easily or get the same kind of leverage. In fact, while he could touch the handle, he couldn't turn it and still keep an eye on the road.

Support vehicle for off-road racing team carries 40 gal in custom-made tank designed to fit around bed-mounted spare tire.

This caused the vehicle to wander hither and yon while he struggled with the valve handle. There were also several times when the engine ultimately died and he had to coast to the side of the road, get out, then reach in and make the switchover.

For some reason, this procedure always infuriated his wife. Especially that time in the mountains of Colorado when the fateful sputter took place on a narrow trail on the way to a ghost town with a rock wall on the driver's side and a sheer drop on the passenger's.

Do You Need a Fuel Gage?—Simply put, you can get along without a fuel gage for an auxiliary tank. But one is convenient to have, especially if you're using an electrical switchover valve. Then you can wire the gage into the same switch so the changeover from one tank to another is made automatically. This is the way it's done on vehicles whose manufacturers offer an auxiliary tank as a factory option. If you don't have automatic switching, there's a good chance you'll forget to switch the gage over and screw yourself up.

There is a logical alternative to having a gage on your auxiliary tank, however. That's to always use the fuel in the auxiliary tank first. When the auxiliary tank runs dry, switch to the main tank. Then you can read the gage and keep tabs on the quantity left.

Locations for Auxiliary Tanks— Popular locations to mount auxiliary tanks include: under the rear end, in various side-saddle locations outboard of the frame and, for pickups, in the bed itself. As you could predict, the easiest installation is also one that uses up the most usable space. For example, a simple cross-bed tank that sits in the pickup bed just behind the cab is easiest to install and simplest to plumb. This is also a practical location because it adds weight near the center of the vehicle where it's least likely to upset handling. Unfortunately, sitting there in the bed, it also occupies space that you might like to use for something else.

Another in-bed location that's more practical is the small tank or pair of small tanks that fit behind the rear wheel wells. These don't eat into usable bed space as seriously, but they do add weight at the very rear. In most pickups, this isn't a problem and, in fact, the extra weight often improves ride quality. However, if your truck has a modest payload, these additional pounds may cause the rear end to sag when you've loaded the back end with a week's hunting gear, including the four cast-iron deer decoys you never go without. In-bed tanks could be located in front of the wheel wells but they'd have to be of considerably smaller capacity because most trucks have more space to the rear of the fender well, especially the long-bed models.

Under the rear end in the place usually occupied by the spare tire is another very popular location for an auxiliary tank. Unfortunately, this requires an alternate location for the spare, such as on a swing-away rack or interior bracket.

Mounting the tank on the side between the frame and exterior sheet metal is also popular. But such tanks are usually of smaller capacity than cross-bed mounts or installations under the rear end.

Where you *don't* want to install an auxiliary tank is under the driver or passenger seat or in the cargo space of

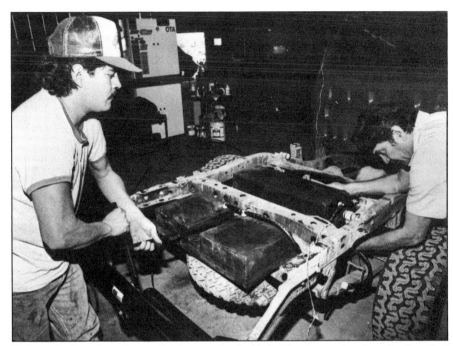

Fuel supply of most popular small pickups can be doubled with unique system from Auxiliary Fuel Systems. Polyethylene tank straps into place between spare tire and bed, which was removed only for photo purposes. Photo by Bruce Smith, courtesy Four Wheeler magazine.

your utility vehicle. This is something akin to carrying fuel cans in the passenger compartment and is simply too great a hazard to consider. It is also illegal in all states. True, many older pickups mounted the standard fuel tank under the front seat, but not any more. A rash of fires and incinerated drivers put an end to that.

Filler Lore— Most auxiliary tanks have their own filler systems. This usually requires cutting a hole in the side of your vehicle in the appropriate place and using the hardware supplied by the manufacturer. This isn't as simple as it sounds, however, because a recent regulation states that a fuel-filler cap must be recessed into the body sheet metal so it can't be pruned off in a sideswipe. It doesn't have to be under a filler door but it must be recessed, which can be inconvenient unless your vehicle has a handy built-in recess you can use.

Other tanks, usually those that snug up either ahead of or behind the rear wheels, are designed so the filler cap is in the wheel well. With this type, you don't have to hack up your sheet metal. But it

does make for a mighty messy filling operation after you've been playing in the mud. If mud is a way of life where you do your off-roading, you can minimize this aggravation by hanging a rubber flap over the filler cap. Regardless, gassing up is still not something you're likely to look forward to when en route to a fancy dress ball at the country club.

Some auxiliary tanks are also designed to fill through the same filler as the main tank. This seems like an excellent idea except that one of the authors had one of those once and was never sure the whole thing worked like it should. What made him suspicious was that although he had a theoretical fuel capacity of 40 gal, he was never able to convince himself that he got more than about 35 gal into the two tanks. With separate filler systems, you know exactly how much fuel goes into each tank.

What he suspected was that an air lock developed in the longer hose to the auxiliary tank and that it simply didn't accept any more fuel after a given point. If there wasn't an air lock in the filler hose to the

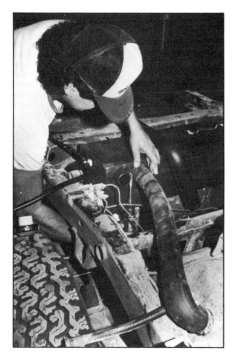

Auxiliary tank is mounted higher than and drains into standard tank. No switchover valve or added fuel gage and sending unit is required. Fill hoses, vents and all required hardware are supplied. Installation can be done from underneath by one person in two hours with simple handtools. Photos by Bruce Smith, courtesy of Four Wheeler magazine.

auxiliary tank, he never figured out what was wrong. The tank's manufacturer was baffled as well, by the way, able to offer nothing more helpful than, "Gee, I never heard of that one before...."

Incidentally, if you have an auxiliary tank and want to check your gas mileage, always check it using the main tank. Why is that, you innocently ask? It's like this: There's a surplus fuel return from the fuel pump and dribbles from the vapor canister and these empty into the main tank, not the auxiliary. If you try to calculate the mileage while using the auxiliary, you're not getting the benefit of the fuel that drains back into the main tank.

INSTALLING YOUR FUEL TANK

Most of the professionally manufactured tanks are designed for do-it-yourself installation and require nothing more specialized than the usual shade-tree mechanic's handtools. The most difficult part of the installation is manhandling the tank into place and holding it there while you get the fasteners attached. Unless you've got a strong friend, this part of the job can be simplified by the use of a floor jack and an improvised cradle.

Otherwise, there's nothing difficult about the installation as long as you follow the sequence recommended in the manufacturer's instructions. Fail to do so and you may end up with the tank bolted into place before realizing that you haven't hooked up the fuel sender, which is on top of the tank and now completely inaccessible.

Routing the fuel lines must also be done with care. These lines are made of plastic or neoprene and you should make sure they aren't resting on anything that will either melt or rub a hole in them. Securing the lines in place with nylon cable ties will help avoid problems.

SOURCES FOR TANKS

When you get serious about extending your range, the best source is usually your local, friendly off-road specialist. If you don't have such an animal, ask the dealer for a recommended supplier. If you're unsuccessful there as well, check out the advertisements in off-road publications. If there isn't a tank ad in the issue you're looking at, call the magazine's advertising department and ask them for the telephone number of a couple of tank manufacturers.

If you have a vehicle for which no ready-built tank exists, you can have one built by your local welding shop. As noted earlier, you do need to have baffles inside the tank to keep the fuel from sloshing but outside of that, the job shouldn't be either complicated or terribly expensive.

In other words, there's almost always a way of increasing your fuel capacity.

13

Skidplates & Body Armor

It is unfortunate that the mechanical makeup of any vehicle puts the tenderest parts down low. The engine oil pan, fuel tank, exhaust components, differential and, on 4X4s, the transfer case, are vulnerable to rocks, stumps and other snags that can jump up and bite you where it hurts the worst. Vital suspension and steering parts are down there, too: spring hangers and U-bolts, tie rods, steering arms, and more. In fact, it's almost incongruous that the all-important engine pan, or sump, that acts as reservoir for the life blood of the vehicle, is nothing more than thin, stamped sheet metal. If the engine oil sump acquires even a pinhole leak, the oil-pressure gage or dash warning light may not register a loss of pressure until it's too late to save the engine.

Newer vehicles often have aluminum housings for transmissions and transfer cases to save weight. It doesn't take a very hard knock to fracture one of these. Cast-iron or forged-steel housings are stronger, but even these cannot stand being dragged over boulders or smacked by some unforgiving piece of landscape.

For heavy-duty skidplate protection, some off-road racers use 3/16-in. aluminum mounted with flush-head Allen bolts. This one is shaped to fend off rocks by sloping down from pushbar and back under engine.

YOU'RE RESPONSIBLE

Before we get into the real meat of this chapter, remember that you're responsible for getting there and back with your machine in one piece. In other words, never depend on your skidplates to save you. Always drive as if you don't have a single skidplate anyplace.

Don't bash into that pile of rocks just because you think you're protected. When the tall rock comes along and there's no way of avoiding it, think about it and decide where you want it to pass underneath the vehicle.

This means figuring out where the most vulnerable parts are and then driving accordingly. For example, if your front differential is the lowest part of the front end, move over to one side and let that rock or stump pass under an area that has more ground clearance. This means

spending some time under the vehicle to study the locations of everything that's most likely to be damaged by contact with an undesirable object.

If you have a choice, always pass over the obstacle on the side where the fuel tank isn't—that is, if it isn't centered. You never know when a tire is going to tip a rock the wrong way and you're going to have to listen to it bang and rumble the whole length of the vehicle. That's the kind of incident that instantly brings you to a full pucker and can wreak havoc with anything as vulnerable as a fuel tank.

In most modern 4WD vehicles, the engine sump is well up out of what should be harm's way and, for that reason, is seldom protected by a factory-installed skidplate. If your vehicle is like this, avoid driving over rocks that the sump could come down on if a wheel slips or a rock shifts.

USE THE OLD BEAN

In the next section, we describe a number of skidplates and other protective devices for your off-roader. Obviously, if you're a casual weekend off-roader, you're probably not really going to need skidplates over the bolts that hold your leaf springs in place. On the other hand, if you're a hard-core back-country rock basher, you might be foolish to be without them.

What we're trying to say is to use the old bean, decide what degree of protection you want and don't settle for anything less.

SKIDPLATES

The term skidplate comes from the fact that they are designed to slide or skid over rocks and other solid obstacles which might otherwise damage vulnerable parts or high-center the vehicle and hold you fast. Harm to vital components

Vehicle manufacturers tend to be stingy with skidplates as illustrated by lightweight shield under transfer-case crossmember.

Rugged aftermarket skidplate by Con-Ferr is designed to protect steering gear and linkage on a Jeep CJ.

Business end of this D-50 could use skidplate protection for engine, transmission, front differential, CV joints, and transfer case. Photo courtesy Chrysler Corp.

can come from not only big rocks but stumps, fallen branches, hummocks of earth, and even small stones that lie on the hump between the wheel ruts or are kicked up by the tires. Damage can occur at low speeds, as when inching around rocks, almost as easily as at a faster pace. Skidplates, then, become very important to trouble-free off-roading, regardless of your driving type or style.

Stock Skidplates—Fortunately for the casual off-road driver, most late-model 4X4s are offered with small, individual skidplates to protect some of the more easily damaged vitals. We say *offered* because they are actually extra-cost options on some makes and models. If you are contemplating buying a new 4WD vehicle, find out if factory-available skidplates are included when you fill out the order form. Factory skidplates can also be purchased at your dealer parts counter, for vehicles for which they are available, and can be modified to fit on trucks and utilities not originally equipped with them.

If yours is a 4X4 for which no skidplates are offered, or a 2WD whose delicate underbelly cannot be fitted with stock skidplates intended for a same-make 4WD, or if you want even more low-down protection than the factory provides, it's time to paw through the aftermarket equipment catalogs. Or, you can take your rig to your friendly blacksmith or metal-fabricating shop, or even get some metal plate and make your own.

As a matter of fact, even if your 4X4 has factory-installed skidplates, it's not a bad idea to crawl under your rig and examine them closely. Decide if they'd really be effective when bashed by a stump, or if they'd do their job when the vehicle dropped straight down on a tall, pointed rock. Some manufacturers tend to skimp when designing such accessories to cut manufacturing costs and save weight.

The engineers probably never envisioned anyone actually driving through the boonies as hard as you want to, so they sometimes settle for nothing more than light sheet metal when armor plate is what's really needed. A hard whack can jam one of these stock plates into whatever it's intended to protect and the damage will be almost as bad as if a skidplate wasn't installed at all.

Suspension & Chassis Skidplates—Depending upon the make of the vehicle and whether it's 2WD or 4WD, there may be important suspension components that need skidplate protection. These might include the front-spring hangers or shackles on vehicles with semi-elliptic leaf springs, spring U-bolts and nuts, lower shock-absorber mounts, and so forth. Even if you don't bend or break one of these on an obstruction, the vehicle can become high-centered because of their shape and location. Small plates can be home-fabricated or purchased to protect these critical pieces and allow them to slide over an immovable object.

The Innocent Bush—The authors were once involved in a photo-and-test session with a full-size 4WD utility vehicle. We

Skidplates take many shapes and require odd cutouts and bends. When making your own, use a cardboard pattern. Shown is a transfer-case skidplate for a full-size Chevy Blazer or 4X4 truck.

Seldom-traveled trails often harbor rut-centered rocks concealed by shrubbery. Even with skidplate protection, wise off-roader lets taller rocks and other obstructions pass under side of vehicle with most ground clearance. Photo by Dennis Casebier.

were rattling along a semi-abandoned trail when we spotted an innocuous little shrub growing up between the tire tracks. No harm in straddling that, the driver mused. Trouble was, the bush had grown up around the nastiest rock in the entire southwest. With a *clang* that echoed off the canyon walls, the center crossmember collected that rock. Then, an unnerving howl began from somewhere deep in the bowels of the rig. Visual inspection showed only a crunched flange on the lower edge of the crossmember. But the grinding persisted whenever the vehicle was in motion. What we later discovered was that the crossmember was bent upward and the transfer case, which it supported, was pushed up against the floor. This in itself did not create a drive-line problem, but the whining sound of the transfer case, normally isolated by rubber mounts, was being transferred to the floorpan and thence throughout the rig like one big echo chamber.

Making Your Own—If a commercially made skidplate cannot be found to protect a critical chassis part, fabricate your own or find someone to do it for you. A welding or blacksmith shop, or anyone who can handle metal fabrication, can turn out a decent skidplate. But there are tricks to making one. Whether you're handy with a cutting and welding torch,

or even if you plan to leave the labor to a commercial service, here are a few points to bear in mind.

Study the component you want to protect and decide how the skidplate should be shaped to not only protect that part from below, but from the front and rear, as well. The skidplate should not be fastened to the component itself, except in the case of the differentials. Doing so would only transfer the shock of hitting an object to that part and possibly do as much harm as if the skidplate didn't exist. Study the proximity of the frame side rails or nearby crossmembers to see if they'll provide suitable mounting places. If they are too far away, are too oddly shaped to be of any help, or if they would require that the plate be overly large, plan on fabricating some heavy-duty brackets. Don't bolt the plate only in front, letting it extend rearward unsupported. It should be securely fastened at both ends and possibly at some mid-point, as well.

Allow a small amount of "crunch space" between the vital part and the skidplate. About an inch should do it; more than this will reduce ground clearance. Angle the leading edge of the plate upward to help the vehicle slide up and over a snag. And put another up-turn or bevel at the rear so you won't hang-up on something when reversing.

Mini-guard is for vehicles with semi-elliptic leaf springs to prevent exposed U-bolts and nuts from getting hung up on obstacles. Stud (top right) is lower shock mount.

Templates—Even if you have a professional shop custom-make a skidplate, you can save some money by making up a template or pattern for it. Do this by trimming, folding and taping heavy cardboard pieces until you get an accurate fit. Once you have it roughed out, the template can be transferred to metal plate and jigsawed or flame-cut to shape.

While it's a sensible idea to provide a skidplate under the engine when the oil pan is vulnerable to the abuses of off-roading, consider making a larger one

Off-road racing Mazda pickup features skidplate with heavy, louvered guard to protect radiator and other up-front vitals from a direct hit.

Another item from off-road race truck is battered but still snug-fitting rear differential guard.

that will also provide protection for nearby and vital suspension and steering parts. Such a skidplate can attach to the front bumper, a push bar or grille guard, angle back and down under the front crossmember or axle, then extend rearward as far as is prudent. It needn't be much wider than the oil pan, yet still safely cover the inboard ends of the tie rods, the front differential and critical steering linkage.

Skidplates for the engine, transmission and transfer case should have *access holes* so you can reach the fill and drain plugs. It's very disconcerting to have to remove a heavy skidplate just to do a little routine maintenance.

Material—Imported and small domestic trucks and utility vehicles can get by with 3/16-in. skidplate material. Full-size rigs might go up to 1/4-in. stock for really abusive off-roading. Aftermarket skidplates, and most home-brewed ones, too, are usually made of cold-rolled or high-tensile steel, and you can use this as well. However, a better, though more expensive, choice is aluminum. The professional off-road racing people lean toward 3/16-in. 6061-T6 aluminum. It's tough, can be formed to nearly any shape, can be accurately cut and drilled, and it's lighter than a similar-sized chunk

of steel. Also, it doesn't need painting, won't rust, and it retains its handsome silverish color regardless of abuse.

We have seen a number of handmade skidplates, and even some professionally fabricated, that were expertly done and solidly mounted. Yet they were bolted with ordinary hex-head fasteners. The head of a bolt or a nut protruding from a skidplate can be sheared off, or so badly mangled that it would take a cutting torch to remove the plate. Also, the vehicle can become hung-up on a bolt head. To prevent this, countersink the mounting holes in the skidplate and use countersunk Allen-head bolts. Flush surfaces are just the ticket for skidding along over Mother Nature's outback obstructions.

If you do follow our advice and use countersunk Allen-head bolts, be sure to carry an Allen wrench of the appropriate size. There may be a time when you have to unbolt that sucker when you're halfway between here and nowhere. In many instances, you can substitute a small, flat-blade screwdriver inserted between the hex "points," but there's no satisfactory substitute for the right Allen wrench.

Catalytic Converters—Vehicles with catalytic converters usually have a heat shield to help prevent the super-hot con-

verter from setting fire to grass or brush. These don't even pretend to be skidplates. Because catalytic converters are dreadfully expensive, you may want to protect yours with a real skidplate. Shape it so that twigs and leaves cannot become lodged between it and the heat shield and the converter.

Even if you leave this component as-is, check it from time to time if your travels take you through tall grass or brushy country. A good pal of ours very nearly lost his brand-new CJ-7 when a fire erupted as he drove along a gravel country road. There were no bushes there for his converter shield to scoop up, but he'd been in some grass earlier that morning. Heat from the converter dried the grass, then it erupted into flame. Only his fire extinguisher saved his vehicle.

Suppliers—Most off-road shops carry aftermarket skidplates or they can point you toward someone who does. But one of the best manufacturers we know about is Con-Ferr, Inc., 123-211 South Front Street, Burbank, CA 91502. Owner Pete Condos is a veteran off-roader himself and was a co-founder of the National Off Road Racing Association (NORRA) way back in 1967. His firm offers a wide selection of skidplates, replacement shock-absorber and spring mounts with

Exterior "body armor" such as diamond-plate rocker-panel guards and nerf bar are available for most vehicles.

An axle truss is designed to prevent flexing or bending of axle housing from high suspension impact loads encountered in off-roading. Combine one with a differential skidplate and you've got the best of both worlds.

designed-in skidplate protection, rocker-panel armor and similar products for a wide array of 4WDs. Incidentally, Con-Ferr has been in business since 1961, which makes it one of the oldest in the business for off-road equipment.

AXLE TRUSSES

The bumps, jolts and suspension overloads of off-roading can bend a solid-type, one-piece axle housing. Because the wheels are some distance outboard of the spring seats on the axle housing, imposed loads can permanently deflect the center of the assembly downward. This is not always visible, but sufficient to misalign the axle halves and create rotational resistance and abnormal tire wear. A bent housing can also put undue stress on the engine and other drive-line components, to say nothing of what it does to axle bearings.

The situation can be prevented in two ways. One of these is to weld steel gussets to the rear-axle tubes and differential housing, a treatment popular with off-road racers. But this can be overkill for the purely recreational off-roader. And if the job is not properly handled by a competent welder, heat from the welding may warp the housing and create exactly the problem that you're trying to avoid. The other alternative is to add an aftermarket axle truss, readily available through off-road shops to fit virtually all

Rear-axle truss with integral differential skidplate clamps to axle tubes of Toyota 4X4s with U-bolts. Installation is only a 10-minute proposition.

one-piece axle housings.

Basically, an axle truss is little more than a pair of steel bars or rods that bolt to the base of the differential housing and extend up and out to attachment tabs near the ends of the axle tubes or to spring U-bolts. When the rods are properly tightened, enough upward force is exerted on the axle housing to preclude its bowing downward. Aftermarket axle trusses can be installed in just a few minutes by the average do-it-yourselfer using common handtools.

Con-Ferr, Inc. has axle truss assemblies that incorporate small but rugged skidplates for the differential housings. Because the bottom of the housing is often the lowest point on a vehicle, and

because it is centered between the wheels, it is subjected to damage by obstructions lurking between the wheel ruts of back-country trails. You can high-center a vehicle, too, if the differential hangs up on a snag. A skidplate here can let you slide to safety, and when it becomes a part of an axle truss, so much the better.

GRILLE GUARDS

Grille and headlight guards, and push bars, are popular aftermarket products for protecting the fronts of vehicles from the hard knocks of off-roading. As their various names imply, they are useful for fending off branches and preventing other low-hanging objects or dense brush

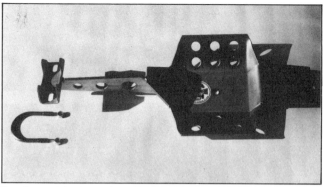

Sturdy combination axle truss/skidplate for solid front-axle Toyota pickups.

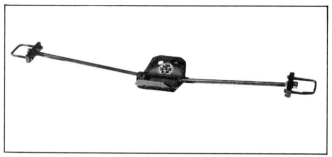

Outboard ends of this axle-truss/skidplate combination for full-size vehicles clamp to spring hangers. Large nuts at either end of truss bars allow preloading axle housing to minimize flexing.

Grille guards are also useful as a mounting place for auxiliary lights, or even a winch. Side extensions can protect headlights from low-hanging limbs or brush.

Pete Condos, off-road supplier since 1961, fits prototype grille guard into place. Optional headlight protectors bolt into place.

from inflicting damage on grilles, headlights and surrounding sheet metal. A push bar lets you push-start a disabled vehicle regardless of bumper height. Some are also suitable for mounting a winch and auxiliary lights.

These protective guards are readily available from most off-road equipment suppliers and mail-order houses. Some guards are universal, while others are designed to conform precisely to the front bumper, grille and headlight contours of specific vehicles. If you are in-terested in one of these, be sure it bolts securely to the frame or other sturdy chassis part and not just to the bumper.

Quality bars will bolt to the frame *and* to the bumper. This will reduce the tendency for the upper part of the guard to spring back on impact and damage the top of the grille or leading edge of the hood. The guards come in various shapes and styles, as you'll see while paging through this book. One will surely strike your fancy.

Most grille guards, especially those that extend outboard to double as headlight protectors, are assembled from several sections of steel plate or tubing. This is so they can be shipped knock-down to minimize freight charges. There's nothing wrong with this. Just be sure to follow the assembly instructions, and if the bolts that hold the sections together seem a little skimpy, ream out the holes and go up one bolt size.

Or, you can *weld* the grille-guard sections together for a really strong unit that won't vibrate apart.

Sportbars & Rollbars

One of the authors extricates himself from an off-roading upset. The truck did not have a rollbar, and had it rolled over onto its top, the extra protection would have been appreciated. Photo by Jimmy Nylund, courtesy Four Wheeler magazine.

Shortly before this book reached its final stages of preparation, one of the authors rolled a brand-new 4X4 pickup. No, it wasn't a high-speed highway accident. Nor was it the result of misjudgment during an off-road leaping antic like you see in the magazines. Nor did it happen during an off-road race. The truck was proceeding as nicely as you please along a rocky shelf in eastern Utah, high above the Colorado River. A curbing-like ridge divided the shelf into two narrow, boulder-strewn paths. The driver had to approach the sheer step-up at a shallow angle, just like the trucks that had preceded him in a caravan, and put the left front tire against it. Then, with just the slightest amount of throttle, the

truck started to climb the obstruction. It was then that it rolled lazily over on its right side to crinkle the sheet metal and break the windshield. The driver climbed uninjured *up* and out through the driver's side window, wondering why his view of the countryside had suddenly turned sideways.

What had happened was a relatively common off-roading occurrence. It is one that even some-time, casual four-wheelers should bear in mind when equipping a vehicle for the rigors of the outback.

The incident points up the need for off-roaders to have an important item of safety equipment in addition to seat belts—a *rollbar*. And which, by the

way, the subject truck did not have. In this particular case, the rollbar would not have been called upon to save a life from inward-buckling sheet metal. But the rig could have just as easily continued over onto its top where its weight could have crushed the roof. Or worse, the truck might have tumbled to the bottom of the river gorge with dire results.

Sportbars vs. Rollbars—The racing fraternity insists on a distinction between a sportbar and a rollbar. The rollbar, professional racing organizations insist, must meet certain stringent criteria including tubing diameter, material type, the manner of welding, how and where the assembly joins the chassis, and so forth. But rollbars for the purely recrea-

Prefabricated bar assemblies are available for virtually every type of off-road vehicle, be it two- or four-wheel drive. This one includes tabs for mounting roof lights. Photo courtesy Smittybilt.

Assemblies may have one, two or three hoops. This double unit of 3-in. tubing has stout downbars that fasten to wheel wells in pickup bed. Photo courtesy Smittybilt.

Rollbars for recreational use are sometimes called sportbars or lightbars. Shown is a three-tube unit with double downbars designed to fit in pickup-truck bed. Photo courtesy Smittybilt.

like the one suffered recently by the author. In his case, the truck had virtually zero forward momentum when it tilted onto its side. Situations such as too-steep a side-hill, an embankment that gives way under a low-side wheel, and similar happenings can cause a 4WD to land anywhere but on its wheels.

Occupant protection against accidental spills are what recreational rollbars are all about. And when installed in the bed of a pickup truck, they're handy to mount auxiliary lights, where legal. Recreational rollbars look good, too, lending any vehicle a definite macho appearance, to say nothing of driver peace of mind when he's off-roading with family or friends.

Types of Rollbars—First are the single-tube bars, usually of large-diameter steel tubing. These have supporting legs, called down-bars, that brace the assembly from the rear. Single-tube bars bolt into a pickup bed, or inside a closed-body utility vehicle, with the down-bars fastened to the rear wheel wells. The entire assembly might be welded into a single structure, but more often it is pieced together from slip-jointed curved and straight sections that bolt together. These come knocked-down to reduce shipping costs.

Then there are double-tube rollbars with twin hoops. If the hoops are spaced several inches apart, they are often joined at the top by sheet metal or steel mesh and called sandbars. These are handy on open

tional vehicle can be a far simpler structure and, if one is purchased ready-made from an aftermarket supplier, capable of a do-it-yourself installation.

The confusion between the terms arose when lawyers decided to help save manufacturers from product liability suits if the driver and passenger got into an upside-down situation and were injured or killed. But in more court cases than

you want to think about, the decision has been that if it looks like a rollbar, it had better work like a rollbar, and calling it something other than a rollbar does not reduce the manufacturer's liability. Lawyers just love it!

Common Rollovers—Most off-road rollovers are not the sort of spectacular crashes you see in the movies or on TV. The bulk of back-country upsets is more

Mangled rollbar on this Jeep CJ-5 probably saved driver's life. Bars are now standard on all topless Jeeps. Photo by Ron Sessions.

Some in-cab bars or rollcages require no cutting or welding for installation; tubes slip together and are through-bolted. Photo courtesy Smittybilt.

rigs such as Jeep CJs and help keep an inverted vehicle from sinking too far into sand, hence the name. Double-tube rollbars are often of smaller-diameter tubing than single hoops, but provide comparable protection.

In-Cab Rollbars and Cages—In-cab bars are prefabricated to fit specific vehicle makes and models. These are formed to closely follow the inside contours of a truck cab or utility vehicle. Some are merely single-bar hoops that run up from the floor inside the rear door jambs, then curve across under the roof just behind the front seats. In a utility vehicle, the in-cab bar may also have down-bars that tie into the rear floor area or to the wheel wells.

Some in-cab assemblies use two hoops, one over the driver's head and another running inside the cab's A-pillars then across just above the windshield. These are tied together with fore/aft tubes that unite the structure into a cage-like structure, hence their name. If mounted securely at their bases, these can provide good occupant protection. The best mounting is with the fasteners running through the flooring and into the chassis side rails or body mounts, similar to how race-truck rollcages are secured.

All in-cab rollbars and cages tend to be a little unsightly, but that's the price you must pay for safety. Also, it's best to wrap the tubing with lengths of tubular padding to prevent bumped heads, shoulders and shins.

If you're thinking of buying a new 4WD, check if you can order it with a factory optional rollbar. The agency parts man may also be able to order a factory rollbar for older models as well. But if you don't like the looks of the factory rollbar or one isn't available for your model, any number of aftermarket suppliers can accommodate you. Stop by your friendly off-road shop. If he doesn't stock a bar to your liking or one to fit your specific vehicle, choose one from his rollbar catalogs and have him order it.

Other Side of the Coin—Despite the added strength a rollbar adds to the cab of a vehicle in the event of an upset, it has its negative points. It's only fair that we look at the flip (pun intended) side of the rollbar argument.

The large-diameter tubing used for the main hoop and down-bars of bed-mounted rollbars makes loading or unloading difficult, at least from the front sides. Too, a rollbar eats into bed space and, unless you have one especially tai-

If you drive like this, better have a rollbar to protect your noggin. Photo by Peter du Pre, courtesy of Four Wheeler magazine.

lored for it, you can't use a camper shell.

Rollbars inside of utility vehicles can also be unhandy. Again, they use up interior space, can partially block the view through some windows and, in the case of two-door vehicles, further hamper the already-hard rear-seat access and egress.

What it all boils down to, really, is your own particular preference. Of course, we cannot ignore the occupant-

Professional racing rollbars and cages must be fabricated from specific material of certain diameters and wall thicknesses. Because rollcage joints must be welded all the way around, cab had to be lifted above chassis after hoop legs were secured to frame.

Racing rollcages cannot be welded directly to the chassis. These downbars end with urethane bushings through-bolted to tabs on frame.

protection aspect of rollbars. It ranks right up there with dutifully buckling our seat belts for even the shortest of trips. But then, how many off-roaders do you know that have rolled a 4WD and had a rollbar save them from injury? Rollbars are good things to have, true, but the odds of having to rely on one while putting up with its general inconvenience is something to consider.

Racing Rollbars & Cages—Race-ready rollbars and cages are an entirely different matter than recreational-vehicle assemblies. And though we don't expect the weekending off-roader to cough up the $1500 or more it costs to have a rollcage fabricated by a professional race shop, noting some of the requirements of race organizations gives a clue to fabrication and how much emphasis they put on safety.

A race-approved rollcage is more than a tubular structure designed to save the driver's noggin. It's a part of the chassis, designed to reinforce the vehicle against the brutal punishment dished out during a race. The sheet-metal or fiberglass body on most professionally built off-road racers can be peeled away leaving a reinforced frame with the front and rear ends united by an inverted truss.

The rollcage itself is essentially a box-like structure surrounding the driver's area. Down-bars run from the rear top of the cage to the frame ends. More bars run from the cowl area in front to the forward frame ends. There are usually myriad diagonal tubes running here and there to form the necessary triangulation. The whole thing results in a girder-like structure to help the vehicle withstand stresses and strains that would reduce a conventional vehicle to junk. Often, tubing is also used for mounting shock absorbers, the fuel tank, a spare tire, and other essential equipment. The bodywork, in most cases, is merely decorative and adds little or no strength to the vehicle.

Though a proper racing rollcage is designed to strengthen a chassis, some flexibility must be permitted, or the race vehicle is apt to break in half. This is done, not by solidly welding the various tubes and down-bars directly to the frame rails, but by mounting them with urethane bushings. Some of the nearby photos show a rollcage undergoing fabrication, just to show you how time-consuming and complex a project it is and why it's so expensive.

Racing Rules—SCORE International (31356 Via Colinas, Suite 111, Westlake

Village, CA 91362) is the largest sanctioning body in off-road racing. Most of the smaller organizations follow their rules and regulations. These are very explicit and while there may be some variation in rollbar and rollcage requirements depending upon the type of vehicle, here essentially is what SCORE tells you:

"Mild carbon steel or 4130 chrome-moly is recommended for all types of rollcage construction. All welded intersections must be stress-relieved by flame annealing. Welds must be high quality with good penetration and no undercutting of the parent metal. No oxyacetylene brazing on rollcage is permissible. No square tubing is permitted.

"Cages must be securely mounted to the frame, gusseted and braced at all points of intersection. Cab- or body-mounted cages must be attached to the body structure by direct welding, but must also be bolted through and attached by the use of doubler plates (one on each side) with a minimum thickness of 3/16 in.

"Rollcage terminal ends must be located to a frame or body structure that will support a maximum impact and not shear, allowing more than 1-1/2-in.

Racing rules forbid gaps in welded rollbar joints. Tube ends must be fish-mouthed with a grinder or cutter for a close fit.

Additional driver protection is offered by X-brace that fits inside door panel on this Class-7 Chevy S-10 race truck. Photo by Tom Monroe.

movement in the rollcage-terminal end.

"Where nuts and bolts are used, the bolts shall be at least 3/8-in. diameter, SAE Grade 5 or of equivalent aircraft quality.

"All rollcages must be constructed with at least one front hoop, one rear hoop, two interconnecting top bars, two rear down braces and one diagonal brace and necessary gussets.

"All rollcage bars must be at least 3-in. in any direction from the driver's and co-driver's helmets while seated in their normal positions.

"Gussets must be installed at all welded *main* intersections on the main cage including diagonal and rear down braces, and where single weld fractures can affect driver safety. Gussets may be constructed of eight 1/8x3x3-in. flat plate, split, formed and welded corner tubing, or tubing gussets the same thickness as the main-cage material. Rear down braces and diagonal braces must angle no less than 30° from vertical."

Despite its legalese jargon, SCORE gets the message through. Safety is first and foremost in racing. And many casual off-roaders should heed this, too. You never know when you might tilt over on your side, roll to the bottom of a sand

Rear frame rails are supported by braces that tie into rollcage. Soft bushings are used at mounting points to allow some flex. Photo by Tom Monroe.

hill, or crunch over on your lid when side-hilling at too steep an angle. So, although there are pros and cons involving rollbars, you might want to give one careful consideration. In the meantime, try to keep the shiny side up!

15

Off-Road Driving

Obviously, not everyone drives their truck-tired Oldsmobile Cutlass down the Baja pensinula at breakneck speed. But even actor James Garner and Cliff Coleman had to keep their Baja 1000 entry "Banshee" on course and drive where it was legal to do so. Photo by James T. Crow, courtesy Road & Track magazine.

The first question a person who has never driven a back-country trail will ask is, "How *do* you drive off-road?" And the question that one grizzled veteran might ask another is, "How do *you* drive off-road?"

To old-time off-roaders, it's like asking how they tie their shoes or comb their hair. They know how to do it, but they learned this skill so long ago that by this time they've forgotten there was ever a time when they didn't know how. They've forgotten that they were once innocent of a whole bunch of specialized skills that now seem like second nature to them.

Ask them how to keep from getting stuck and they'll say, "Well, you kinda feel your way along and don't break traction." Which is exactly what you do but is of no help at all if you haven't had the experience.

The bottom line is that being an expert off-road driver comes with experience. And the only way to get this experience is to go out there in your off-road vehicle and learn. All of us, when we first started out, pulled dumb stunts. For example, on his very first off-pavement expedition, one of the authors shoved the transfer-case lever to 4H and innocently drove off the hard road toward the nearest sand dune. And promptly got stuck. He didn't know that, in those days, you also had to get out and lock the front hubs.

Learning by Doing—The point is this:

In off-roading, you learn by doing. Oh yes, there are many do's and don'ts to driving in mud or sand or snow or whatever. There's also the mechanical side, such as learning when to shift into four-wheel drive, when to air your tires down and how to get unstuck once you're in over your wheels. These are all good, helpful hints and are things you need to know. In fact, this book was written to tell you just that.

But what we can't do, of course, is take the place of good old-fashioned, hard-won experience. That, you've got to get for yourself.

Are you a person who does everything logically and in a well-thought-out sequence, preparing yourself as well as

Off-*pavement* driving is a better term when using existing trails, but there are still many techniques to be learned, and habits to be formed, before hitting the dirt.

When properly equipped, four-wheelers can tow trailers through the outback where the driver of a conventional car wouldn't dare tread.

possible before actually doing it? If you are, here's a course of instruction for you to follow before your first venture into the outback:

First, get out the owner's manual for your vehicle and study it, becoming familiar with the operation of the controls and learning everything the manufacturer can teach you. How does the four-wheel-drive system work, for instance? Do you know how to operate the transfer-case shift lever? Do you have manually locking hubs or automatic ones, and how do they work? Or are there no locking hubs at all? Does the manufacturer suggest more frequent maintenance if you've been driving off-road? Good information, all of this.

It's also a good idea to spend an hour or so lying on your back looking underneath your vehicle. The purpose is to learn where everything is, particularly those pieces that are vulnerable to damage from rocks, stumps, elephant skulls and other obstacles you may encounter along the trail. Where's the fuel tank, for instance? Is it tucked up out of the way where you don't have to worry about bashing it with a rock? Or, if it isn't, does it have a protective skidplate under it? How about the oil pan? Is it vulnerable? Or the steering linkage? Or the transmis-

Automatic-locking front hubs (left) are replacing manual hubs like that at right, but be sure which type are on vehicle you're driving. Photos by John Lawlor

sion or transfer-case housing? What's the lowest point on the underside? Usually it's the exhaust system. Where is it located? If you know where the lowest point is, you have that better chance of keeping it away from danger.

As we say, all of this is good stuff and gives you information about things you ought to know.

Now that you've accumulated all of this theoretical knowledge, the next step is to find an open field or unpaved parking lot and put your vehicle through its paces. Drive around, turn left and right, stop and start, shift into and out of four-wheel drive. Get to know your vehicle, in other words, and get a feel for the difference between driving over unpaved terrain and your typical hard-surfaced street or highway.

Safety—Always snug down your seat belt and make sure your passengers do, too. This is a basic and fundamental practice for any kind of driving. Second, al-

109

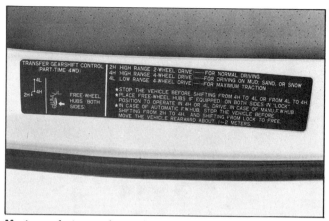

Most manufacturers place a decal similar to this somewhere in vehicle's cab to suggest when to use 4WD modes and how to operate transfer case.

Develop a sense for your vehicle's ground clearance and where lowest parts are. Don't straddle a rock or tree stump unless you are certain you won't damage something.

Always drive with your thumbs outside steering-wheel rim. This way you won't injure yourself if a front wheel strikes an obstacle and spins the wheel out of your grasp.

If you're new to off-roading, find a place to practice turning and going up and down hills. *Don't be overconfident.*

ways hold the steering wheel with your thumbs outside the rim. Hitting a rock or other obstacle with a front wheel can rip the steering wheel out of your grasp and the spokes can do bad things to your thumbs.

The next step is to find some easy off-pavement trails to practice on, gradually working up to more difficult terrain. What you'll be doing at this point is learning to "read the road." This means learning to judge the terrain ahead of you and how fast, in what gear and on which path you should proceed.

Taking it Easy—However, if you're like most of us, the first thing you'll do when you get your off-road vehicle is head out into whatever kind of country you had in mind when you bought that

beauty. Naturally. Who ever reads the instructions first?

And if this is what you do, fine. But do let us give you a few sage words of counsel. First, take it easy. There's an unfortunate tendency for the less-experienced driver to go faster than is either prudent or necessary off-road. Yes, there are times when you do need to gas it. But you have to learn when those times are. At least 99 percent of the time, slower is better. Start slow and build up speed as you build up experience.

One of the first lessons to be learned in off-roading is to be flexible about time. Don't think of time and distance as hav-

ing a locked-in relationship. On an Interstate, you can schedule every stop on your journey and come within a few minutes of your planned arrival time after a 500-mile day. Out there in the great nowhere, there are times when you'll think you've done a terrific job if you have a 50-mile day. Heck, we've seen trips where we would have been tickled to death with a one-mile day!

Second, in the words of an old-timer we've traveled many a good off-road mile with, "Do it elegant." By this, he means always drive smoothly. Never spin a wheel if you don't have to. Don't abuse the machinery. Don't rush into

One of four cardinal rules of off-road driving: *never spin your wheels unneccessarily.* You stand a chance of digging yourself down or, if the ground is hard and rocky, of cutting your tires.

If you don't have friends with 4WD vehicles, there's bound to be a club in your area. Ask to go along on a trip as a guest, then join up if they're friendly folks who like to do the things you do.

situations before you have evaluated them. And when in doubt, stop and think it over. Then proceed with caution.

Come to think of it, these may be the most valuable words we can give you on the subject. Do it elegant.

Go With a Buddy—We'd like to make one more suggestion in this regard. When you first start out in the wonderful world of off-roading, always go in the company of at least one other vehicle. If you've got a buddy whose skill level is about the same as yours, you can learn together. And that's always more fun. But the real reason is that with a buddy—and a towstrap—you can travel off-road with much greater impunity than if you're alone.

Alone, even if you're prudent and don't take any foolish chances, you can get seriously stuck. Which isn't a lot of fun when you're 40 miles from nowhere, the creek is rising and a pack of wolves is closing in on your campfire.

This is logical and basic stuff. And we don't want to bore already experienced off-roaders who may be reading this in hopes of sharpening their own expertise or rediscovering forgotten techniques. So, we'll move to more interesting things after listing the four cardinal rules of off-roading.

It looks calm and serene in this dry wash, but vehicle in rear is *high-centered* on embankment. A friendly yank set things right. Always travel with a buddy.

1. Always snug down the seat belts.
2. Always put your thumbs outside the steering-wheel rim.
3. Never apply the brakes just as you strike an obstacle.
4. Never spin your wheels if you don't have to.

WHEN TO USE 4WD

One question that will be bandied about around back-country campfires long after the marshmallows are gone, is when to shift a vehicle into four-wheel drive; that is, if the rig is a 4WD and doesn't have a full-time system. Some drivers like to snick the transfer-case lever into 4H (four-wheel drive, high range) as soon as they leave pavement. They feel safer this way, because if they suddenly encounter a swath of soft stuff, they have the traction to get on through to the other side. If they do mire down, there's always 4L (four-wheel drive, low range) to get them out.

Some makes of 4WDs require stopping or at least slowing before engaging four-wheel drive. On other makes with manual-locking hubs, someone has to get out and set them. Momentum and late braking may have put the vehicle well into the slippery stuff, and it's disconcerting to get out in the cold or rain and twist the hub levers. If you shift into 4WD right off, you won't have to put up with this.

Proponents of the other school recommend staying in two-wheel drive until it's absolutely necessary to shift. This way, they argue, if and when they mire down, they can rely on four-wheel drive to get out by backing to the harder surface they just passed over or by going through to the far side. They also argue that the less four-wheel drive is used, the less the wear and tear on the machinery and the better the fuel economy.

Directional Stability—All of this may be true, but it's also true that four-wheel drive provides better directional stability on dirt. With all four wheels driving, the forces are divided between the axles, and the rear end won't slide out on turns so easily. Sudden veering to avoid an obstacle will be more precise and all four wheels will be affected by engine braking when you lift the throttle, not just the rears which can induce skidding.

Another school of thought is that you should use four-wheel drive at every opportunity. You paid a lot of money for the 4WD option on your vehicle so why not use it every chance you get?

2WD vs. 4WD—In a comparison test of two otherwise identical trucks, except that one was 2WD and the other 4WD, the two-by led the four-by over a long and arduous route, the remnants of an abandoned railroad right of way. The trail wandered through an arid western desert, dropping now and then into sandy arroyos once crossed by trestles. On occasion, it knifed through old cuts now littered by rocky rubble. The 2WD, making its way as nice as you please in third gear, suddenly ran into a patch of soft sand. The alert driver felt the truck begin to bog down so he deftly dropped to low gear and gassed it to maintain momentum. Shortly, he was safely on the other side.

The 4WD, following a few minutes behind, was in two-wheel drive because the trail had been an easy one so far. The pilot wasn't paying as much attention as he should have. When he reached the sand, he lost his momentum and stopped but not until after the rear tires had dug themselves a nice pair of holes. He got out all right but not until he'd climbed out to lock his hubs, shoveled a little, then pulled himself free in four-wheel drive. During all this, the 2WD driver was watching from a comfortable seat on his tailgate and laughing.

There are two morals here. Three actually. One is that one driver was paying attention to what he was doing and the other driver wasn't. Another is that the cunning and watchful driver of a 2WD can often go where the inattentive driver of a 4WD cannot. Third, of course, is that the 4WD driver would have been better off using four-wheel drive from the outset of his journey.

Actually, deciding when to shift into

You don't need four-wheel drive on a hard-packed surface like this. But if you do, you'll have better directional stability, especially over washboard surfaces, and be ready for softer ground that may lie ahead.

Use low range on steep hills, whether heading up or down. Low range can minimize clutch slippage when going uphill and provide more compression braking when coming back down.

Many abandoned railroad rights of way are historically interesting, pass abandoned settlements, and can be a challenge to drive. But check first with local sheriff or ranger to see if trail is open to public use. Many are, but not all!

Sand dunes up ahead! Better put it in 4WD, low-range. Photo by Dennis Casebeir.

four-wheel drive boils down to a matter of personal preference. When you've gained the experience that only many trips into the outback can teach, you'll have had enough encounters with the unexpected, and with your vehicle, to know when to reach for the transfer-case lever.

Low Range—Something else you need to decide is when to use low range. We think that low range is one of the best features of four-wheel-drive, especially with the more moderately powered small trucks and sport-utility vehicles.

What low range does is increase torque to the wheels, giving you more go-ahead, get-down-and-grunt go-power. It does this by sending the transmission's output through a reduction gear that usually just about doubles the final-drive ratio. What

Trail can quickly change from hard and smooth to sandy, rocky or muddy just as quickly as it can change from level to steep up- or downgrade. If route is new to you, go easy.

Low range is absolutely essential in certain places. Worse than driving up the capital steps is this rocky gorge where progress may be measured in *feet* per hour instead of *miles* per hour.

Sand can be fun if treated with respect and you're absolutely sure of what you're doing.

Or sand can be treacherous. The grains under this tire have been "rearranged" sufficiently that some jacking and digging are in order.

you do is yank your transfer case into 4L and all the gears in your transmission are multiplied by the low-range ratio.

Some off-roaders only use low range when they're bogged down and can't make headway in any gear in high range. That's not making the best use of a good thing, in our opinion. One of the good things about low range is that it lets things happen slowly. And there are times when going at the slowest possible pace is absolutely the best way to do it, such as when crawling through rock or any other kind of really rugged terrain. In low range, you can grind your way up, onto and down off those big obstacles. This not only helps qualify you for our award for elegance, you're also much less likely to drop down on a great jagged rock and graunch up your sheet metal or poke a hole in something vital.

Steep Hills—Low range is also what's needed on a really steep grade, of course. Shove it into low-range first gear, let out the clutch and let it creep, where in high range you'd be slipping the clutch (with a manual transmission, of course) trying to keep from killing the engine. And the smell of fried clutch is not one of the fine odors you like to remember from your off-road adventures.

Low range also provides greater engine—compression—braking. When

you're heading down a steep slope, for instance, where you don't want to brake and take a chance of the wheels sliding, low range is what you need.

It doesn't sound right, but we also believe it's possible to make better time in low range than in high range when the trail is made up of a combination of slow and some not-so-slow stretches. With four (or five) gears in your transmission, you aren't limited to a creep when you're in low range. In fact, in most small trucks and utilities, fourth gear in low range produces approximately the same final-drive ratio as second gear in high range. So you've got good off-road cruising speed when you need it, but you've also got those lower gears that'll bring your speed right down to a crawl when that's what the road demands.

So hooray for low range. Use it every chance you get.

SAND

Sand has been the bane of mankind since the automobile was invented. There may have been more vehicles stuck in sand than any other substance. Why is this? Why is sand, which is merely a lot of small pieces of rock or the remnants of seashells, so soft? Tires don't sink into larger rocks. In fact, nothing gives a firmer surface on which to

Tire with aggressive tread is intended for mud, but wide cross-section works just as well in sand where tread has little to do with flotation.

drive than rock.

A sand grain is as solid as its parent material. But the granules come in various shapes. Depending upon the material of which it is composed and how it was worn by the actions of wind, water and other grains abrading it, a grain can be shaped like a cube, round or jagged. If all the grains on a sand patch were cubed and neatly arranged, like boxed sugar cubes. the surface would support a vehicle. But if the cubes were piled willy-nilly as they are in Nature, there'd be space between them and pressure would rearrange them, crumble the edges and force them closer together. Rough grains would have even more air between them and be more easily disarranged under weight.

Press a heavy object into sand and the area bearing the weight will sink down in relation to the surrounding surface. A tire will leave a track in sand because as the weight moves over the surface, it is rearranging the grains into a more compact form and forcing some of them aside. When this occurs, a tire cannot roll because of sand piled ahead of it.

Penetration—A sharp object will penetrate sand more readily than one that is blunt. And the blunter the point the more force required to penetrate the surface. Penetration depth is a function of the force applied and the contact area. The old Model T Fords used tires with a cross-section of 3-1/2 in. and a tread width less than that. So the famous Flivver got stuck in sand a lot. A newer tire with a tread width of, say, nine or more inches will not sink into sand so easily. That early Ford tire had a surface contact patch, or footprint, of about 10 in. The 40 sq in. of all its tires supported 2000 lb or 50 lb per sq in. A modern tire with a 9-1/2-in. tread width will put down a footprint of roughly 80 sq in. A 3500-lb vehicle with a total footprint of 320 sq in. will present only 11 lb of weight to each square inch or approximately 1/5 as much as the Model T. Or, put another way, it will have five times the flotation.

Still, vehicles old or new, big or small, and no matter how much or how little power they produce, will always get stuck in sand. Too much throttle and the tires spin, scooping sand out in their tread grooves and settling down until the chassis rests on the surface. Too little throttle and the vehicle loses its momentum because it cannot climb up and over the "bow wave" of sand ahead of the tires. Tread pattern has little to do with slogging through sand, outside of special paddle tires made expressly for the purpose and which are useless on harder surfaces, except that a well-worn tire with little or no tread left works best under most circumstances. Large diameter tires help in sand since they present a longer footprint than a small-diameter one. However, the widest possible tread

Always carry a reliable tire-pressure gage. When airing-down, all tires should be close to same pressure. Owner of this big rubber uses a clip-on air-release chuck to help prevent dirt getting into valve stem.

Aired-down tires increase flotation capability and help soak up some of off-roading's bumps and grinds.

width is the best all-around answer for sand.

Low Range and Sand—Sand is another place that you can make good use of low range. With low range, everything happens so much more gently. When you mash the throttle, the wheels turn more slowly than when you're in the same gear in high range. Which means you're less likely to break traction and dig in. And digging in is what you don't want to do when you're in sand.

Airing-Down—Instead of buying a special set of sand tires, there's a simple way to increase the traction of the tires you already own. Just let some of the air out of them. Airing-down, it's called. Not all of it, of course, but enough so the sidewalls bulge out. This both lengthens and widens the footprint to increase the square inches of surface contact and distribute the weight over a greater area. Tires with a recommended street inflation pressure of 28-30 psi can be run in sand at 16-18 psi without problems and some off-roaders drive blithely around at 12 psi. A friend who lives full-time in Baja California on a beach at the end of a sandy road keeps the 10.50-15s on his Wagoneer at 5 psi and has had no prob-

lems to date. This, however, may be overdoing it or, rather, *under*doing it.

When you head out on an unfamiliar trail through country that's apt to present sand somewhere along the way, you might as well drop your pressure as soon as you leave the pavement. A rule-of-thumb is to go down to about half the tire's street pressure. Use a tire gage when you do this because you want all your tires to end up with the same pressure. If you don't have a gage, although every off-roader should carry one, use your watch. Push the valve stem in with a small screwdriver or a stick (never *remove* the valve core, it may get dirt in it or be lost forever in the sand), and time it. For a 28-in. diameter 9.00-15 tire, 30 seconds will reduce the pressure from 30 psi to 18 psi. On a larger 31-in. tall 10.50-15 which has a greater air volume, it will take 60 seconds to drop from 30 psi to 16 psi. Tires of other sizes will deflate proportionally. You might want to time one of your own tires at home before you head for a weekend in the boondocks.

Softer Ride—Airing-down has other attributes. It will ease the vehicle's ride and reduce the drumming that comes through from a ruffled surface. The side-

It takes special vehicles with paddle tires to tackle a steep-sided sand dune. But if you try it in a conventional 4WD and get stuck going up, you can usually back down.

Evening approaching on a lonely Baja beach before tide rolls in. Safest place to drive is at high-tide line at left of photo.

Sand carried by water runoff is generally coarser, thus harder, than blown sand. But it pays to be cautious and this truck is moving at a moderate pace in low range.

Take it easy through puddles. The overexuberance of this off-roader might have bogged him in mud over his wheels.

walls are soaking up a lot of the vibrations that can come up through the suspension to rattle your teeth and loosen the screws on your sunglasses. Soft tires are easier on the vehicle than fully inflated ones and you'll find that handling and directional stability are improved, too. The increased footprint and more resilient rubber grips the ground better and you can steer where you want to go more easily and accurately.

You must avoid sharp objects like rocks or stumps when you're off-roading aired-down, however. Soft tires make the sidewalls more vulnerable to damage when you strike an obstruction and the tire might even depress enough that the rim cuts into the sidewall. Always drive conservatively when you're aired-down, and watch where you're going.

Airing-Up—Don't forget to air-up when you're back on pavement. If you don't have a pump or inflator with you, head at moderate speed for a service station. Prolonged, fast driving promotes heat build-up which accelerates tire wear and can even cause tread separation.

Wet Sand—Sometimes sand is harder if it is damp, or it can be softer. It all depends upon the texture of the material and how much water it contains. There's a particularly nasty beach in Mexico that is nearly flat. When the tide comes in, the water sweeps several hundred yards inland. When it goes out, the surface appears to dry out but underneath the sand is very saturated. You can drive over this stuff, properly aired-down of course, for the surface is reasonably hard, and you'll leave only faint tire tracks behind you. But if you stop, the weight on the tires presses down and this forces the water up and around the tires and turns the surface into the softest mess you'll ever encounter. A jack is no good for it will just sink out of sight. When you're stuck there, you're stuck for good. The more someone works around a

Often, only way out of silt is to jack vehicle up and pack brush, limbs, rocks or anything handy into holes made by tires. Process may have to be repeated over and over.

Soft sand of these dunes may mean airing-down to as low as 5 psi and using low range to keep a slow but steady pace up the slope.

mired vehicle in this stuff, the wetter the surface becomes. After an hour's labor with a towstrap or winch from another vehicle, you'll be slogging in sandy water above your knees.

This is not an isolated instance of what amounts to shoreline quicksand. For the record, this otherwise attractive beach fronts the northern reaches of the Gulf of California (Sea of Cortez) along the Mexican state of Sonora.

Blow and Wash Sand—There are basically two different kinds of sand out there: blow sand and wash sand. Blow sand is the kind that's carried by the wind and sometimes drifts across the trail or builds up into spectacular dunes. Wash sand, on the other hand, is the type that was delivered to its present location by moving water. So this is what you find in a sand wash or along a beach. And there are also blow and wash sand combinations such as the low dunes you find back behind a beach.

As a general rule, blow sand is made up of smaller grains and is softer and less easy to negotiate in an off-road vehicle. This means that even lower tire pressures may be required. We've seen blow sand that required even large tires to be run at a flabby 5 psi before the vehicle would dependably travel through it.

Wash sand is generally made up of heavier, coarser grains and can usually be traversed at a "normal" inflation pressure (roughly half the manufacturer's recommended pressure).

Silt—And then there's silt. Silt is something else again. Not sand, exactly. But something like sand. Except worse.

Silt—the Australians call it bull dust, probably because cattle like to roll in it to clean their coats—is a byproduct of muddy water and it can be more treacherous than even the worst kind of sand.

The main problem results from the fact that silt is deposited in layers by muddy water that has spread out over an area after a heavy rain. Once the water has drained away through the ground or evaporated and it's dry again, what remains on the surface is a very soft powder. Over the years, this powder can build up to incredible depths and, even worse, an occasional rain can create a crust on top of the powder. That's what makes it really treacherous. You're merrily riding along on this crust when all of a sudden your wheels start breaking through the crust and into the soft, dry, powdery silt.

When that happens, you can be in serious trouble. Or, if you're lucky, you may be able to jack and fill, jack and fill your way to shore. And if you're not lucky at all, you may have to shovel your way to firmer ground and hope that, somehow, you can work your way back up onto the surface again.

Thinking About It—Before driving off into soft sand and then wondering what to do, it's never a bad idea to stop before you get into it and study your best approach. How deep is the sand? How

soft is it? How far are you going to have to drive in it?

If you're just going to cross a sandy wash and get right back onto firm ground again, that's one thing. But if you're going to stay in this wash, or play in the dunes, that's quite another.

If you're just going to cross the wash, then you'll probably find it sufficient to back up, work up to a moderate pace in a mid-range gear and motor on across, letting your momentum do half the work.

But if you're going to be driving through the stuff, then you need to take a more serious approach. Walking out into the sand can be helpful. If your foot leaves a reasonably clear footprint, you're probably going to have no trouble (assuming tires are aired-down to half the normal highway pressure). Just get into low range, shift into a gear that's low enough that you won't bog down, drive at a moderate pace and don't do anything abrupt like trying to make sharp turns.

If, when you make your test walk through the sand, the sand slides right back into your footprints and fills them up, then you may need to get serious about this bit of sand traveling. This is soft stuff. If you're only going a short distance, you can probably rush it and go through on momentum ("rush it" is a comparative term, you understand). But keep a steady pace, don't stop and don't turn suddenly.

If you're going to travel through this soft stuff for any distance, you're prob-

117

Stealth off-road guerilla? Hardly. Owner of this Toyota 4WD almost got over his head in mud.

Mud filled tread grooves of this Land Cruiser and while it doesn't *appear* to be stuck, it took winch on CJ in background to literally slide it to drier ground.

ably going to have to reduce your tire pressures to 10, 8 or even 5 psi, depending on your vehicle and the size of its tires. Then it's low range, steady pace, no abrupt changes in direction and, oh yes, it also helps if you sit at a higher pucker.

Final Words on Sand—Sand, wet or dry, is best attacked at a moderate speed, without losing momentum, and without veering too sharply. A hard turn will scrub off speed and if you shift to a lower gear to compensate, the surge of torque at the wheels may bog you down. Follow as straight a line as possible, keep the rpm up without laboring the engine in the gear you've selected and avoid pools of water. With any luck at all, you just *may* get through. If you don't, there's luckily a section in this book on getting unstuck.

MUD

Mud comes in many consistencies and is called by all sorts of names. There are marshes, swamps, fens, bogs, mires, everglades, sloughs, swales, moors and mudflats, among other things. Some of it is sticky, some of it is soft, but all of it is bad. Mud might be a thin slime over a firm underbase, or it can present a seemingly solid crust on top but be almost bottomless underneath.

The consistency of mud is a function of the dirt of which it is composed and the degree of saturation. But one thing is

sure. Mud is liquified soil and can be one of the most effective barriers ever faced by a motor vehicle. Most muds have a lubricating quality almost as good as 30-weight oil.

There is no hard and fast rule for driving through mud. You cannot always air-down the tires, for a wide footprint in some types of mud will only squish that much more of the stuff behind, ahead of, and beside the tires, which is a great way to become stuck. If the mud is a thin layer over a firmer surface, full- or even over-inflated tires with a thin cross-section are best because they'll cut through the muck and get traction on the harder base. This works well in snow, as well.

One problem in coping with mud is that it tends to adhere to the tires and quickly fills the tread grooves and cancels their contribution to go-ahead traction. Some mud is so sticky it will cause a tire to "grow" as layer after layer builds up on the circumference of the rubber. Other types of mud can be so thoroughly saturated with water that the dirt particles are in suspension to the point where the consistency is more like dirty water than wet soil. In this case, treat it like a puddle and determine its depth before plunging ahead.

Getting Muddy—It's a sure-fire bet you're going to come face to face with some form of mud in your off-road travels. It may have been formed by rain

and water runoff. It may lie along the banks of a stream, a seashore, or it may have lain since time immemorial as a swamp or other form of inundation.

And when you get into the stuff, rest assured you're going to get good and muddy, from slogging through it to get to your front hubs or lying prone trying to connect a towstrap so some good Samaritan can pull you out.

Avoid the Stuff—The best bet with mud is to avoid it altogether. Beyond that, negotiate as little of it as possible by skirting the edge of a bog instead of crossing it, fording a stream at its narrowest point, or straddling a water-filled wheel rut. Above all, don't drop into four-wheel-drive low range, stand on the gas and charge ahead.

If you can, stop before the trail you're following becomes too muddy. Climb out and take a close look at the situation. Your footprints will give you an idea of how soft it is and its composition. Poke a stick into the mud to see if there's a harder base underneath it. If you finally decide to tackle it instead of backtracking toward home to wait for a drier time, shift into low range and move ahead cautiously. You'll want a little momentum, of course, and do keep engine rpm up. As long as you're moving and it doesn't feel like the mud is sucking at your tires and you have a good grip without wheelspin, keep up the steady pace and don't stop

Hapless off-roader wandered onto a surface of fairly hard mud, then left wheels broke through crust into softer ooze below with a consistency of axle grease.

Churning wheels turned gumbo into thin chocolate pudding. Jeep Cherokee was freed only after several hours' work by two other vehicles, one with a winch.

until you're across it. If you do stop or lose traction, you may just quietly sink in the west like the proverbial sun

Most deep mud has the proclivity of sticking a vehicle more soundly than any other type of terrain in which you're buried to the same depth. This is because a vacuum forms under and around the tires and grips them through suction. Couple this with mud-filled tread and you're not going anywhere.

"Dry" Lake Mud—One off-roader met up with a very strange form of mud on a California dry (supposedly) lake. It was just a film, but it was super-slick. The hapless driver had driven out of a well-defined track and stopped. When he tried to go again, his truck wouldn't move. The tires weren't depressed into the surface, but the tread grooves of the tires were full. The perplexed off-roader found he could push the truck sideways, backward and forward as easy as shoving a chair around on casters. But he couldn't get back to the harder ground he'd strayed from. Only a tow by a friendly passer-by got our friend back to where the *terra* was *firma*.

The Ultimate Mudder—Driving in mud is a real art and we've known drivers who were real artists at it. One of the most impressive demonstrations we've ever seen of mud driving was on a photographic expedition in Wyoming where our host was a local rancher who took us

Sometimes, only way out of a sticky situation is to hook towstrap onto another vehicle.

out in his two-wheel-drive pickup. Yes, two-wheel drive.

This old boy understood mud. He knew exactly when to crawl, knew when to creep and knew, too, when he could get that tiny bit of extra traction that would shove us on through a bog that we would have hesitated to put a 4WD into. It was beautiful to watch.

A highly developed skill like that only comes from years of in-the-mud experience and we can't tell you any more how

to do it than we can tell you how to grow hair.

Back at the ranch, we asked him why he didn't use a four-wheel-drive vehicle. He thought about it for a minute and then said, "Heck, I don't go anyplace where I'd really *need* four-wheel drive."

Cleaning Up—If you had a fun weekend mudding around the outback, take a hose to your rig as soon as you get home. Rinse away all that stuff that has caked around the suspension and drive-

Nowhere do rocks demand more slow-going than on the Rubicon Trail near Nevada's Lake Tahoe, site of famed Jeeper's Jamboree.

Sometimes, rocks can be a benefit. Gulleys cutting across a trail can hang-up a vehicle by its front or rear bumpers. If you don't like the looks of one, throw in some rocks and make your own "road" across.

line parts. Wash out the wheel wells and douse the engine compartment if mud has splashed in there, too. Mud can surface-dry but stay damp underneath, and when it gets into the nooks and crannies, it quickly promotes rust and corrosion. Also, some soils contain a high degree of salts and other minerals which also accelerate the rusting process.

Don't forget to rinse off your wheels, inside as well as outside. Mud caked in the decorative slots or holes, or stuck around the rims, can dry quickly and stick there to produce the worst out-of-balance condition you've ever felt.

We can't help but tell the story of a four-wheeling caravan that encountered wet clay in the deepest reaches of Sonora, Mexico. They got stuck, then they got out. But in doing this they got mud on everything. The wheels were caked with it, inside and out. Trouble was, the stuff dried quicker and harder than anything they'd ever seen—short of adobe brick. They actually had to *chisel* it off their wheels and drive shafts before they could drive at anything over 10 miles per hour.

ROCKS

If you've been on, or seen pictures of,

the Rubicon Trail near Lake Tahoe in Northern California, then you know what rocks are all about. Big rocks, from basketball-size to some as large as the vehicles that try to climb over or between them, are par for the course. Few are the rigs that come through the Rubicon unscathed in terms of broken drive trains, damaged suspensions, mangled sheet metal or all three. Add deflated egos to the list.

Going Slowly—The right way to tackle heavy rocks is slowly, down in four-wheel drive and low range with the engine at idle or barely above. It takes experience and careful judgment to decide how large a rock you can straddle without scraping a differential or a skidplate. Or how to keep from squashing down on one with the fuel tank or other vulnerable part. If a nasty rock is unavoidable and you don't think you'll clear it, aim one front wheel directly at it. When the inevitable contact is made, and if all goes well, the wheel will climb up and over then drop heavily on the other side. This puts the rock under the edge of a front fender or rocker panel. If the rock is tall enough you'll hear the *graunch* of bending sheet metal. Or the upsetting rumble as the frame or floorpan rolls the rock

along underneath where it can squash a brake line or fuel line.

Massive rocks are not for sissies. If you absolutely have to give the Rubicon or one of its many counterparts a try, you're pretty sure of bending, breaking, scraping or flattening something. But this is what he-man off-roading is all about and some enthusiasts point with pride, instead of chagrin, to all the dings and bashes they've managed to collect.

When you're in an extremely rocky region, shift into low range and keep your foot off the clutch with a manual transmission. Give just a little gas as you approach a boulder, then let off and allow the idling engine do its work. Drop off the far side the same way—foot off the clutch and at idle. Where even an idle is too fast, some purists will switch off the engine when a front tire contacts a really big fellow. Then, leaving the transmission in first gear, they'll turn the ignition key to crank the engine over. Not enough to start it, just enough to move a few inches. Or they'll disconnect the coil wire and run the engine with the starter for a longer distance. A starter motor backed with a healthy battery produces gobs of torque; add this to low range and you'll be amazed at how much power is

Even though its wheels appear to be firmly planted, this Ramcharger is high-centered on a boulder. Without a companion vehicle toting a towstrap, fix is to jack the thing up and either remove the obstacle or build ramps under the tires and drive off. Photo by John Lawlor

Land Cruiser is almost lost in spray from a water crossing taken imprudently. It's best to stop, get out and assess situation, then climb back in and proceed cautiously.

generated without hurting anything. Don't stay on the starter for more than 30 seconds at a time, however, or you may burn it out.

Negotiating large rocks with an automatic transmission requires a somewhat different technique and, some say, your chances of getting hung-up are increased. When a front tire rolls up against a rock and the vehicle stops, you have to give it enough throttle to get the transmission to start turning the drive shafts but the surge will probably come in a burst and send you up and over faster than you want. The way to overcome this is to apply the brakes lightly. Hold the left foot above the brake pedal then ease down on the throttle with the right foot. When you start to move but it seems too fast, stomp lightly on the brakes. Let braking effort be the deterrent factor to forward progress rather than the rocks themselves.

High-Centered—Other than tipping over sideways or breaking something mechanical, about the worst that can happen in rocks is becoming high-centered. This is where some part of the chassis is resting on a rock, the axles all awry, with one or more wheels clawing at thin air. A full transfer-case lock-up and limited-slip gears in the differentials may be enough to pull you through. But maybe

not. One way out is to jack up your rig until it's lifted above whatever is hanging it up, then stack rocks under the free-spinning wheels to give them something to bite against when you let the jack back down. Form a ramp with the rocks so the tires can roll down a slope rather than falling off which will, of course, just high-center you all over again.

Another way to get free is to resort to the winch if you or a companion vehicle have one, or hook up the towstrap and wait for a friendly motorist to come by. A final recourse, all else failing, is to try digging under the rock that is creating the problem so it can settle downward and, with luck, bring the tires in contact with Mother Earth once again.

Rock-Straddling—Rocks that periodically jut up between the wheel tracks you are following, or which poke up through mud or sand, are another matter. Straddle them if you've the chassis clearance. Otherwise, steer to one side or the other, even if it means leaving the ruts you've been following. One backcountry addict tells the story of how he barely tipped a rock with his front differential in a sand wash. It didn't break anything, but the tap uprooted the rock to wedge under the rear-axle housing which brought him to an ignominious stop. Then, when the rock was removed, the

truck had to be shoveled free of the sand. Thirty minutes were lost when a slight veer to the right or left might have steered our friend away from trouble.

WATER CROSSINGS

There are many things the well-equipped vehicle can do, but one thing it can't do is float. It is inevitable that at some time during your off-roading career you're going to encounter water. It will be in the form of a puddle, a stream or small river, or at the edge of a lake or ocean. If there's no other way around it and you have to splash on through, there are some things you should know.

If standing water is blocking the trail, the bottom is apt to be soft. Swamps and marshes are two examples of this. Even if the water has only recently arrived, as from rain or runoff, chances are it has soaked into the ground underneath and turned it into a morass.

If there's running water in your path, the chances of getting across are a little better because moving water tends to wash away the fine silt and leave only the larger-grained sand or gravel that *might* support the weight of your vehicle.

In either case, the first thing to do is determine the water depth. Even a narrow stream or a shallow-looking puddle may be hiding a hole large enough to put you in up to your doorhandles. Don't feel smug if there are tire tracks going in one side and coming out the other. They may

Most vehicles can negotiate fairly deep water if not driven too fast. Otherwise, water spray can drown engine. Photo by John Lawlor.

If you have to ascend a hill at an angle to maintain speed or avoid deep gulleys, do so at only a slight angle and keep a steady throttle foot. Photo by Peter du Pre, courtesy of Four Wheeler magazine.

have been made by a rig with greater ground clearance than yours or the water level might have been lower when that other off-roader preceded you.

Unless you can see the bottom and that it is composed of stones or heavy gravel, don't drive into it as though it wasn't there. And under no circumstances should you back up to get a fast run at it and trust momentum to carry you through. It won't!

Stop and Look—As in all other cases when driving into the unknown, be wary. Stop at the edge of the water, get out and take a look at it. Wade across, in fact, and stomp your feet to judge how hard the bottom is. If you don't relish getting wet, and cannot convince your companion to slog his/her way across while you follow with the vehicle, throw out a stone. If it makes a friendly "shplit" sound when it lands, the water is probably shallow. But if it makes a solid "ploop," it's deep. Toss more stones to fall along the course you intend to follow and some to either side as well. If you're satisfied it's "shplit" all the way across, shift into four-wheel drive (if you haven't already done so) and proceed slowly. Splashy water crossings may seem like fun and there are always photos of these in magazines. But the journalists seldom admit they drowned the engine doing it.

Go Slowly—Drive slowly into water and remember that just as much is thrown

or splashed up underneath the vehicle as gushes out to the sides. Few vehicles have really adequate inner wheel housings and engine shielding. It doesn't take much water to put a distributor or alternator out of commission. Even water sloshed over the front bumper can spray back and into the electrical system from the engine fan.

As long as your front wheels don't suddenly drop out from under and your rig keeps churning along, stay easy on the accelerator and head for the far side. But if one or both front wheels begin to sink or you feel them hit an obstruction, stop and take stock if the situation. Back up a few feet then come ahead on a new course to the right or left of the first one. If the wheels don't start to settle or there is no bump this time, keep working your way ahead. But if a deeper channel has cut the stream bottom, wade in to see how deep it eventually gets and how wide it is. If you don't think you can drive any further, don't waste time sitting there. Running water can wash out the finer particles under the tires and down you go.

Arroyos and Washes—Deep arroyos and the long washes and gullies that prevail in desert country should be avoided if they contain water. If the water is really rushing, it can have enough force to turn a vehicle downstream or flip it over even when it's shallow enough to only reach

the rocker panels. If it has begun to drizzle as you approach an arroyo and it's already carrying a dribble of water, there may be a cloudburst nearby and a wall of water may be rushing your way. Even if you could get across, don't try it. Chances are there's another, bigger arroyo somewhere on the other side which will stop you for sure. Then, when you turn back, you may find the first one overflowing its brim. Being stranded until the water subsides is not much fun.

How Deep is Deep?—The bottom-line question to all of this is, how deeply can a vehicle be submerged without damage and bringing it to a halt? That depends upon the vehicle, its ground clearance and other factors. If you don't mind getting your floormats wet, you can put the tip of your exhaust pipe under water momentarily—if the tailpipe exits at the rear bumper and you don't shut the engine off. The tailpipe curls up and over the rear axle so the water can't flow forward. Exhaust pressure will merely gurgle at the outlet. But if the engine is stopped, or you have a side-exiting exhaust ahead of a rear wheel, cooling of the exhaust system can suck water into the catalytic converter and muffler and damage them.

In fresh water, it does no permanent damage to submerge the brakes, although stopping will be erratic until they've dried out, helped by driving slowly with the brakes lightly applied. Salt water is another matter. In this case, flush the brakes with fresh water under pressure (as from a garden hose), pulling the wheels and brake drums if you can. If you don't do this, the brake parts will begin to rust and corrode very quickly.

Beyond this, as far as water depth goes, don't let the engine fan tip the water and spray it into the electrical components. On manual transmissions, water can get into the clutch and cause it to slip. Also, a vent on top of the rear-axle housing (and the front one in 4WDs) will admit water if it's submerged and some automatic transmissions are vented, as well. If water gets into these, drain the lubricant as quickly as possible then replenish it. Neither manual nor automatic front hubs like water either, though they are sealed against the elements. When you get home from a deep-water outing, though, it's a good idea to dismantle the hubs, wipe away any traces of moisture, then relubricate them. Drive a little way in 4WD and give the grease a chance to coat the machined parts that may have become wet.

HILLS

Off-roaders have a positive affinity for hills. An abrupt elevation change in a short distance can be fun, present a challenge and show off driving prowess. Heading up can help gain a higher vantage point from which to survey the surroundings. Going downhill can be fun, as well. But there's one thing to remember about hills. They can be dangerous. An uphill run can be steep enough to make you feel like you're going to roll over backward. But while this isn't impossible, it's not likely to happen because you'll lose traction and, hence, upward progress before disaster occurs. Going down a steep incline can be scary, too, but it's unlikely you'll roll over frontward. But what you *don't* want to try is ascend or descend a hill on an angle, or side-hilling as it's called.

Depending upon the degree of slope and the texture of the ground, you'll probably spin your wheels going up. If the hill isn't too steep, not very high and you've nearly made it to the top, you can always roll back to the bottom and have another go at it. A harder running start may give you enough oomph to go up and over. If you still can't make it after a second or third try, give up. It's smarter to be at the bottom of a hill and upright with intact sheet metal than to be otherwise with everything bent.

Rolling Back—If you're following a well-defined trail that ascends a hill you can't make, roll back to the bottom and consider the situation. Just because your buddy made it up in a big-tired Jeep CJ doesn't necessarily mean you can follow him in a heavier Wagoneer with stock rubber. You're not admitting defeat by not scratching up the hill; you're displaying concern for your passengers, yourself and the vehicle. This makes you a very prudent off-roader.

If you can climb only part way up a hill until the vehicle simply won't go any farther, or you've decided you'd rather be back down where it's nice and flat, there are things to remember. If you have any forward momentum at all, don't use it to try and turn around to head back down. This is side-hilling and it causes more roll-overs than anything else. Stop where you are, then back straight down. Stay in the tracks you made coming up and, for heaven's sake, don't lock up the brakes no matter how much speed you generate. You're in 4WD, of course, in low range and reverse. Just press the brake pedal in little, soft jabs while the idling engine provides most of the holding power.

Always keep in mind that a vehicle can safely handle a steeper down-slope that it can climb an up-slope. If you're on a ridge or plateau and think you'd like to be at the bottom, think about the climb back up. Use logic and judgment before dropping into a valley; can you make it out the way you went in?

Inclinometers—Those little accessory tilt-meters they sell at off-road shops are fun to watch as you wander around the outback, but they are actually quite meaningless. Some resemble a carpenter's level with a curved glass tube and a little ball or a bubble to indicate the tilt. Others use a needle with an incremented scale. You can fasten one to your dashboard and see how far off level you're tilting to one side or the other, or install it on one side and the indicator will move as you go up and down hills. But even though some manufacturers even install them as standard or optional equipment, an inclinometer can't tell you when you're about to tip over. The makers of these gadgets have no way of knowing what make and model of vehicle they'll be installed in nor how that vehicle is modified with oversize wheels and tires, a body- or chassis-lift kit, or what sort of load you're carrying on an outing. Things like these raise a vehicle's center of gravity and this is the basis of roll-overs. A car or truck may fall over sideways if it's canted more than 40°, or it may reach 45° before it falls. If you want to play with an inclinometer, be safe and don't let it exceed 30°.

If on a past outing you've successfully survived a 35° tilt on a hard surface, don't be so sure you can lean this far on the side of a sand dune or anything soft. The vehicle's weight shifts toward the low side in a leaning situation. On something soft, the low-side tires will press into the surface and, without warning, you'll have more lean than you can handle. If you have a tilt-meter, use it only for amusement and see how nearly level you can stay rather than how far you can lean.

Be Cautious—So the basic rule about side-hilling is, don't. However, if you do get into a situation where you have to travel across a slope rather than straight up or straight down, proceed with great caution. This is another of those places where it's a good idea to walk the trail before you drive it. Study the slope as you take your walk and pay special attention to the surface you're going to travel over. Obviously, if your uphill elbow keeps dragging the ground, you stand no chance of driving across it. Also, if the surface is not firm and there's much of an angle at all, you're almost certain to end up in the valley; a valley from which there may be no return. Or, you might apply the old-timer's rule about it being too much of a side-hill when the person on the low side keeps trying to crawl into the lap of the person on the high side.

Even if there are already tracks across the slope, it's wise to be careful because a recent rain, or a recent lack of rain, may result in the surface providing less traction than when those tracks were originally put there.

When you're traveling across a slope,

Hillside trail is a bit too skinny for camper-equipped 4x4. Driver will have to bear to his left to avoid the low-side erosion and let cactus gouge his paint job.

It's always wise to walk ahead and check terrain if you can't see around a bend or beyond a sharp rise. Photo by Paul Lord.

keep a steady pace and don't make any sudden changes in throttle opening. A sudden application of the throttle can break traction and start your long descent into the deep unknown.

If, when you're traveling a side-hill, you feel the vehicle begin to slide, don't mash the accelerator, hoping to jump across before you disappear down the slope. Instead, get off the gas and immediately turn your front wheels down the slope. That will keep you from going over. No, don't turn straight down the slope, not at first. Try to sneak across on a descending angle.

If it's even too steep for that, you may have to point it straight down the hill to keep upright. That may result in your driving all the way to the bottom, but at least you'll arrive there on your own four wheels rather than on the roof. If you crank your wheels the other way and try and turn up the slope, you'll almost certainly end up in the same place but with a lot of bent sheet metal around you.

NARROW TRAILS

One of the more potentially dangerous trails is one that's been cut into a hillside. Old mining roads, logging trails and other abandoned routes through hilly terrain have often been cut as a ledge above a stream or canyon bottom to stay above running water during seasonal rains. Un-

maintained roads like these may be partially blocked on the inside by a small landslide or a nasty boulder, forcing you to move nearer the off-side edge. Or erosion and rain may have cut rivulets into the bank. In either case, a trail may become narrower than it was when you started out. If the bank crumbles under the weight of your vehicle, you might find yourself tilted to one side with a wheel clawing at air, or down in the canyon wondering what happened.

Watch the Edge—The object here is to stay as far from the outer edge as possible, even driving with your inside wheels up on the high-side embankment where you'll crab along at an angle. If a rockslide means you'll have to move nearer the edge and it doesn't seem there's room to get by, get out and shift the dirt or rocks around if you can, or at least rearrange some of the obstruction so you can drive over it.

Take a Look—This is a prime case of *not* wanting momentum to carry you through. Go as slowly as you can, and this means using low range to give yourself maximum control. Before the route narrows so much that you're scraping the doorhandle on one side and the tires are kicking dirt over the side on the other, stop. If you can get out of your vehicle, do so and walk the road ahead. See what lies along the paths the front tires will

take if you keep going. Check out how much margin there will be between the outside ones and the edge. Stomp hard near the edge to see how firm it is.

If the road curves out of sight not far ahead, or disappears into a thicket or stand of trees, walk up and see what's around the bend. The trail might become even narrower or be cut all the way across by erosion. Or it might widen out and emerge into a level clearing giving you a choice of turning around or proceeding. If you don't think you should continue, however, and obviously you can't turn around where you are, backing out of the situation is your only recourse. Just be careful doing it.

BEACH AND BOAT LAUNCHING

Driving along a beach or the edge of a river is fun and a little different than negotiating other forms of sand. Here you usually don't *have* to enter the water unless you're faced with a shallow inlet or the arm of an estuary. But where it's permissible, driving a shoreline is great if you aren't intimidated by sand, mud, the threat of a rising river or incoming tide.

When paralleling a beach, it's safest to straddle the high-tide line which is generally marked with bits of seashells, seaweed or other flotsam. Nearer the water, there is apt to be mud or wet sand that could slow your progress or stop you

These folks launched their boat then found out the hard way what driving on unfamiliar beach can do. They eventually got out just before high tide. Photo courtesy Trailer Boats Magazine.

Launching a boat from a beach without an improved ramp will get you away from crowds, but can also lead to trouble. If the sand is hard at mid-beach and at least firm at water's edge, fine.

Air-down tires and use low range if you're not sure you can get boat in water—or get it out again.

No, this isn't trick photography. It snowed in Death Valley and caught some desert-loving off-roaders off-guard.

completely. And if the water rises before you get free, kiss your 4X4 goodbye. Also, it's often very soft above the high-tide line where the finer sand blown by inshore wind is as dry and soft as talcum powder.

Judgment—Many times the best running along a beach is up a ways where the sand has flattened out. You'll have to use your judgment where it's best to drive. Sometimes the dry, loose sand is softer up here than down by the high-tide line but it's also a lot safer because getting stuck is the worse thing that's liable to happen. Down where it's wet, you not only take a chance on getting trapped by the tide, you also get the underside of your vehicle coated with salt, which en-

courages corrosion.

If you're going to run the soft sand, you'll probably need to air-down your tires to dune-running flabbiness. You'll also have better control in low range.

Boat Backing—Backing a trailered boat across a shore without an improved launch ramp can be risky but not impossible. In such a case, you are moving from dry inland soil to possibly damp terrain beginning at the high-water mark, then into lapping water which may or may not have a soft bottom. The thing to do is stop well above the high-tide line and walk down to the water, examining the situation as you go. If you don't leave much of a footprint anywhere, jam a heel down hard. You may be on a crusty surface

with bottomless muck just below.

If the ground between your rig and the water seems satisfactory, turn the vehicle and trailer around so the stern of the boat is taking dead aim at your launching site. A straight line is the shortest distance between two points and the less beach-crossing you have to do, the better. This is where having a front-mounted trailer hitch is handy. You can watch the trailer's tires as you head toward the water. If they are making an ever-deepening track, stop and drive out. But if you can't drive out because you're headed up-slope now instead of down, unhitch the trailer and get your rig to higher ground. If your towstrap or winch cable will reach from the truck to the trailer, fine. If not, at least

All-terrain tread and full inflation pressure give this truck mobility, but snow tires or chains are the best bet in wintery weather.

Wide, high-flotation tires are great for rocks and sand, but they're not good in snow. Sticky stuff has plugged the tread grooves leaving very little traction, and tire width keeps them from cutting through to harder ground that's underneath.

your vehicle's not in danger and you can worry about the boat and trailer later.

On a boat-trailering expedition into Mexico once, we picked a launch site on a near-level beach at a bay. The tide there can reach 28 vertical feet, enough to drown a vehicle parked well inland. What the group decided was to leave the boat on its trailer near the water during low tide, then let the incoming tide simply float it off. Just the opposite was done to reload the boat later on.

SNOW AND ICE

Winter brings a mantle of gleaming snow to many parts of our country. It's picturesque and invites winter-sports enthusiasts to get out their parkas and skis and enjoy the frigid outdoors. Trouble is, you also have to drive through snow and over ice. And if anything is the enemy of a vehicle, this is it.

Like mud, snow comes in many consistencies. It can be light and fluffy and barely cover hard ground beneath it. It can also be light and fluffy and have ice under it. It can be hard-packed or soft, wet or dry, and can be mean enough to fill in the holes and ditches and hide boulders and tree stumps with no visible surface evidence. While few things are prettier than a fresh snowfall that turns the landscape into a postcard scene, it can be a real headache and a trip-killer when

you have trouble negotiating it.

A four-wheel-drive vehicle really comes into its element in snow. In fact, many easterners and dwellers of high country buy 4X4s as a matter of course, simply to get from point A to B on icy, slush-covered pavement. Some have no conception of how they're used for recreational fun and games in less-inclement climes. With one pair of wheels pushing and the other pulling, the 4WD driver has far better control over steering, braking and acceleration.

Tires—Tires play a major role in how successful a vehicle is in snow. Some devotees insist that a tall, skinny tire pumped up to maximum inflation pressure is far superior to a fat, soft one. A narrow cross-section tire will cut down through the snow and get a grip on the harder, denser surface below. Wide, soft tires will want to ride on top of the snow because of their greater footprint and they'll lose traction when slush begins to build up in front of them. This is one of the few off-road situations where you *want* the tires to sink into the surface. Also, an open-tread tire, one with significant spacing between the tread blocks, encourages self-cleaning and will throw the snow off better than a tighter tread which will hold the snow and fill in the grooves. And with no grooves, no go. Also, thinner tires are easier to steer out

of ruts while fatter ones will fight to stay in the tracks and perhaps lead you where you don't want to go.

Braking—Braking on any slippery surface, whether it's snow, ice, wet clay or fresh owl droppings, requires a special technique. When you want to slow down, lift your throttle foot and let engine compression participate in retarding your forward motion. Then, pulse the brakes. This means applying them with gently increasing pressure until that split second when you feel a wheel lock and a tire begin to slide. You can't steer a sliding tire, you know. The instant the tire begins to slide, get off the brakes, let the wheels turn again and make any steering corrections that are necessary. Then gently brake again, repeating the process, off and back on, off and back on. This will slow you down and also let you keep going the direction you wanted to go in the first place.

Naturally, if it's really slick, you're already in low range and driving at a very cautious pace. But the important message here is not to just jump on the brakes, lock up the wheels and begin that long heart-stopping slide into the nearest obstacle. Stay cool, pulse the brakes and be elegant.

Driving Tips—The biggest mistake that off-roaders make when they get into snow is not engaging four-wheel drive soon enough. When you see the first little patches of snow on the ground, or a few random flakes are beginning to fall, shift into four-wheel drive and leave it there. No matter if small patches of snow or ice are alternatively spaced with stretches of pavement or other hard surface, keep that transfer-case lever right where it is. The "wrap-up" or binding forces that occur in 4X4s equipped with part-time systems when they are driven on asphalt or concrete roads, will disappear when the axles and wheels play catch-up on the slippery spots. If you wait too long to shift into 4WD, it may be too late and you're liable to find yourself off the side of the road in a ditch.

The second major problem inexperienced snow drivers have is knowing when and how to use the brakes. You cannot steer, speed up or slow down if the wheels aren't turning and when this occurs, you'll wind up everyplace except where you want to be.

Low Range—Always keep speed on the conservative side when driving in snow, by using a lower transmission gear than you would at the same rate on pavement, and shift to low range if it's really bad. When you want to slow down, lift your throttle foot and let engine compression provide the braking. This puts a positive, yet easier, resistance on the wheels than jabbing the brake pedal, and your chances of slowing safely, instead of skidding, are greatly enhanced. In other words, scrub off speed through four-wheel drive, the transmission and the engine.

Getting Started—Don't nail the throttle when you want to get going in snow. This will only promote wheel spin and when this happens, and the roadway has the slightest crown or you're on a slant, all you'll do is slide rather inelegantly sideways and into a snowbank or ditch. Judge how much throttle you can give without spinning the wheels, for as long as you have a bite on the surface, you'll move out slowly but deliberately.

Skidding—One of the hardest things for a novice driver to learn, regardless of the surface under him, is steering *into* or toward a skid. Even experienced highway drivers find this hard to learn when they first tackle the snow country. If the rear tires begin to slide in either direction, steer the front wheels the same way. If the rear wheels start to slide out to the left, turn the front wheels left. If the rears start to go right, steer right. Turning opposite the skid—steering right when the rear end goes left—will cause a spin-out and leave you either facing in the opposite direction, or up against a tree or embankment.

Pathfinding—When deep snow covers the ground, you can usually tell where the paved roads go because of banks or other marks defining the edges. In some mountain areas, the road departments have thoughtfully placed poles at intervals to mark the right and left sides. These are usually for the convenience of snow-removal crews, but you can use them as well. If you're in your own neck of the woods, you'll know the local geography well enough to get about even though the right-of-ways may not be too sharply defined.

Winter off-roading through a snowy wonderland. Four-wheel drive can get you there and back, but snow and ice require careful driving.

Covering of snow can be as beautiful as it is hazardous. Some areas that seem inviting may be private property or are otherwise restricted to vehicular travel—whether posted or not. If it's unfamiliar territory, check with a local off-roader.

But off-road it's another matter, especially if you're out for a day of recreational driving and the region is not especially familiar. Snow covers rocks, stumps, fallen limbs and other obstructions, and drifts can fill in the ditches and holes. Even a mild snowfall can leave a surface as a gently undulating expanse while the ground below is littered with all sorts of bad things. This means that you should be very cautious in the outback after a snow if there are no other vehicle tracks around. Unless you really know an area, or are with someone who does and have tracks to follow, don't go.

In some areas of federal lands, such as parks, forest preserves or other tracts set aside for some reason, winter-driving regulations may be different than at other times of the year. Where there might be a whole series of roads open to 4WD driving during mild months, snow can bring temporary closure to many of these. They may be limited to sleds, skis, snowmobiles or other uses and are hence closed to all four-wheel vehicles. Even if such an area is not posted, check at a ranger station or visitor center for guidelines to permissible access roads and trails.

STUCK!

Let's face it. Somewhere out in the great beyond you're going to get stuck. It's unavoidable and, come to think of it, there's no shame in it. In fact, some of the best campfire stories involve being stuck. Or, rather, getting *un*stuck. As a very wise off-roader once observed, "Being stuck is like being pregnant. You either are, or you aren't."

But there are different kinds of being stuck. Like sitting at a fork in the trail and not knowing which way to go. Or having two flat tires with only one spare. Or even losing your ignition key. But we're here to talk about the kind of stuck when your rig is mired down into something unforgiving or being high-centered with one or more wheels in the air.

If you stop to analyze it cooly, being stuck is merely a matter of tire traction being overcome by resistance. The way to get free, of course, is to either improve the traction or reduce the resistance, or both. This is simple, looked at logically, but getting stuck often gives vent to irrational thoughts and the obvious solution is sometimes forgotten. Stay in the car for a few minutes when you first become stuck. Smoke a cigarette if that's what it

Sooner or later, you're going to get stuck. Photo by Ron Sessions.

Getting stuck in sand is a common problem that's easily overcome.

Jack vehicle until wheel(s) is level with surface, then partially fill hollow with sand and cap it off with a layer of brush or rocks. Let jack down and drive away.

takes to calm you down. Let your pulse return to normal before you do anything else. Then calmly get out, walk around the vehicle and really study the problem.

One thing to remember is that you're not really stuck until you've used up all of your vehicle's options. You've shifted into 4WD, you're in low range and you've aired the tires down to a paunchy 8 psi or so. Now, if you can't move, you are well and truly stuck. Unless, of course, you have a winch, the theory and use of which is discussed in Chapter 10, or your off-road buddy is just behind you and already unlimbering his towstrap.

Suggestions—There are many ways out of your dilemma. Of course, each stuck situation has problems all its own and there is no given set of rules to cover all

the many possible situations. But here are some general suggestions.

Sand—Of course you've exercised all of your vehicle's options, you're in sand and the vehicle will not move. Take a look around. Are the tires really stuck or is the chassis hung-up by something underneath? Often it takes only a little extra power to get free of a sandtrap. Your rig's engine may have the power, but added resistance caused by a hummock or brush catching onto the chassis is enough to hold you fast. Dig out, drag away, chop down or otherwise eliminate the snag. If you still can't move and your only contact with the ground is the tires, then it really *is* the sand that has you trapped.

Getting free is a matter of trying successive attempts at getting unstuck in their order of difficulty. There's no reason to try the hardest solution first if the simplest one will work. If you're with a companion, either in your vehicle or accompanying you in his, have him (or, if you're lucky, them) hand-push while you try to drive in whichever direction seems the best suited. Don't lunge down on the throttle in low gear. Ease down on the gas in second. If this effort fails, back off the throttle the moment one of the wheels begins to spin or you'll dig yourself into a worse situation.

Bouncy-Bouncy—Have your friends bounce their weight up and down on the rear bumper while you work the throttle. (The driver always seems to have an easier time of it than his helpers!) The jounce and rebound of the suspension

will sometimes enable the tires to get enough of a bite to move free. No luck? If your vehicle is heavily loaded, dump everything out on the ground to lighten the load. If this doesn't work, then pile everything back in and somehow add some extra weight. Still stuck? There are other tactics.

Towstrap—A towstrap is great if there's another vehicle nearby. Chains also work but are not really recommended because they do not give when the slack is taken up. A suddenly tightened chain can break a link or tear off whatever it's fastened to. A rope is satisfactory if it has the heft to stand the strain and provided the ends are properly tied or looped around suitable attaching points.

The best towstraps are of woven nylon or other high-strength material. These can withstand loads up to several thousand pounds and have the elasticity to literally yank a vehicle free as if it were on the end of a huge rubber band. To use one, make sure each end is securely fastened to each vehicle. Don't just loop it around a bumper or anything with sharp edges, for this will only cut into the strap. Tie or loop the strap around a solid, preferably round-edge part of the chassis as the axle housing or frame side rails. If such a vehicle has its own chassis-mounted towhook, that's the best place of all. Move the free vehicle until 1/4 to 1/3 of the strap's length is slack. Now, with everyone standing well out of the way, accelerate the free vehicle hard in the appropriate direction. The strap will come taut and, usually in a slow surge,

Some 4X4s come from the factory with handy tow hooks. If not, they can be purchased at off-road shops and bolted or welded in place. Used with a towstrap, one can help get you unstuck.

Never use a hitch ball as a towstrap anchor. A sudden yank by the pulling vehicle can sheer the ball shank and send it through the air like a missile.

If a vehicle has a Class II trailer-hitch receiver, stuff the towstrap loop into it then slide the lockpin through. It's a splendid towstrap anchor and allows a straight pull by a rounded object and won't cut strap material.

the mired vehicle will pop free.

Jacking—The next attempt is more troublesome and will take time. Get your jack out. We assume you've read Chapter 9 on proper off-road jacks and how to use them, and you're suitably equipped. Raise the rear of the vehicle or other chassis point until the suspension droops and the wheel(s) come up out of the holes they've dug. If the jack will rise sufficiently high that the wheels are elevated above the surface, fine. Scoop sand back into the holes then pack something fairly solid under the tires: rocks, brush, boards, anything the tires can get a grip on. Then let the jack down. If you do this to the rear wheels of a 4X4, you usually don't have to do the front ones, too. But it's a good idea to shovel out gently sloping ramps ahead of the tires in the direction you want to go.

Get back in the driver's seat, warn everyone away so they won't be hurt if the tires fling debris up, and give it a try. Go easy on the throttle. Just press it gradually until one of two things happen: Either you begin to move or the wheels spin and churn out whatever you packed beneath them. If you do move, keep a steady throttle and don't make sudden changes in direction until you reach safe ground. If you move only to the limit of your packed brush or boards then sink in again, go through the jacking routine once again. Repeat as often as necessary.

Mud and Snow—Mud, slime and other bad forms of ooze, including snow, can be attacked much like sand. Just remember that traction has to be improved and resistance decreased. If the stuff is piled up ahead of the chassis and suspension parts, it has to be dug away. If only the tires are mired, try digging gentle ramps in the direction you want to go. Traction is often less in mud or snow than in sand because the goo fills up the tire tread grooves making the surface slick with no biting ability. You can't do much about this but you can follow the same general steps as with sand.

Talk your buddies or neighboring campers into pushing while you work the throttle and steer, but warn them against standing in line with the tires or they'll get a bath. Ask them to jump up and down on your rear bumper. If your tires are aired-down, reinflate them to full pressure if you have the means. A narrow footprint may let the tires sink deeper into the surface and get traction on a harder base below. The next step would be to use a rope or towstrap and another vehicle to pull you free.

Finally, get that jack out. Raise the wheels far enough so you can cram limbs or shrubbery beneath the driving wheels. Let the jack down, slide into the seat, and have at it. But use the throttle gingerly. If you get some momentum, don't lift the throttle and, above all, don't panic. Head

toward hard ground and don't make any sudden moves or changes in direction.

When All Else Fails—If your vehicle isn't equipped with a limited-slip or locking-type differential, one wheel of a two wheel-drive vehicle will spin uselessly on ice or mud while its mate rests on a harder surface without doing anything. On a 4X4, one wheel on each axle may spin while the other two sit idly by. This is because the action of a differential sends power to the wheel with the least resistance, the one in the mud. What has to be done, though it isn't easy, is prevent the free-turning wheel from rotating so engine power goes to the one with the greater traction.

Look under the vehicle near the rear-brake backing plates. On most cars and trucks, the emergency-brake cable is exposed between the end of its sheath or flexible housing and where it enters the back side of the brake assembly. Make sure the emergency brake is off, then from underneath, pull on the cable to the free-spinning wheel with pliers. Clamp it there with Vise-Grip pliers or similar tool. Now get in, fire up, and try to move once more. Often the high-traction wheel will have sufficient bite to move the vehicle while the braked wheel just slides along. This troublesome technique has worked in a surprising number of cases. Once on solid ground, of course, remove the clamp.

If there isn't access to the brake cable, you could remove the wheel and brake drum from the side with traction and disconnect the cable. Put everything back together and try driving while you work the emergency-brake handle on and off. This is a lot of trouble and you'll get dirty in the process, but it may be better than remaining stuck.

Shoveling—There's more to say on the subject of sand. You're stuck and the vehicle won't move. What usually brings you to that final halt is that you've dug your tires far enough into sand that the vehicle's weight is resting on the suspension or frame instead of the tires. This lets the tires spin freely and what you have to decide is whether you're going to raise the road, lower the vehicle, or both.

If you decide to raise the level of the road, jack up the offending wheel(s) and build up the road underneath the tire(s) until the vehicle's weight is back on the tires where it belongs. If you're going to lower the road, dig out underneath until you can see daylight from stem to stern and, again, the weight is back on the tires. It usually works best to do a combination of both. Jack and fill and also dig out a little.

But don't do what a friend of ours did. He got separated from the rest of his group, got stuck in sand and then discovered his jack wouldn't work. So he couldn't do anything but dig. By the time we found him several hours later, he had his truck sitting in a big shallow hole that was about two feet deep. It took two of us and two towstraps to haul him up and out.

One More Tactic—We mustn't overlook one other trick that sometimes works in mud and sand. Try gently applying the brakes at the same time you add a little throttle. We've seen this work on a 4WD vehicle with automatic transmission. What happens is that the brakes offer just enough resistance to keep the free wheel from spinning and lets both tires get a marginally better grip. We've never tried it with a manual box using low range and first or second gear, but it's certainly worth a try.

Rocks—Being hung-up in a rock pile or on a nasty boulder is no fun, but there are ways out—or off. You know the problem by now, not enough traction to overcome the resistance. You have to im-

prove the first and decrease the second. Having someone push or using a tow-strap tied to another vehicle isn't the answer. If the rock is under the front crossmember, for example, pulling the vehicle forward may cause it to slide off the rock, which could then puncture the oil pan.

What's needed here is to raise the vehicle with the jack and remove the rock. But this is often easier said than done, because big rocks are usually quite immovable. Raise the vehicle anyway, then build a pyramid of small rocks under the tires. When you let the jack down, the tires will rest on the little platforms you built and, with any luck at all, you can simply drive down and off of them.

If that fails, raise the vehicle by its bumper to the jack's upper limit, then push it off to one side. This is best with a tall mechanical jack. It's possible to work the vehicle sideways in a succession of lifts and pushes until the chassis is away from the offending boulder—if there's room.

Reminders—Because being stuck can frequently be a serious problem, it's worth repeating that panic is never the answer. If you tend to be the nervous type, shut the engine off once you're certain you're stuck and sit there for a few moments. Then get out and rationally assess your problem and think of as many plausible solutions that you can. Try the easiest ones first and save the more laborious ones until later. Using common sense and old-fashioned logic is better than rushing headlong into a hastily conjured project you're not sure will work. An off-roading friend who is a very inventive sort once mired himself on a very soft beach. Faced with an incoming tide and finding nothing nearby to pack under his wheels, he calmly removed the tailgate from his truck and shoved it under a wheel. It ruined the tailgate, naturally, but at least he didn't lose his vehicle completely. Or himself.

WASHBOARD

In desert country, the ground is generally bone-dry and the roads hard. Old trails, mine and ranch roads head out into the wild drab yonder in a series of ambling straightaways connected by turns of varying degrees. Traffic, sparse

though it may be, has latticed the surface into a regular pattern of small, evenly spaced ridges. This is the classic washboard road and is formed by little hops of tires as they propel the vehicles along. The worse they get, the more that tire-hop is compounded and so on, until driving on them will rattle your teeth.

Really bad washboard roads will induce enough vibration to loosen bolts, do the same for the screws in your glasses, make a cigarette pack do a little dance on the dashboard and leave you not knowing just how fast to drive. Speed is a factor on how jibbery a washboard road feels. Sometimes 20 mph is too fast and 60 mph isn't fast enough.

If you pussyfoot along on washboard, the tires may ride up and down over the undulations and make you seasick. A somewhat faster pace will make your rig drum until you wish you'd brought a set of earplugs along. At a heady rate, the tires are clipping only the tops of the serrations and while things may quiet down, vehicle stability and directional control are reduced because you're in the air more than you're on the ground.

If you can't find a comfortable speed on washboard, air-down the tires and let the sidewalls soak up the vibrations. If you still aren't satisfied, try driving on the left side of the road. Study washboard closely and you'll see that one side of each little ridge slopes gradually while the other side is steeper. This is caused by the direction of traffic. Going "against the grain" on the wrong side of the trail often lessens the drumming. Just watch out for oncoming traffic!

BERMS

Dictionaries describe a berm as a ledge or shoulder along the side of a paved road. But off-roaders know them along dirt roads as well. A berm may have been built up by the road grader that originally scraped the route, or it may have been formed by dirt kicked aside from passing vehicles. A berm can also be the edge of deep wheel ruts worn below the natural ground surface.

Somewhere out there you're going to encounter berms. But this is not necessarily bad. In fact, berms can be great if you know how to make the most of them. About the only problem they create is

Washboard roads set up enough vibration to loosen bolts, eyeballs and teeth, if yours are the portable variety. Sometimes 20 mph is too fast and 60 mph isn't fast enough.

Once back on pavement, don't forget to air-up your tires.

when you try to steer off the trail and encounter a berm at a shallow angle. This will tend to deflect the wheels back into the ruts. Don't be intimidated. Simply slow down and lurch over the berm at a steeper angle.

It's because a berm will tend to keep your rig on the trail that it is an asset. You can "lean" on a berm in a curve, letting the outside wheels ride against it, and you'll go around like you're on rails. On a long straight, they'll guide you like a luge going down a bobsled run as you ricochet slightly from one to the other.

Sometimes a two-rut trail will have a hump or center berm between as high, or higher, than the edge berms. On a standard-height vehicle, this can be a problem. The trick here is to ride up on the berm, the wheels straddling one or the other of the tracks with one pair up on the outer berm and the other up in the middle. It isn't graceful and you'll have a tendency to fall back into the lower wheel tracks, but fight the steering wheel and stay up there until better conditions come along.

BACK ON PAVEMENT

When your great trail trek is over and

it's time, alas, to head for the barn, there are certain procedures to follow when pavement looms ahead. You have to undo all of the things you did before heading out. These appear elsewhere in this book, but they merit repeating here.

Shift out of four-wheel drive. The actual steps for doing this depend upon the make and model of your vehicle. On some, those with a part-time system and automatic-locking hubs, come to a stop. Shift the transfer case lever into 2WD. Then put the transmission in reverse and back up a few feet. The hubs will disengage automatically and sometimes the clicks are audible. Then all you have to do is drive away.

With manual hubs, you must stop, shove the transfer case into 2WD, then get out and twist the hub-locking levers into their "free" position. Now get back in and motor off into the sunset.

On the various other systems, just do the opposite of what you did when you first hit the dirt. The steps are explained on a sticker somewhere in the passenger compartment, of course, but they should be quite familiar to you by now. Just don't forget to do them.

Airing-Up—If you had aired-down

your tires, now's the time to do something about this. If you have an electric air pump that plugs into the cigarette lighter socket, a "chuffer" that screws into a sparkplug hole, a bicycle pump, or an inflater hose that reaches all of your tires from the overinflated spare, now's the time to use it. Unless you've timed the procedure at home using your own particular inflation device, you cannot time reinflation with your watch as you may have done when you aired-down. You need a gage. Use it to make certain all four tires are pumped up to their recommended inflation.

If you carry no portable means of airing-up, head for the nearest service station or garage as soon as you hit pavement. But drive there at a moderate speed. Low-pressure tires will quickly build heat on hard surfaces and you don't want a tread separation this close to the end of your trek.

If you did some night driving on your cruise and took the covers off of your auxiliary lights, put them back on. Some states don't permit extra lights to be uncovered on public highways.

16

Maps & Navigation

"I know that road is here....somewhere." Photo by Dennis Casebier.

MAPS

No matter how well-honed your off-road driving expertise may be, when you wander further afield than your home area, you're going to need maps to guide you. Even knowing that the sun rises in the east and sets in the west, or relying on an inherent and uncanny sense of direction, a good map of the back country you want to explore is crucial to a successful adventure. In fact, your very survival may depend on it.

If you plan to do no more off-roading than occasional forays to a favorite trout stream or desert oasis, and you've been there many times and know the route like the back of your hand, a map may show you things you've never noticed before. There may be a more scenic, alternate way to get there, or perhaps a primitive campground just over the next hill that you didn't know existed. A map can show you these things and more.

By definition, a map is a drawing or other representation, usually on a flat surface, showing a certain geographic area with its countries or other regions, cities, mountains, and so forth. North is usually toward the top, south at the bottom, and west and east at the left- and right-hand sides, respectively.

Maps come in all shapes, sizes, degrees of detail, scale (the distance on a map proportional to the true distance; as one inch to 10 miles), and generally show major geographical features such as lakes, valleys, hills and more. The types of maps we're interested in will also show roads; perhaps only major traffic arteries like interstates and state highways, or on down to routes of less importance to the casual user as secondary roads, rural lanes, scenic byways and, hopefully for the adventurer, abandoned roads and trails.

State Maps—The degree of detail shown on maps is a function of its scale. Some highway maps, for example, have a scale as small as one inch to 20 miles, meaning that every pond, little hill and trail is not large enough to be illustrated. State route maps are generally intended to show the major paved highways and roads for conventional vehicles anyway, so the off-roader will need one only to show the most direct way to a region.

If you live in Arkansas, as an example, and are planning a first-time trip to the Olympic Peninsula in Washington, a Washington highway map, or even one including several of the western states, will be handy. In fact, if your outing is to be this extensive, avail yourself of a U.S. road atlas which will have all states in individual page form, and usually show portions of southern Canada and northern Mexico, as well.

State road maps, atlases, travel guides and other useful publications for travelers are available through map oulets, book stores, travel agencies and automobile associations. Many are dispensed by vending machines or over-the-counter at service stations.

County Maps—Better than state maps for showing detail are county maps, though there is little standardization among their legends, scale, degree of detail, even their sizes, or whether all driveable roads and trails are shown. An experiment by a group of four-wheelers to drive as much off-road as possible between the Province of Quebec in eastern Canada and New Orleans on the Gulf of Mexico, 1600 miles as the crow flies, netted them 74 county maps from nine states. These ranged from 12-in.-square maps of counties almost as large as Texas to a five-footer for one county scarcely larger than a football field.

Many of the maps showed highways, streets and byroads without route numbers or other designations, while others had them named or numbered, but were not so identified when we got there. By and large, though, they proved useful to the expedition, whether revealing heavi-

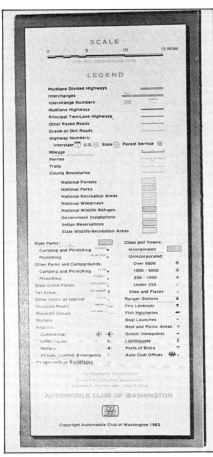

Key to understanding any map is its legend. This one includes its scale (one inch on map represents six miles on ground) and various lines indicating road surfaces from multi-lane divided highways to trails. Geographic highlights are also indicated by symbols.

At one time, maps were given away at service stations to help promote travel and hence fuel sales, but are seldom free anymore. Depending upon the source, state and county maps sell for $1 and up. The off-roading group mentioned earlier got maps in advance of their trip by phoning chambers of commerce at state or county capitals and requesting them. Some were sent without charge, evidently to promote tourism in the area. Others required an advance payment and still others arrived accompanied by a bill.

It won't hurt the off-road traveler to acquire a county map, regardless of its detail, for the area he or she wishes to explore—if one is available. Some counties simply do not provide them, or may combine several adjoining counties onto a single map. County maps may also be acquired from unexpected sources, such as real-estate agencies, and logging or mining companies. The best regional maps we've seen for some eastern states are prepared and sold by Alfred B. Patton, Inc., P.O. Box 857, Swamp Road & Center Street, Doylestown, PA 18901. Presented in a large format by county, they are known as plan-dot maps, Type 10. These are used by real-estate agents to show prospective customers the exact lay of the land, *all* routes including hiking and nature trails, as well as larger structures and other useful features.

The Automobile Club of Southern California, an affiliate of the AAA, produces its own outstanding county maps for roughly the southern third of the state. While other motoring organizations also prepare maps for their members, "The Club," as it's locally known, is mentioned specifically because it also offers the best outing map of Baja California bar none, together with two guidebooks to be used in conjunction with it. The Club's Baja map is regularly updated by field mapping units who prowl the peninsula every two years or so, and by the use of satellite photos.

Mapping of Baja California began in the 1920s as a service for more adventuresome Club members. At the same time, signs with village names and distances were posted at wilderness trail intersections. These famous signs have

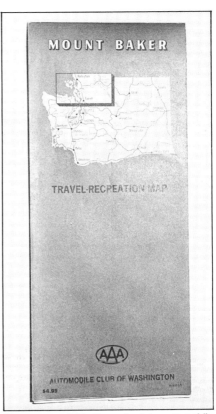

Maps are available through state automobile clubs for areas not defined by county boundaries. Shown is travel-recreation map for the Mount Baker region in Washington.

long since disappeared as rare collector's items, as have older Club signs erected throughout southern California. But each new edition of the Baja map is cherished by thousands of member-travelers, most of whom wouldn't be caught south of the border without it. The Baja map and guidebooks are *free* to current Club or AAA affiliate members.

USGS Maps—For accurate standardization of size, presentation, detail and route depiction, the most exhaustive series of maps published are available through the United States Geological Survey—USGS. Virtually every square foot of the United States is covered in scales ranging from approximately four miles to an inch down to 2000 feet to an inch. Best of all, they accurately show land forms and elevations above and below sea level by contour lines in increments of 40 or 100 feet. Once accus-

ly traveled routes only, or denoting by various colors or shadings of solid, dotted, dashed or cross-hatched lines the types of roads from thruways to farm lanes, abandoned and even *proposed* roads. This exercise gave a splendid cross-section of the kinds of county maps available throughout the United States. Most of them proved to be relatively up to date, which is more than can be said for many federal and state maps.

County maps are available through a state or county chamber of commerce, the local highway or transportation department, by mail order from private map retailers, at service stations and travel agencies, and from auto clubs or local tourist centers.

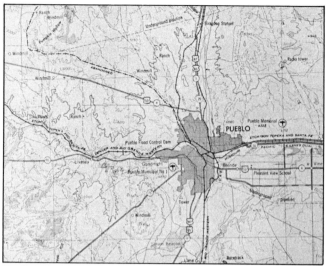

Section of United States Geological Survey (USGS) topographic map titled "Pueblo" covering an area 110 by 70 miles. Scale is 1:250,000, adequate for finding dirt roads and trails although smaller-scale maps are available. Note trail leading northwest from city marked "Abandoned." Make your mouth water?

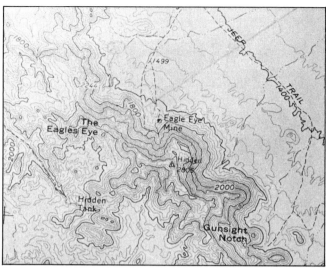

Portion of a quad map with a scale of 1:62,500 or roughly one inch to the mile. Lighter squiggly lines represent land contours at 40-foot intervals. Where lines are closely grouped, ground is steep. "Jeep," meaning recommended for 4WD only, trails are represented by dashed lines.

tomed to reading and using these topographic, or "topo," maps, a user can read the shape and appearance of the terrain almost three-dimensionally. Where the contour lines are widely separated, the ground slopes gradually; where they are closely spaced, the terrain is steep.

Topos also show *every* highway, road, street, trail, path or other route, lakes, streams and rivers, and such man-made creations as major structures, dams, bridges, mines and windmills. Virtually everything that exists on the ground at the time a given map was prepared is represented. Using a topo map is like observing the ground from an airplane.

Topo Map Preparation—And that's exactly how most topos were prepared—by satellite photography for the later maps and aerial photogrammetry for most earlier ones. Unfortunately, federal funding cutbacks have prevented an updating of the majority of topos, including some originally prepared by ground-surveying parties in the early 1900s.

This is not all bad, however, for outdated topos will show old roads, little-remembered town sites, railroads no longer used, now-overgrown cemeteries and other abandoned developments which are the goals of many off-roaders. Of course, while land contours probably have not changed much over the years,

the older maps cannot portray modern routes or other improvements, and it's sometimes difficult to orient yourself. But because USGS maps cover areas defined by latitude and longitude, and often include township, section and range lines, a relationship can be made between a topo and a recent state or county map if they also include lines of latitude and longitude.

Using an Older Topo—An example is the USGS topo map labeled Vicksburg, Arizona, shown in part in a nearby photo. It indicates one off-roader's goal, an unusual topographic feature known as the Eagle's Eye. It is a huge, natural hole through a precipitous mountain, visible from a great distance. Because a topo is prepared as though one were looking straight down at the ground, the Eagle's Eye does not show—it is horizontal. But the site is identified by name on the map and the dense crowding of the contour lines indicate that the mountain is steep indeed.

An off-roader wanted to drive as near the Eagle's Eye as he could, even up to it if possible, but was unfamiliar with the terrain. When he acquired the topo, he found that Interstate 10, from which the Eagle's Eye is visible in the distance, was constructed long after the topo was produced. But from landmarks and the loca-

tions of nearby towns, he penciled-in his own I-10 and thus determined his access to the Jeep trails the topo *did* show and, eventually made his way there.

Scales—Three scales are commonly used for USGS topo maps. The smallest and least detailed is 1:250,000, or about four miles to an inch, and represents 1° of latitude by 2° longitude. The next size is 1:62,500, or about one mile to an inch, four times the magnification of the first, and representing an area 15 minutes—1/4°—square. Lastly is the 1:24,000 scale with 2000 linear feet to an inch for an area 7-1/2 minutes square, or 1/8°. The 15-minute and 7-1/2-minute topos are also known as quadrangle maps, or *quads*. Quadrangle-map detail is so good that you can almost watch your vehicle move across the map as you drive.

Either scale of the two quad maps, while depicting in detail virtually every rock or bump in the trail, covers just a very small physical area, about 70 square miles in the southern reaches of the United States and some 50 square miles near the Canadian border. The difference lies in the fact that lines of longitude converge at the North Pole, from their spacing at the Equator, due to Earth's curvature. The distance between lines of latitude remain the same everywhere on the globe.

Long-abandoned railroad right of way shown on USGS map was not passable. Any true off-roader following the berm, though, would simply bypass this steep-sided washout and keep going.

While this sign serves to warn casual motorists in their sedans, off-roaders will head for 15-mile mark just to see *how* deep sand really is.

So, while USGS maps are great for planning an off-road excursion, it will take several adjoining ones to cover an area you can drive in a day, or even in several hours. If you want to explore a fairly substantial region, you might need a dozen or more topos. And they're not free. At this writing, the 1:250,000 topos are $3.60 each and the quads run $2.25. If the Jeep travelers who plotted that route south across the eastern United States had relied solely on topo maps, they'd have spent over a thousand dollars acquiring them.

Topo Map Indexes—To select topo or quad maps for an area, you'll need an index sheet for that state. These are available free. Sheets for states west of the Mississippi River come from the Western Distribution Center, USGS, P.O. Box 25286, Federal Center, Denver, CO 80225. State indexes east of the Mississippi come from the Eastern Distribution Center, USGS, 1200 South Eads Street, Arlington, VA 22202. Private map firms may stock some, but not necessarily all, of the index sheets, and major cities generally have a USGS map outlet among their federal offices. If you can't find the index sheet you want, simply write to the appropriate USGS distribution center.

One side of the index sheet will show the outline of the state covered with a grid, each square representing the specific 15-minute or 7-1/2-minute quadrangle map. A separate chart of the larger-scale topo maps is also given. On the reverse side is a list where the individual topos can be seen, as at public libraries, schools and universities, or where they may be purchased: private map outlets, blueprint companies, recreational and outdoor-equipment companies, book stores, and so forth. Not all such agencies will have all topos for a given state, so if you can stand the wait, order them from the USGS directly. Be sure to include a check or money order for the required amount.

Finding an exact topo map from an index sheet may not be easy because the state outline includes no topographical features or other landmarks. However, you can coordinate the index with a state or county road map and come pretty close to the topo you want. Alternate topos are also available for National Parks, Monuments and other federal areas, and these often conform to the boundaries of those sites, rather than to latitude and longitude. These will also be given on the reverse side of the index sheets for those states that include them.

BLM, Forest Service Maps—If there is one shortcoming of all the maps discussed so far, it is that none of them show which areas are private property and which ones are open to public use. An old trail or abandoned road that you might be rightfully driving along may suddenly cross into private property, with or without a "No Trespassing" sign. Or it may cross a federal area, such as a military reservation or missile test site, or a region reserved as a wilderness area or designated for limited-use only. Fortunately, there are at least two additional sources for federal maps.

The agencies issuing these maps are the Bureau of Land Management, (U.S. Department of the Interior, 1800 C. Street NW, Washington, D.C. 20240) and the Forest Service (U.S. Department of Agriculture, 14th Street and Jefferson Drive, Washington, D.C. 20250). Writing either office for their maps of certain areas will probably bring you a referral to the nearest regional office to whom you'll once again have to write for the maps you want.

BLM and Forest Service maps, though not available for every part of the U.S., will generally show which sections or specific areas are open to vehicle use, which are privately owned or otherwise closed, which parts are limited to such users as hikers, three-wheelers or snowmobilers, and so on. These maps

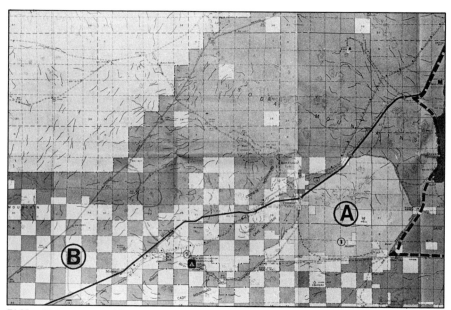

BLM vehicle access guide with shaded sections representing "Open," "Limited" and "Closed" areas. Even though trails are shown through all designated areas, you cannot necessarily drive on them.

Some off-limit areas are marked by signs, others may not be. Be *sure* you go off-roading only where it's legal to do so.

are not as well-detailed as the topos, but are useful when used in conjunction with them. Many do not show topographic features in anywhere near the detail of the USGS maps, and neither agency has such maps for every tract under their jurisdiction. But many regions, especially those considered to be "high-use" areas, are covered in considerable detail and are frequently updated.

The vast California Desert District, for example, contains many millions of acres of public lands interspersed with private holdings, areas under lease for ranching or mining, and other off-limit or limited-access areas. The desert is riddled with hundreds, if not thousands, of miles of unpaved roads and four-wheel-drive trails—an off-roader's paradise. Lying as much of it does within a weekend's range of 12 million people, many of them avid recreationalists, the region has been carefully mapped. These maps are called *vehicle access guides,* and are available free for the asking from local BLM offices.

Many other parts of the United States are similarly covered by BLM or Forest Service maps and access guides. It always pays to investigate the local off-roading situation by studying maps before dropping into four-wheel drive and blindly heading out—and finding a rang-er hot on your heels.

Park Service Maps—The National Park Service is another good source for special guides and maps. These are commonly available at park-visitors' centers. To cite an example, the USGS topos will show all sorts of old trails in Death Valley. But the region within the Monument is greatly restricted as a means of preserving the resources there: ghost towns, mine sites, original wagon roads, as well as habitats of endangered plants and animals. Use-maps, area guides and other helpful literature concerning the vehicular do's and don'ts in Death Valley are stocked at Monument headquarters at Furnace Creek. The same restrictions apply to other federal, state and sometimes county monuments, parks, forest preserves and similar regions.

BIA Maps—Many people do not realize that the Bureau of Indian Affairs has jurisdiction over vast areas of the United States and that travelers are usually encouraged to drop in. These lands are held in trust by our government, not for the general public but for the individual Indian tribes. Tribal councils sometimes make old roads and trails within their reservations available for use by off-roaders. In some areas, camping, fishing, hunting and general exploring are permitted—even encouraged—by the

Indians. Many tribes have established good campgrounds, visitor and interpretation centers and other facilities.

The larger Indian reservations are in the West. For example, nearly 1/4 of Arizona belongs to the Apaches and Navajos. There are others in California, Nevada and other western states. And smaller tracts are in midwestern, southern and eastern states, as well. Write the BIA (U.S. Department of the Interior, 1951 Constitution Avenue, Washington, D.C. 20242) and request maps and guides for the region in which you're interested. An alternate source is the American Indian Travel Agency, Suite 550, 10403 West Colfax Avenue, Lakewood, CO 80215.

Cautions—It should be mentioned that no map or access guide, no matter how well it depicts the geography in other respects, can show you what a trail is actually like to drive on. Even the excellent USGS maps fall short in this respect. Often the cartographers have seemingly labeled routes quite arbitrarily with the notations "Jeep Only" or "Impassable." Why is this? Is it too sandy, muddy or rocky? Is it so overgrown with brush or trees that vehicles cannot get through? What about trails you've been over during the summer? Are they driveable in the winter as well?

While BLM, Forest Service, Park Service and BIA maps generally indicate abandoned townsites, this off-roading hobbyist specializes in pinpointing building locations by comparing century-old photos against land forms.

Outdoorsman's compass includes a folding sight for taking bearings on distant objects and locating oneself by triangulation.

Unfortunately, there's no way to learn the true condition of an old road without actually going there and seeing for yourself. But, after all, that's the fun of off roading, isn't it? Heading off into the unknown and returning with tales of how a "Jeep Only" trail was a piece of cake in two-wheel drive with an expert handler behind the wheel, is the stuff of an off-roader's dreams. Or negotiating what was labeled as an "Impassible" path, weaving its way through a forest, was a cinch for a narrow imported truck or a short-coupled Jeep CJ while a full-size Bronco or Blazer was stopped in its tracks. These are stories for campfire-telling. Maps often tend to discourage the use of conventional vehicles in difficult terrain where a low-slung passenger car might high-center itself or drag its tail crossing a ditch. But for the properly equipped off-roader, maps are like a carrot on the end of a stick inviting the adventurer farther and farther into the outback. All parts of our country, and those of our neighbors to the north and south, are worth exploring. Knowing how to read and use maps are the keys to unlocking the unknown.

COMPASSES

A compass is a useful instrument when working with maps, especially the USGS topos. With a compass, you can determine not only the direction you're heading, or want to head, but pinpoint your location by reference to landmarks or other topographical features.

The Chinese are credited with inventing the compass centuries ago. It is so simple that few improvements have been made in the last 100 years, other than manufacturing methods. In essence, a compass has a magnetized needle which aligns itself automatically with the magnetic field surrounding the earth. The needle will always point northward no matter where you are—except at the North Pole where every direction away from it is south—providing a constant reference for determining direction. Directly opposite of north, of course, is south and at right angles to this line are east and west, the four cardinal directions. Compasses are round and are marked off in degrees with 360 making a full circle.

North—Both of Them—The trouble is, there are two norths. True, or geographic, north lies toward the North Pole, which is the earth's axis. Magnetic north is the direction a compass needle actually points due to the concentration of magnetic forces near, but not exactly at, the North Pole. To confound matters even more, magnetic north is not a constant for it gradually shifts from one location to another. At present, it is in the general vicinity of Hudson Bay in the Northwest Territories of Canada.

If you stand on the east coast of Maine, the magnetic north indicated by the compass needle will be 12° *west* of true north. From a Southern California beach, it would lie 14° *east* of true north. Because magnetic north continually shifts its position, these readings will change as time goes by. Presently, magnetic and true north are aligned along a wavering "zero" line that extends from about Tallahassee to Lake Michigan.

Magnetic Declination—The difference between true and magnetic north is termed the angle of magnetic declination. The farther *west* of the zero line you are, the greater the angle of declination *eastward* from true north. Conversely, the farther *east* you are of the zero line, the greater the angle of declination *westward*. To make accurate compass readings, you must know the angle of declination at your location. This angle is printed at the bottom of every topo map. Sporting-goods stores and other recreational-equipment outlets that sell compasses will also have isogonic charts, or declination maps, for determining the angles of declination for all parts of the country. Instructions accompanying a quality compass will usually have such a chart, as well.

The annual change of declination is relatively small, and the degree depends upon your location. But it is sufficient to throw precise bearings off, especially if the declination map or topo you are using is several years old. Most such maps are dated, however, so you can calculate the degree of declination at the present time.

Let's say you're in southern Arizona where the magnetic declination is 13° east of true north. Here the annual variation is three minutes west. With 60 minutes of arc comprising 1°, this means that in 20 years the magnetic declination at the same spot will have changed by 1° to 12° east. A shift of 1° in 20 years may not seem like much, and most sportsman's compasses cannot be read that closely. But if you were 1° off on a journey of several hundred miles, you'd be dangerously far off course.

Other sections of the country will have more or less of an annual variation to be added or subtracted when calculating magnetic declination. Check the declination on the topo you'll be using in the field and apply the annual variation to see if there's enough of a difference since the map was printed to warrant going through the mathematics.

Deviation—Another factor that can influence a compass is termed *deviation*— the degree of compass error due to influences such as concentrations of metal, incidental magnetic forces or electrical disturbances. Some of these can be overcome by removing the interferences or moving the compass away from them. High-quality compasses have adjustments to help offset them.

We do not intend to force-feed you on navigation or compass theory. Rather, we are citing some of the factors governing a compass to point out that a high-quality instrument can be a real asset in unfamiliar territory. The garden-variety or dime-store compass, the type with a suction cup that you can stick on the windshield or dashboard, will only indicate a generally northward direction at best.

There are really good automotive compasses over a wide price range that have adjustments for deviation. Many of these also have a liquid-damped needle to minimize the effect of vehicle vibrations on accuracy. But another type of compass may be better suited for off-road exploring, as we shall see.

Types of Compasses—Automotive compasses are intended to be permanently mounted. This is fine if all you want to know is which way is north and the direction you're heading. But far

Pair of binoculars is another useful tool to carry along when wandering in the outback.

more versatile is a portable or sportsman's compass with a movable, calibrated dial and a sighting system for use in obtaining other directions called *bearings*. A compass attached to a vehicle cannot be used in this way.

Because a sportsman's compass can be influenced by the metal in a vehicle and its electrical equipment, it should be used well away from such error inducements. This means that to use one, you have to park and walk a few feet away. Hold the compass steady in your hand or set it on a flat surface—not your metal hood or tailgate but on a picnic table or anything non-metallic.

A good hand compass and a topo map for the area are the best tools available for finding where you are and the direction you want to go. Each is useful by itself, but they are better when used in conjunction with each other.

Start by spreading out the topo map and orienting it so that its indicated true north (top of the map) corresponds to the actual north from where you're standing as determined by your compass. Align the map to true north by placing the compass on the map over one of the *meridian*—longitudinal—lines printed

on it. Now, adjust the map and compass for the declination angle between true and magnetic north that's printed on the bottom of the map. If your location has a declination of 15° *east*, twist the map 15° in the opposite direction, or *west*.

Triangulation—To find out where you are, pick out a couple of landmarks shown on the map and which are visible from your location. These might be a peak, a lake or any other prominent feature. Try and spot one off to your left and another to the right, or at least 30° apart. Use two that are as far away as possible for greatest accuracy.

Without moving the compass, line up its sight with the peak to your left and note down the direction to it in degrees. Let's say it stands 270°, or west, of where you are. Draw a light line on the map through the peak at 270°. You are somewhere along that line. Repeat the process for the lake which you find to lie 40° from your position, or northeasterly. When the 270° and 40° lines are extended to meet each other, their intersection is your location. To check yourself, add a third or even a fourth landmark and go through the process again.

This is known as *triangulation*—a form of navigation using fixed points from which to draw bearings. Now that you know where you are on the map, you know which trail to follow, and how far it is to that elusive goal you came so far to see. You can also figure out how far away, and in which direction, the highway is, just in case you want to bail out.

BINOCULARS

It's a good idea to pack a pair of binoculars when preparing for a cruise into the outback. There are too many brands and types, as well as degrees of magnification, to dwell on them. But as a point of reference, binoculars of 7 X 35mm will optically bring an object 1000-yards distant to 578 feet.

Binoculars are useful for studying the far-off landscape around you and to give close-up looks at how a road cuts into a canyon or climbs through a pass. They can also help you accurately pinpoint the landmarks you are using for triangulation by bringing out features too far away to be seen with the naked eye, but which are marked on the topo maps.

Camping

Camping off-road can be a lot of fun if you plan ahead and camp in scenic places.

We've gone the full route on off-road camping. We started out curled up on the ground in a borrowed sleeping bag, warmed our can of beans over an open fire and scrubbed out our war-surplus mess kits with sand just like they teach you in the Army. And we thought we were having fun.

On a recent camping trip, the most strenuous part of the routine was cranking up the pop-up camper on the back of a four-wheel-drive truck. We also slept on a 4-in. foam mattress, drank chilled beer from a gas-electric refrigerator and heated dinner on a two-burner gas stove while listening to a James Taylor tape on the stereo. And we still thought we were having fun.

So we've made the whole trip from stark simplicity to something approximating sybaritic luxury and made stops at most of the other places in between.

One of the discoveries we made fairly early in our camping career was that we prefer to be comfortable. Admittedly, the tailgate of your truck or utility vehicle is an acceptable temporary place to park your bones, but it's still a poor second to a real chair. Also, while there are people who can sleep on a pile of used bricks, we've learned that we're not like that. We always feel better the next day if we've had a decent night's sleep.

We should also warn you that we're traveling campers. We don't go traveling to camp. We go traveling to travel. But make no mistake, camping is still a major part of the pleasure we get from treating ourselves to a weekend or a week out there in the great nowhere.

PACKING

One of the best features of camping out of a pickup truck is that there's room to take along the equipment required to be comfortable. For us, that includes sleep-ing cots, plus amenities like an ice chest, stove, gasoline lantern, folding chairs, folding table, folding toilet seat, boxes for food and supplies, plus a basic tool-box, High Lift jack and essential emergency gear. Why travel light if you don't have to?

Traveling Light—On the other hand, it's also possible to travel light and still be comfortable. One of the authors made many a pleasant camp when he was using his Baja Bug as his official off-road traveling machine. This required that some equipment be downsized, but it didn't mean having to sleep on rocks again.

For example, instead of a cot with springs and a mattress, there was a light-weight steel-frame canvas cot. Instead of a giant-size ice chest, there was a modest-size one. And in place of the king-size sleeping bag, there was a back-packer model with a stuff-bag that was

139

If you really want to be comfortable, haul your trailer to a scenic location and use it as a base camp for serious off-roading, or plug in your color TV and watch the World Series.

Water containers survive better if they're square-cornered and carried in their own plywood box. Photo by James T. Crow.

Camping out can be as easy or as hard, as comfortable or as miserable as you make it. This Bug easily carries enough lightweight gear for two during sojourn into Baja desert.

smaller and lighter but still comfortable.

By the way, if you need justification for carrying a lot of gear in your truck or utililty vehicle, think of it this way—you need to carry the extra weight because your four-by rides better with a load in the back. And that's true. You get the springs a little more stretched out and their action isn't nearly so harsh. Also, if you take along enough gear to fill up the floor of the bed, the whole load tends to

stay where it's put rather than shifting around and trying to get out. So there!

PACKING

As for getting your camping stuff ready to pack, there are certain rules to be followed. First, everything goes in a container, with nothing loose to roll around, get lost or fall out. And everything must be organized. For the kind of camping we do, this means one box devoted to paper

goods and related supplies, such as paper towels, paper plates, paper bowls, a roll of aluminum foil, an extra roll of toilet paper, and so on.

Another box houses the cooking gear: a set of nested pots, pans, skillet, coffee pot, cooking utensils, a can opener, corkscrew, and the like. And don't forget the condiments and special seasonings.

Depending on the length of the journey and availability of supplies along the way, there will also be one or more boxes of food.

Packing Boxes—Many years ago, the best packing cartons for off-road travel were cardboard boxes originally manufactured to hold a dozen quarts of beer. These heavy-duty containers were fastened together with heavy staples and well-designed sturdy lids, not the typical wimpy corrugated paper cartons that are glued together and fall apart at the first hint of rain. Alas, a cheaper way was discovered, the beer cartons went away and we've been looking for the perfect packing box ever since.

The most satisfactory solution we've found is to build your own packing box out of plywood. These can be custom-tailored to fit whatever you want to carry. But it still lacks the versatility and virtual indestructibility of the old-fashioned beer carton.

One widely used packing box is the molded-plastic milk crate. This has the

A rough trail can really stir your camping gear around, so box related items together and either wedge them tightly in place or secure them with rope or bungee cords. Photo by James T. Crow.

It's good practice to load the heavy items forward, and the more destructible things, too. There's less up-and-downing in the front of the bed than at the rear.

twin virtues of being almost indestructible, as well as being readily accessible. The most convenient source is the tempting stack out behind your supermarket—although these include a painted-on warning that it's a legal no-no for you to even possess them—but they're also available at those sell-you-anything stores like Akron, Cost-Plus, and the like. Their great disadvantage, as far as we're concerned, is that they offer neither dust nor rain protection.

Water Containers—As for water, it's our experience that one-gallon plastic jugs are far superior to containers holding larger amounts. The smaller jugs are easier to fill, lighter to load and more convenient to use around camp. We regularly use those rectangular one-gallon bottles in which "spring" water is sold and carry them four to a custom-made box. These aren't indestructible, but they're easily replaced at virtually any outpost of civilization.

Maybe all of this seems over-organized, but it's ultimately simpler this way. The vehicle is much easier to pack if you have a collection of rectangular cartons rather than 12 times that many irregularly shaped packages.

A friend of ours always keeps everything in its individual package. As a result, he has to move everything to find anything. And he often can't find it even after that.

LOADING THE VEHICLE

There's also something of an art to loading the vehicle. The best system we've devised is to gather up everything we're going to take on the trip and stack it alongside the vehicle. Then we start the loading process, heavy to the front, light to the rear.

This is so fundamental to us now that we can't believe there was a time when it wasn't. But one of us recalls one early camping trip when he and his companion put the Styrofoam ice chest next to the tailgate of their Jeep Wagoneer so it would be handy when they wanted to get into it.

Smashed Eggs—After the very first rough stretch of road, they discovered what seemed to be eggs running out from under the tailgate. And that's what it was; smashed eggs. The ice had leaped up and down, not only breaking the eggs, but destroying the foam cooler, as well. So they not only lost their eggs, they also had no way of keeping anything cool for the rest of that trip. And a camping trip without cold beer is like a trip without sunshine.

So, heavy stuff such as the ice chest, water containers, toolbox, and so on, go to the front. So does anything that's vulnerable to damage by getting tossed up and down. As you know, the rear end of your vehicle is at the long end of the pendulum, and not only travels up and down a much longer distance, but also at a much greater rate of acceleration. There's much less movement near the vehicle's pivot point. So, delicate stuff such as your gasoline lantern, electron microscope and star-scanner telescope go toward the front. Period.

To the rear goes the light, indestructible stuff, like your sleeping bag, cots, folding chairs, and the like.

Incidentally, it's also been our experience that it takes two or three days for the load to shake down. We used to try to get everything in exactly the right place before we left home. Now we follow the general rule about heavy to the front when we first pack and let the load fine-tune itself as the trip goes on. After a few days, everything seems to find the place it wants to be.

COVERED VS. UNCOVERED

Perhaps the next decision is whether to cover the load or to leave it uncovered. We've tried it both ways and after years of experimenting, we're now exponents of the uncovered load.

Small Tarps Useful—A pair of small 6 X 8-ft tarps is useful in any number of ways: as a ground cloth to put your cot on and avoid cockleburrs in your socks; a windbreak when it's windy; a cover when it rains; and as something to lie on while working on a broken whatever. If it means getting unstuck, one can be used

To keep dust out, this tight-fitting tonneau cover, held in place by Velcro strips, beats a tarp secured with rope or bungees.

as a traction improver in the sand. They are also useful to cover the load when it's wet, but not when it's dry.

Sure, things get dusty if you don't cover them. But they also get dusty if you *do* cover them. In fact, in our experience, if you throw a tarp over the load, it seems to get dustier than if you don't. We've noodled this through, however, and decided it's a result of negative pressure. When you cover the load, the wind passing over the bed creates a negative pressure that sucks dust in through every available crack. And most vehicles have a lot of cracks. So, what you do when you cover the load is trap the dust under the tarp. If you leave the load uncovered, the dust is more likely to be sucked on out of the bed and left behind.

There are times when you do want to cover the load, of course, such as when it rains. Most newer trucks have had their aesthetics cleaned up and their aerodynamics improved by eliminating the old-style tiedown hooks around the outside lip of the bed and devising some kind of substitutes inside. This is fine except when it rains, and then you find that there's nothing to hook your rope or bungees to cover the load. If you put them inside, you simply encourage the water to drain onto the floor of the bed and soak into your camping gear. Yuck. One solution we've found is to put the tarp over the load and down over the outside of the bed, then stretch bungees cords all the way across and down to hook under the side panels. This works fine and everything stays dry, but the bungees can wear away the paint if

they're allowed to vibrate in the wind and thrum against the sides. You can avoid this by padding the bungees at the critical points. Unfortunately, you usually don't know it's happening until it's too late.

Heavy Plastic Bags—And what about those things you do want to seal up so they don't get dusty or wet, like your sleeping bag? We recommend placing these items in a *heavy-duty* plastic garbage bag, sealed with a wire wrap. Don't use thin-film garbage bags because these tend to go to pieces from being whipped by the wind. Plastic bags like these are also convenient as dirty-clothes containers, to house your heavy jacket and sweaters, and are even useful to keep garbage in. And don't forget to bag that genuine calfskin attache case you never travel without.

Long Bungee Cords—If you're driving an open-bed truck, you need something to keep everything from jumping out on the road. For this purpose, we take along about six long bungee cords. These are versatile and can be arranged to control almost any load. Sometimes, you need to cross them, sometimes run them straight across, and there have been times when we've woven them fore and aft as well as side to side.

Lacking bungees, you can use a rope or heavy cord to keep your load in the truck. Speaking of cord, that's something else we always try to carry a supply of. Ordinary heavy cord is strong enough to tie down almost anything that's loose. And it's especially helpful when you need to anchor a tarp or replace the boot lace the packrats carried off.

WHEN TO CAMP

Hunting for a place to camp in the dark is zero fun. That's the way you end up sleeping in the town dump. At least we have. So, something you need to establish as part of your camping routine is what time of day you're going to begin your search for the perfect campsite.

The rule we've come around to is to start looking for the perfect place about an hour before dark. But if it's still an hour and a quarter before dark and you see a good place, stop immediately. Don't assume there's an equally good place on ahead. There usually won't be.

The next rule is this: As darkness settles down over you like a vampire's cloak, lower your standards in direct proportion to the amount of light that's left. With a full hour's daylight left, you can be choosy. When the sun has already disappeared behind the hills, you can't. Consider yourself lucky if you find a place that's flat enough that you don't have to stake yourself to the ground to keep from rolling off a cliff.

It's always more satisfactory to stop early in the day. This gives you more time to appreciate nature. It also provides adequate time to gather the rocks for the fire ring and drag in the wood needed for the evening campfire. Without these things, no camp is complete.

WHERE TO CAMP

Everybody has his own favorite kind of camping place. Ours is a place that's sheltered by big rocks, has a view of both sunset and sunrise, comes with clean, coarse sand underfoot, and is flat and level. But wait, there's more. We prefer one with a babbling brook and a convenient source of firewood. Then, there are other aesthetics such as coyotes that howl in the distance at night and birds that twitter in the morning. Two things we don't want are snakes or other human beings within 50 miles, especially human beings or snakes with transistor radios.

The minimum requirement is a place that's reasonably level and also large enough to accommodate both the vehicle and the appropriate number of cots or sleeping bags.

Wherever you decide to camp, consider what may happen if a natural disaster or two takes place during the night. One

No campsite is complete without a campfire, especially if it gets chilly. Unless you're trucking in your own firewood, camp near a convenient source of supply.

There's camping and then there's *camping*. Spending the night with hundreds of others on a dusty, dry lake bed is about as much fun as sleeping in a shopping-center parking lot.

of us once made a camping trip to an area where the desert bordered the sea. He and his companion knew that this particular location was subject to occasional freaky high tides, so part of their plan was to park their Jeep on a hummock, figuring it would remain high and dry if the water rose. Also part of this plan was to sleep on lower ground near the Jeep so the high tide, if it came, would awaken them. The high tide came and went without dampening them. But in the middle of the night, the author's companion got to worrying about the Jeep slipping its handbrake and rolling down over him. So he got up and drove it to lower ground. In the process, he ran over the ice chest, thoroughly crushing all of their groceries and drinks.

Friendly Glow—Given a choice, it's always cozier if there are big rocks against which you can build your fire. The fire has a much friendlier glow when it's reflected off something than if its beams are sent out to be lost in the reaches of outer space.

If there aren't rocks or other types of protection, we prefer to set up camp with the truck behind us. This at least provides some feeling of shelter.

When possible, it's nice to orient the truck in a north-south direction with room on one side for your evening camp where you can watch the sunset and space on the other for you to establish your sleeping quarters so you can enjoy the sunrise. Maybe this seems like a lot of

If you camp near tidal waters, don't forget to check tide table before picking camping spot. This group stayed dry but just barely.

trouble, but it's these fine points that make the difference between being a good camper and being a great camper.

Your truck also makes a good windbreak and that's another specialized condition you should know about.

WHEN IT'S WINDY

Wind can be one of the banes of the camper's existence. While we realize that there's no perfect solution to protecting yourself from the wind, we have also evolved a few procedures that can make the difference between getting a little

sleep and spending the whole night in misery.

Protecting yourself from the wind's direct blast is the first essential, of course. If there's only a little wind, just letting the vehicle act as a windbreak is sufficient to make life tolerable. One way is to set up the head of your bed against one of the wheels and let it protect you. This isn't a bad idea in any kind of weather, actually, because it also gives you a place to prop your head while you have that first cup of coffee in the morning.

When It's Really Windy—If it's really

If it's windy and it seems that it'll keep blowing from the same direction, rig your tarp as a windbreak.

When the weather threatens rain or you don't like the morning sun in your eyes, anchor the tarp over your cot.

windy so the breeze whips your socks right off your feet as it whistles under the vehicle, you can use a small tarp or tarps to increase the efficiency of your windbreak. Ordinarily, this can be done by anchoring the upper end of the tarp to the vehicle and holding down the bottom side with an assortment of whatever—ice chest, chairs, food boxes, chests of unburied treasure, and so on.

With such an arrangement, you've at least got a pretty snug place to sit. And when bedtime comes, you put your cot there, as well. Provided the tarp is well anchored—and the wind doesn't shift—you are pretty well protected.

If it's hopelessly windy, or the wind keeps shifting, or if the windbreak is merely acting as a trap for blowing dust and sand, your next move may be to sleep inside the vehicle. You probably already know that a truck bed and a utility vehicle's cargo area two of the world's worst places to try to sleep if you don't have a sufficiently thick pad under you for insulation and to rest your bones. One experienced camper we know routinely sleeps in the bed of his pickup truck, not so much for wind protection but because he has a highly developed aversion to sharing his sleeping bag with creatures having more than two legs. What he does is empty the bed of the truck of everything else, then shovel in enough sand to fill in between all the grooves in the floor. The sand eliminates the ridges,

gives him a little padding and also provides a measure of insulation against the chill. Sort of like sleeping in a huge kitty litter box, without kitty.

Like most off-road campers, we've also spent nights in the cab. This never works very well as a place to sleep, with steering wheels, seat belts and shift levers poking at you, but is sometimes preferable to getting wet. A small tarp over your sleeping bag is generally a better solution.

Anchor the Tent—If you have a tent and it's windy, it's always a good idea to use the vehicle to break the wind before it gets to the tent. One of the authors remembers a night when the wind came up and he and his companion didn't bother to move the truck and tie the tent to it. The tent billowed and snapped and kept them awake most of the night, of course, but nothing untoward happened until morning when he let himself out. He'd been sleeping on the upwind side and as soon as he departed, the wind got under the tent floor. This was followed by a muffled clatter and mumbled expletives as the tent, chairs, cots and companion were all rolled into a ball.

RAIN

What do you do when it rains? You put up the tent you always bring along in case that happens.

And what do you do when you didn't bring the blasted tent because it never

rains this time of year? The obvious answer is to sit up in the cab of the truck all night, but there are other measures that you may be able to take.

If there's only a light rain, a tarp directly on top of your sleeping bag is a satisfactory solution. However, if there's more than a little rain, capillary action sees to it that you get wet by delivering water through the canvas wherever the canvas is touching anything. As a result, your sleeping bag can weigh 40 pounds by morning. Which isn't much fun.

Make a Lean-To—Even in a good, hard rain, we've slept dry and comfortably under a lean-to created by anchoring the up end of a small tarp to the side of the vehicle and tying the other end to the foot of the cot. This doesn't work so well if the wind is blowing at the same time, you understand.

We've also known people who have put the tailgate down and used that as a sort of roof over their miserable heads. This obviously works better if you have something you can use to cover the crack between the tailgate and truck bed.

If you're thin enough and your vehicle sits high enough, you may also be able to sleep underneath. This is only practical if the rain didn't start until after you parked the truck so the ground is dry underneath. It won't work if you're on a slope where a rushing stream soon tries to share your sleeping bag with you. Also, you have to remember that you can spoil your whole trip and your rig's exhaust system if you forget where you are and sit up suddenly.

In any eventuality, there are basic precautions to be observed. One of the authors was sleeping under a muddy vehicle and had a slab of cold, wet mud slide down onto his face in the middle of the night. Come to think of it, that may have been when his hair turned white.

EATING, DRINKING

If you're going to be civilized, you need an ice chest. The more efficient, the better. The most effective ice chest we've used is Coleman's traditional steel case over molded foam with a plastic liner. These come in dark colors, which isn't the best possible choice if you're trying to make your ice last the max length of time. So if we're going to be using it in the bed of a truck, we've routinely used a can of spray paint to change the color to white and also added a layer of insulating foam on top of the lid.

Making Ice Last Longer—If you are going places where it isn't possible to replenish your ice supply, there are measures you can take to make it last longer. First, chill all the food and drink in your refrigerator overnight. Also, cool down your ice chest by dumping in a couple of trays of ice cubes, adding an equal amount of water and letting that stand all night.

When you do have to add warm containers to your ice chest, remember that metal cans transfer heat better than glass bottles and require less ice to reduce their temperature. If you're restocking on the trail, add your new items in the morning when they're likely to be at minimum temperature rather than later in the day when the ambient is higher.

Use Block Ice—Block ice lasts longer because it has less surface area. For greatest longevity, leave it in one piece. Don't break it up. Also, don't let too much water accumulate in the bottom of the chest. A little water in the bottom helps keep things cooler, especially potables. But too much water—more than about an inch deep, say—needlessly accelerates the ice's transformation back to water.

Other basic rules for making the ice last include such common-sense prac-

tices as not opening the chest any more often than you need to and not keeping it open any longer than necessary.

When we were camping a lot in Baja California and there wasn't any ice available for a stretch of over 500 miles, we found it possible to keep ice for a week by using two chests. The second chest was strictly for ice and was only opened to take a chunk out to put into the other chest. On one trip, we used dry ice between the blocks in the storage chest to further decelerate the melting process. Unfortunately, such heroic measures are no longer necessary, even in Baja.

Conversely, if you're traveling through civilized country where there's plenty of ice available, you can cool things faster and keep everything colder by breaking up the block ice or using cubes and letting water accumulate.

Water Discipline—Incidentally, if you're maintaining any sort of water discipline, you can capture your meltwater in a water jug and use it for washing dishes, bathing, topping up the radiator, putting out forest fires, and the like. Also, it's easier on the ol' back if you carry a plastic hose to siphon off excess water with the ice chest in its regular place rather than having to remove the cooler from the vehicle to drain it.

COOKING

Cooking is another camping specialty that we've been through all the way from A for aigs to Z for zausages.

One of the authors remembers early in his camping career that he took great pride in fixing exotic meals. He recalls a fine dinner for four that included a fresh garden salad, filet mignon with mushroom sauce, fresh asparagus and julienne potatoes. Plus babas au rhum for dessert. His friends were greatly impressed at how civilized it was to go camping with him. But probably no more impressed than he was.

He's gotten over that and his cooking has gotten much simpler. He's now a firm believer in the one-pot, one-dish dinner that can be served with crackers. Stagg Chili Laredo, for instance. Or Progresso Beef Minestrone. About as exotic as he ever gets anymore is Neal Allen stew, which consists of one small can of corned beef, one can of chili beans and

Time-honored place to cook is on tailgate of your off-road vehicle.

one can of Ortega diced chilies all heated up to a bubbling mess. He's famous for his Neal Allen stew. Almost as famous as Neal Allen. Try it sometime.

For breakfast, we're advocates of cold cereal and milk, and a simple sandwich at lunch will do just fine. And if time's a factor, we make the sandwich at breakfast and eat it while still moving. On the other hand, there have been times when a rich, heavy lunch followed by a two-hour nap seemed like the best possible activity to undertake. Be flexible.

We also recall the time when we were hungry for a warm lunch and in a hurry to get someplace. So we decided to try a trick we'd heard about, that of heating a can of stew on the exhaust manifold. We cleverly wired the can to the manifold and motored onward, pleased with ourselves at being so clever and efficient. Problem was that we hadn't heard about the trick of poking a hole in the can to allow for expansion of the stew as it got hot. The smell of cooking stew from the exploded can made us even hungrier.

Put It Away—One of the important rules is to not leave food or dinner scraps where their enticing odors may attract critters. Where there are bears, it can be *dangerous* to have food around where it can be gotten at. The traditional system in bear country is to hang it from a tree branch where the bears can't reach it. But even where there aren't any bears, it still isn't a good idea to be careless in this regard.

One of the authors laughed when he was warned by other campers not to leave plastic water jugs out where the coyotes might get them. The next morning, he found all the water jugs gone. Scouting around, he found one about 200 yards away, empty and with teeth marks around a ragged hole. Obviously, the coyotes in that area had learned that the scent of polyethylene meant water or other good things to drink and were now zeroing in on all such containers.

Protection from Insectivos—A regular part of your camping equipment should include protection from insects. If you camp in summer, you're going to need it. The type of protection you need depends on the kind of camper you are. Most full-size camping tents include nylon screens to help exclude insects but you'll find it impossible to keep them all out when you're going in and out, setting up the tent and getting ready for bed. So you use a bug killer in an aerosol spray can and kill off the creatures that are waiting for you inside. You do this *before* you go into the tent, you understand, then wait for the insecticide to do its magic and the air to clear before entering.

If you're sleeping outside, you may want to rig a mosquito netting over your sleeping bag or cot. Again, use a killer spray to eliminate those that are lurking inside and avoid touching the netting from the inside, which allows the skeeters to stab you from the outside.

Whether you're sleeping inside or outside, with a mosquito bar or without, an insect repellent should be part of your regular camping equipment. We've used Cutter's for years and swear by it for protection from mosquitoes and the various no-see-ums that can make your night

When heating lunch on exhaust manifold, don't forget to poke hole in can (arrow) to allow steam pressure to escape.

When you don't want to bother with a cot, put a tarp on the ground for some insulation and to discourage the crawlies, then use a foam rubber pad under the sleeping bag to soften the lumps.

miserable if you've forgotten it.

Disposables Handy—We also believe in using plastic glasses, paper plates and plastic utensils whenever possible. It is much more satisfactory to throw things away than wash them, provided you stow the trash properly for later and *legal* disposal. We do hate anything flimsy, though, and consequently recommend the heavy-duty airline-quality plastic utensils, if you can find them.

Our reasoning is that simpler is better. We don't go camping to sample exotic culinary delights. We go to relax and enjoy ourselves. Using an hour to fix dinner and another hour to clean up afterward is a lot less fun than taking 10 minutes to fix it, two minutes to clean up and then occupying the rest of our time doing important things like watching the moon rise, telling unlikely stories and staring into campfires.

The one area where we do go to some

trouble is to make sure there's coffee. Instead of heating water for instant coffee one cup at a time, we make coffee a thermos-full at a time. This is a stainless-steel thermos, you understand, having long since despaired of keeping a glass-liner thermos alive for the length of one whole camping trip.

Before going to bed, we fill the thermos again and this is the morning heart-starter. If the thermos is full, the coffee doesn't develop that strong, stale flavor. That only happens when it's exposed to air.

This container of coffee makes a major contribution to one of the great pleasures we get from camping. That's savoring the smell of good, strong coffee while watching the sky turn light and morning return to the world, giving every promise of letting us sneak in one more day before the apocalypse.

Yes, that makes it all worthwhile.

18

Survival

If it's at all possible, you should really try to survive. Perishing of hunger, thirst, cold, heat, snakebite or blood poisoning out in the great nowhere has to rank as one of the least desirable ways of winding up an otherwise fine off-road trip.

Admittedly, neither of us has ever been in an all-out live-or-die survival situation. One way or another we've always gotten the truck out of the mud, the engine started, the unlikely repair accomplished and dodged the bullet one way or another.

Maybe that's been pure luck. On the other hand, the fact that we're probably a bit better prepared for an emergency than most off-roaders may have something to do with it. There are certain basic precautions that now, after all these years, have become more or less automatic.

Buddy System—Your best assurance of avoiding disaster is to travel with a buddy in another vehicle. This is fundamental. If you're going someplace that's genuinely isolated, where a mechanical breakdown could result in disaster, be extremely cautious about traveling by yourself. Even the newest, most meticulously cared for vehicle can expire of a completely unforeseeable failure. The kind of ailment that all the ingenuity in the world isn't going to fix. If you've ever been out there beyond the last telephone pole, you've no doubt reviewed in your mind all the things that could go wrong—the broken crankshaft, the sheared distributor drive, the broken timing chain.

So, the first key to survival is to have a faithful buddy in a good, stout vehicle of his own. The remote possibility of both vehicles suffering a terminal ailment on the same trip provides a reasonable margin of safety.

Leave Word—If it's impossible or impractical for you to be accompanied by someone in another vehicle, the next-best thing is to leave word with some responsible person. Make sure he or she

Survival depends upon your vehicle and on *you* when you're irretrievably stuck miles from nowhere. Of course, it helps if you're Parnelli Jones and a radio-dispatched pit crew is on its way to fetch your Bill-Stroppe prepared Bronco. Photo courtesy of Road & Track magazine.

Traveling in pairs is the best insurance you have for getting home again. If one vehicle breaks down or becomes stuck. The other can usually get it out. Photo by John Lawlor.

knows where you're going, when you plan to be back and what to do if you don't show up.

If you're traveling on public lands, you can always file a travel plan at the park, national forest or Bureau of Land Management headquarters. If that isn't possible, you can check in and out with the local police headquarters, sheriff sub-station or town marshal.

Because water is absolutely essential to survival, remember that a canteen is easier to carry than a handled container.

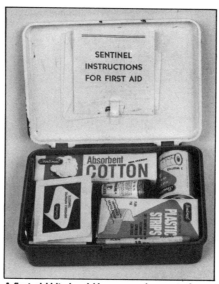

A first-aid kit should be as much a part of your off-road vehicle as a spare tire. This small "overnight" pack contains most basic supplies. Photo by John Lawlor.

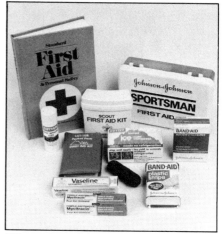

This sportsman's kit by Johnson & Johnson is more complete. And, by all means always carry a first-aid booklet. All the bandages, medicines and remedies in the world won't help if you don't know how to use them.

If you do check in, always be sure to check out. Otherwise, if the system works the way it's supposed to, emergency crews may be out looking for you after you're already on your way home. This wastes both time and effort and makes it less likely that the search-and-rescue team will be eager to help the next time a back-country traveler doesn't check in when he's supposed to.

At the very least, leave instructions with a friend or neighbor so that person knows what to do if you're not back by a certain time. Your communication should include how much leeway to give you and what authorities to notify if you miss your leeway date.

SURVIVAL EQUIPMENT

In the next chapter, we'll cover the spares, tools and gadgets you should be carrying for a vehicular emergency. We'll also give you enough helpful hints to see you through all but the complete disasters. What we're going to suggest here is the really basic survival stuff that you shouldn't be without, a list that's short but important. It consists of:

- Water, food
- First-aid kit and first-aid manual
- Map(s)
- Appropriate weather protection
- Fire-making material

Water is Essential—There's an old saying among survival folk that you can live four minutes without air, four days without water and four weeks without food. The moral of this story is to carry an adequate quantity of water for the kind of trip you're making. The rule of thumb is to carry one gallon of water per person for every day you're going to be beyond the last oasis or other dependable source of potables.

Even then, a vehicular calamity can extend even the best-planned trip by a day or more. This means that a local source of undetermined purity might have to be resorted to. In which case you should follow the instructions on the purification-tablet container that's part of your first-aid kit or boil the water at least 30 minutes. Thirty minutes? That's what it takes if you want to be as sure as possible that you've killed the baddies.

For survival in a warm climate such as the desert, you can get along without food. In fact, even if you have plenty of food, it's better to eat sparingly because the more you eat, the more water your body requires to carry out the process of digestion.

Don't stint yourself. Drink when you're thirsty. Setting yourself up for dehydration or heat exhaustion by trying to do without water may create a problem you don't need.

If it's cold, however, in addition to water, you also need food to create the calories required to keep you from developing hypothermia. So, you should have a supply of high-calorie energy food with a high percentage of fat such as nuts or, better still, the mixture of nuts, raisins and other good stuff that's known among backpackers as trail mix or gorp.

First Aid—Always carry a first-aid kit, preferably one that's a step or two above the basic $2.98 variety from a cut-rate drug store. Most important is a good first-aid manual, one that you get from the Red Cross or at a camping outfitters. It's possible for you to apply your ingenuity and create a bandage by wadding up your shorts and using racer's tape, but it's hard to fake it if you don't have the least idea what to do. Literally, a good manual can be a life-saver because it includes what-to-do instructions for the more common problems such as broken limbs, sprains, serious cuts, burns, and so on.

In addition to the manual, your first-aid kit should include at least the following: several Band Aids of assorted sizes, cotton, gauze, adhesive tape, a small selection of moderate-pressure bandages, disinfectant, an elastic bandage, aspirin or its acetaminophen equivalent,

There are pros and cons about the effectiveness of snakebite remedies. But it might be a good idea to carry a kit anyway if your travels will take you near the habitats of venomous types.

If you're caught by unseasonal cold and aren't prepared for it and face an impassable trail, find someplace to get out of the weather. Guard against hypothermia and frostbite.

laxative, Lomotil or its generic equivalent, burn ointment, water-purification tablets, moleskin, a pair of tweezers and a small pair of scissors. Got that?

If you want to be the medic whenever anything happens on the trail, talk to your physician and secure his advice about what you should carry. Get his cooperation in prescribing such things as pain pills, antibiotics and other prescription-only drugs you may need.

Snakebite—We're of two minds about snakebite kits. On one hand, why not carry one? On the other, the most recent thinking regarding snakebites is to *not* slash the fang punctures and suck the blood. The current word is to apply cold to the affected area, keep the victim as quiet as possible and get help pronto. Maybe you should check with your family physician for his recommendations.

Honestly, though, the best advice about snakebite is to avoid it. This is easy to say, but there's no doubt that caution is your best assurance of not getting bitten by a snake, scorpion or any other poisonous creature. Don't put your hands anyplace you haven't already inspected with your eyes. Don't reach over a blind ledge, for example. On a hot summer night, don't wander around without your

boots on—and stamp your feet if you are out walking to give the creatures fair warning of your approach.

The only person we've ever known who was actually bitten by a rattlesnake was a girl who panicked at the sight of the snake, spun around, lost her footing and momentarily sat down on the snake's tail as it was trying to get away. You can guess where she was bitten. Fortunately, she was working on an oil-exploration crew and within minutes was on her way to a nearby hospital by helicopter.

She was lucky. Although the snake did gets its fangs into her, she got a light injection of venom and suffered little more than an bad scare, an upset stomach and a sore you know what.

In our own experience, we've never encountered an aggressive rattlesnake, scorpion or spider. In every case, given a chance to do so, the creature will slip away, being no more eager for a fang-to-fang confrontation than you are.

On the other hand, if you startle a rattlesnake by putting your hand in front of it—or by sitting on it—you may be sure that the rattler will defend itself in the best way it knows how.

Maps—We've already talked about maps, page 132, but here we're talking emergency and survival. In these highly civilized times, there's no excuse for not

having a map that covers the area where you are. A map—the best map you can get of the area—is one of the most basic survival tools. Being stuck or broken down can happen to anybody, but to drive yourself off the edge of the earth because you didn't bother to bring a map and don't have the least idea where you are going is simply inexcusable.

Travel Log—One of the best ways to keep track of where you are and where you went wrong when you got lost is to keep a travel log. This is especially important in country where your map is less than perfect. Your log doesn't have to be elaborate, but it needs to include such basic information as how many miles/tenths you went, what direction you turned, any major landmarks that you would recognize if you saw them again, and so on. Such a log not only makes a nice souvenir of the trip, it can save your bacon if you're in unfamiliar country and have to get out on your own.

Cold Weather—Whether it's winter or summer, you should be prepared for survival by having appropriate weather protection. In winter, this means such things as warm gloves, something you can use around your neck as a scarf, a cap that will keep your head warm, warm clothing and a winter-weight sleeping bag and/or wool blankets. Don't go off into

149

the great outback without them.

The most insidious danger to a motorist who is broken down and waiting for help is *hypothermia*—traumatic loss of body heat. This is the body's way of shutting down to preserve what's left— and indeed hypothermia is now used in some forms of surgery because body functions such as breathing and heart rate are slowed down. But it's not something you want to do accidentally.

The symptoms of hypothermia are lowered body temperature (though you may be past the stage of actually being conscious of the cold), sleepiness, semi-consciousness, mental confusion, slow breathing and slow pulse rate.

The treatment for hypothermia is to increase the body temperature. But this must be done *from the inside out, not from the outside in*. This means *don't* immerse the patient in warm water, pile on heavy wool blankets or massage the limbs. That will draw blood out into the extremities and not warm the visceral core. Obviously, warming the innards is what's important.

First Aid for Hypothermia—If you're stuck out there and waiting for help to arrive, there isn't a lot you can do for a person with hypothermia beyond putting hot-water bottles (or your ingenious equivalents) in the armpits and crotch and trying to get the patient to drink liquids. If the person has lost consciousness, the chance that you can save his life isn't very good. What the person needs is expert medical care, which consists of replacing the patient's blood with warmed blood and other complicated procedures.

Obviously, the best solution is to avoid hypothermia and the way to do that is to keep yourself warm and not to let yourself remain inactive for long periods of time. If you don't have enough clothing, blankets, or whatever to keep you warm, be ingenious. Try ripping up the carpeting and stuffing it inside your jacket and pants to provide additional insulation, or use the insulation padding glued to the underside of the hood. Then do a series of exercises on a regular schedule to keep your bodily functions going. Don't just sit there and let it happen to you.

Immersion Foot—It's also important to keep dry, especially your feet. Even if it isn't freezing, you can get *immersion,* or trench, foot from having wet feet for a prolonged period. There are two stages: First, the feet are very cold, pale and with no perceptible pulse. The second stage is just the opposite, the feet are red and swollen and throb painfully with every heartbeat.

When the feet are in the first stage— cold and pale—they need to be gently dried and then very gradually warmed until circulation is restored. If warmed too quickly, gangrene may develop.

If the second stage has been reached and the feet are red, swollen and painfully throbbing, then the exact opposite treatment must be given. After gently drying them, the feet should be judiciously cooled to restore normal circulation.

Frostbite—This is the actual freezing of the tissue so blood circulation no longer takes place. There's more than one school of thought as to the best treatment, but current thinking is that the body core should be treated first to get its temperature restored to normal, then the frostbitten area treated.

The treatment for frostbite consists of very gradual warming of the affected limb, beginning with immersion in water about 50—60° F. Water temperature is then increased by about 10°F every five minutes until a water temperature of about 100—105°F is achieved.

Once this gentle treatment is complete, the afflicted person should be kept warm and quiet, and with the injured limb elevated, if possible.

No matter what kind of damage has been done by the cold, treatment should be conservative, not radical. For an amateur, there's an unfortunate tendency to try to do too much. Too often, that's worse than doing too little.

Hot Weather—In summer, the primary essential is protection from the sun. This includes a hat for your head plus a shade-making cloth for your body. The shade-making cloth can be a small tarp, space blanket or whatever. Don't forget that you'll also need an adequate supply of light rope or heavy cord to tie it in place. Lacking an appropriate shade-maker, you'll be reduced to spending your time in or under your vehicle, and that can get very tiresome.

Keep Your Body Covered—Also, wear your hat and keep your clothes on. Sunburn can add a complication you don't need and can also lead to other heat-related problems.

Heat stroke occurs when you lose too much salt from your body. The symptoms are dizziness, a ripping headache, nausea and high body temperature. If you get these symptoms, get out of the sun as soon as possible and try to cool your body. Lie down with your head and shoulders raised slightly. Drink water, if you have it. Take a little salt, too, but only if you have plenty of water. Do not drink any stimulants such as coffee or tea.

Heat stroke is *very* serious. Don't fool with it. It can kill you.

Heat Exhaustion—You may or may not suffer from heat exhaustion before you have heat stroke. The symptoms are similar—dizziness, headache, nausea— but instead of a high body temperature, you feel clammy and may suffer from chills. If you have heat exhaustion, lie down with the head slightly lowered and sip a mild saline solution containing one teaspoon of salt per glass of water. You can also drink mild stimulants such as coffee or tea. If you're having chills, put something warm over you to keep warm.

Dehydration—Simple dehydration is another danger when it's hot. The early symptoms are feeling sleepy, losing your appetite and having your body temperature go up. You can cure dehydration only by drinking water. If you have these early symptoms and don't replace the water your system has lost through perspiration, you may find it difficult to breathe and may lose the use of your limbs. If you get to this stage of advanced dehydration, you're in serious trouble.

Quest for Fire—Whether it's winter or summer, you're going to need a way of making a fire. There was a time when one of the authors thought he'd solved this problem by purchasing a couple of 98-cent plastic cigarette lighters with a transparent fuel reservoir. Problem was that the first time he tried to use one, the fuel was gone and in *both* lighters. He never figured out why. But from then on, he went back to being sure he always had an extra box of matches. Plus, he kept another little stash of matches in a waterproof match safe he bought from L.L. Bean a dozen years ago.

If your match supply has dwindled and you need to save what you have left to touch off that signal fire when you hear the airplane engine, there are other ways. You can create a flame by using the cigarette lighter from your vehicle, putting it in contact with something readily combustible, like paper, and blowing on same to encourage the propagation of a flame. That's assuming your vehicle's battery is still has a sufficient charge, of course.

IF IT DOES HAPPEN

What do you do if you get into a situation where your vehicle is inextricably stuck, unfixably broken or you can't move for one reason or another? The first thing to do is to avoid panic. It's all right to curse yourself for being an idiot, you can even stamp your foot and say, "darn" or "heck." But don't go rushing off in all directions.

Second, once you've swallowed the first rush of panic in accordance with the instructions above, the next thing to do is set-up camp, make yourself as comfortable as possible and wait until the next morning before making any serious moves. By waiting until morning, it's possible that you will come upon a solution to your problem and can get on your way again. On the other hand, even if you haven't, you'll be rested, reasonably refreshed and much better able to make some intelligent decisions about what to do next.

Assess Your Chances—During the night, you'll no doubt assess your chances for survival. If you took our advice and filed a travel plan with a responsible person, telling them what to do if you weren't back by a certain time, just wait it out and survive until the rescue squad arrives.

However, if nobody knows where you are, your chances of survival are somewhat less. Still, unless you've stranded yourself in a really isolated corner of the universe, the chances of being found are pretty good. Especially if you do what you can to improve those chances.

Next, take inventory. This is important. Make a list of all the things you have that can help you survive. How much

A compass will be useful for determining direction. This one is adjustable against magnetic forces when installed in a vehicle. A hand-held compass is handier for hikers.

Use a mirror to flash a help signal to an airplane or a distant source of assistance. If you don't have one that is portable, use the vehicle's. Unbolt it to reflect the sun's rays where you want them.

water? How much beer? How much ice that will melt and make how much additional water? How much water-packed canned food do you have? What's the status of everybody's health? Does anybody need special treatment? How's your fire-making capability, whether it's for warmth or for use as a signal?

Use Your CB—If you have a CB radio, turn it to Channel 9, the emergency channel, and transmit a plea for help on a regular schedule, such as every hour on the hour. Make your message brief and to the point. Give your name, the kind of emergency you're in (stuck, broken down, injuries, etc.) and as much useful information as you can supply that will assist somebody in finding you. The best time to make such calls is just after dark and at dawn. Radio reception is best at night so that's when you have the best chance of somebody picking up your distress signal. As limited as the range of a CB is, you're really shooting in the dark and depending on "skip" and luck. But it's certainly worth doing because there is a surprisingly large number of people who monitor Channel 9, especially in the more remote areas.

Stay With Your Vehicle—Unless you know exactly where you are, how far it is to a source of help and are sure you have the physical stamina to walk out, **ALWAYS STAY WITH YOUR VEHICLE.**

It may be difficult for you to do nothing and simply wait for help to arrive, but in almost every instance, that's the best thing for you to do. When you make the decision to go for help on foot, there's an unfortunate but almost inevitable tendency to be overly optimistic. As a result, you tend to underestimate the distances, overestimate your strength and underrate the difficulties you'll encounter.

Leave a Note—If you do leave your vehicle, leave a note for those who eventually find it, telling them your name and the name of anybody who goes with you, the time and date you left, which direction you went and your hoped-for destination. That may help them find you before it's too late.

Also, if you decide to walk out, take your map, stick to established roads and always keep yourself oriented as to the direction you're going. Walking in a circle is too common to be funny. Maintaining a given direction is relatively easy, assuming you have a pocket compass. If you don't, be damned sure you know where the sun came up and where it is now in relation to where it was then. If you're in the woods, moss tends to grow on the north side of a tree. If you're in the desert, the north side of a cactus may be less well developed than the other sides. But check several before you let yourself be convinced that north is really in that direction.

Sometimes even an animal's survival instincts aren't adequate. When you're going off-roading a serious distance from habitation, don't overlook the possibility of a medical emergency and taking all the steps you can to prepare for it. You certainly don't want anybody to end up like this.

If you have your hand compass and topo map with you, find out where you are before venturing out. Make sure the compass is away from any magnetic influences such as the truck, and orient the topo map toward the north.

Where do you try to walk to? There are two schools of thought. One says that you should try to walk back to the last point of civilization you passed on the way in. That way, you have a finite objective which, with luck, you may be able to achieve. The other school says that you should spend the first day scouting, then return to camp. Walk to the highest point in each direction and see if you can sight a source of assistance. This may keep you from walking 20 miles in one direction when there was a source of assistance only two miles in another. It will also give you a handle on just how likely it is that you'll be able to walk far enough to attain any worthwhile goal.

Make Your Vehicle Visible—These days, if a serious search is mounted by the authorities, it's more likely that you'll be spotted from the air before you're found by ground-search teams. You can help this process along if you'll make your vehicle as visible as possible. If you have a can of spray paint, put a big HELP on the roof. If you don't, use strips of toilet paper held down with rocks. Or rip your boxer shorts into strips. If your vehicle isn't clearly visible from the air,

put your "help" sign in the open with an arrow pointing in the direction of your vehicle. Also, wave your arms a lot.

Even though you've made a "help" sign, you should also be prepared to make a fire that will generate sufficient smoke to attract attention. This is especially effective if you're in a forest where there are firewatchers. For this purpose, you can use a mixture of engine oil and gasoline or, if you remember to let the air out so it won't explode, you can set a tire afire. A burning tire will put out a column of black smoke that's visible for miles. Be careful with any fire you make, however; starting a forest fire can only add to your problems.

You can also use a mirror you've removed from the vehicle to flash a signal at an airplane or at a potential rescuer who is too far away to hear your shouts or notice your frantic waving.

What to Do While You Wait—Waiting to be found isn't a lot of fun. As we mentioned earlier, don't try to do without water. Drink when you're thirsty. If it's hot, stay in the shade and don't make unnecessary expenditures of energy. Tend to your "help" signs and be ready to make smoke and flash signals, but do as little thrashing about as you possibly can.

If it's cold, it's very important to keep yourself warm and avoid hypothermia. If you get your feet wet, do what's neces-

WIND CHILL FACTOR			
Actual Temperature (degrees F)	Humidity (%)	Wind (mph)	Effective Temperature (degrees F)
105	20	7	81
90	40	7	75
40	30	1	36
40	30	6	22
40	30	7	16

sary to get them dry. If there's snow, stay out of it as much as possible. But do create a "help" sign and be ready to touch off a signal fire.

MAKE UP YOUR MIND TO SURVIVE

Survival is partly a matter of physical condition. You'll probably last longer if you're young and strong than if you're old and feeble. But it's also a matter of making the best use of what you've got.

Be determined. If you're absolutely resolved to live through this experience, you've got a much better chance than if you let yourself be racked by doubt.

We've all heard incredible stories about unlikely survivors. There's the one about the person who lived through an airplane crash and walked down the mountain to safety, and another about the person who hung onto the floating wreckage and was still afloat when everybody else had sunk, and still another kid who didn't freeze to death when everybody else did.

Sure, luck has something to do with it, but the pure grit of simply refusing to give up is undoubtedly your best insurance that you will survive.

PROBLEMS IN THE COLD

Problem	Symptoms	Treatment
Hypothermia	Lowered body temperature	Warm body from inside out
	Sleepy, semi-conscious, confused	Put warm objects in armpits, crotch
	Slow respiration, pulse rate	Have victim drink liquids
		Obtain expert medical treatment as soon as possible
Immersion Foot (Trench Foot)	Wet feet for prolonged period	
	Stage I: Feet cold, pale and with no pulse	Stage I: Dry feet, then warm slowly, gently
	Stage II: Feet red, swollen, throbbing	Stage II: Immerse feet in cool (60F) water until symptoms are alleviated, then dry feet and keep lightly covered
Frostbite	Flesh very cold, white, no feeling	Warm body core by drinking liquids
		Keep victim quiet
		Elevate affected limb
		Gradually warm affected part by immersing in cool water (50-60F), then increasing water temp 10 degrees every 5 minutes until temp of 100-105 degrees is reached

PROBLEMS IN THE HEAT

Problem	Symptoms	Treatment
Heat Stroke	Headache, dizziness, nausea	Move patient into shade
	Skin hot, dry	Cool head, body with baths, rubdown
	Face flushed	Put patient on back, raise head, shoulders slightly
	High body temperature (over 100F)	No stimulants
	Loss of consciousness	Cool drinks if victim is conscious
Heat Exhaustion	Headache, dizziness, nausea	Put patient on back with head level, lowered
	Clammy, pale	Mild saline drink (1 tsp salt/1 glass water)
	Loss of consciousness	Mild stimulants (tea, coffee)
		Cover patient if chilled
Dehydration	Sleepy, loss of appetite	Have victim lie down in shade, rest
	Elevated body temperature	Drink water to replace moisture lost
	Breathing difficulty, loss of coordination	

Tools & Quick-Fix Tips

19

OK, OK. You saw it on the cover of this book. But keep in mind that splashing through a creek is a quick way to drown the engine. Make sure you pack enough spares and tools for a quick fix or it may be a long walk home. Photo by John Lawlor.

There is absolutely no doubt about it. Sometime during your off-roading career, you are going to get stuck. And it will happen when you're the farthest away from home or any other form of civilization. Maybe it has already happened to you and you still quake at the thought. But never mind. Being stuck when you're miles away in the boonies is merely a fact of back-country life. Anyone who calls himself a veteran off-roader has been in the same fix and it's nothing to be embarrassed about. It's how you handle the problem that will make a great campfire story, or cause you to hang your head in shame.

When Something Breaks—We are not talking about the sort of stuck you read about in Chapter 15 where your rig is mired down in sand, or is impaled from underneath by the only rock in the neighborhood with your name on it. The kind of stuck we mean is when something vital

on your vehicle has broken, a fuel line has become plugged with *yukk,* or you've broken a fan or accessory-drive belt and don't have a spare. This chapter is about the type of stuck where the weather is fine, the birds are singing, the trail is level and hard, yet you're immobilized by mechanical gremlins.

Maintenance—Certainly, you number yourself among those who tend to their vehicles according to the recommendations set forth in the owner's manual. You change the oil at the suggested intervals—more often under dusty conditions—and you see that tuneups are done on schedule. You also rotate your tires when signs of wear occur, periodically check the condition of hoses, lines, belts, have your rig lubricated at the proper times, and otherwise follow good housekeeping rules. If you do this, the kinds of trouble that stem from neglect aren't going to catch up with you

when you're deep in the woods. Just to be sure, though, take the trouble before you head for the trail to at least check the fluid levels of the engine oil, radiator coolant and the battery.

If you perform these checks regularly, you won't have to carry along enough extra oil to pull off a complete change in the wilds. But do carry a one-quart can of engine oil as insurance against the engine burning more than you counted on, or to replace what was lost between the time you holed the pan on a rock and plugged the leak.

Understand that by following maintenance schedules and keeping track of components subject to wear and deterioration, you'll suffer fewer mechanical problems along the trail and your treks will be nearly trouble-free.

Murphy's Law—There is no way to foretell what might go wrong with your off-roader until it happens. If you predict a flat tire because of the nature of the terrain you'll be wandering over, then count on breaking a drive shaft. Or if you're famous for knocking a hole in your radiator and carry every known cure along with you, then it's certain you'll break a spring. It's very much a Murphy's Law sort of thing when you're romping over hill and dale. You won't have a spare for whatever breaks. Or, what you expect to go wrong won't.

Solutions—The answer to these problems is to equip yourself with tools, spare parts and mechanical survival equipment. But the trick here is in deciding what to take, knowing how to make-do with it, and what to leave behind.

Obviously, you don't have the space to haul along a professional mechanic's roll-away toolchest every time you go weekending. And you can't carry enough spare parts to construct a clone of your vehicle. If you did that, there'd be no room for your in-laws, and you wouldn't want to leave *them* behind, would you? So it is necessary that you understand that the successful off-roader has to be

Boulder driver is so cautiously inching over can crush a fuel or brake line when vehicle settles down on other side. Know how to make an emergency repair for problems such as these. Photo by John Lawlor.

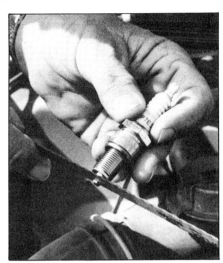

Hacksaw blade is about 0.016-in. thick and can be used as a feeler gage to check sparkplug gap.

resourceful. He, or she, has to know how to make one tool do the work of three, and how there's almost always some kind of temporary fix for a part for which you have no replacement.

This means you should travel light, yet be ready to cope with an emergency using the tools at hand for a multitude of purposes. A screwdriver, for example, can be used for lots of things besides unwinding screws. Opening a can of oil with one means that you can leave the official opener/pour spout at home.

Similarly, take along a hacksaw blade. It's great for sawing either metal or wood, but one can also replace a feeler gage. A blade is approximately 0.016-in. thick, so you can use it for gapping plugs or setting the points on an older vehicle. But leave the hacksaw frame at home. It'll clutter up a toolbox. Just remember to wrap the blade ends with duct tape or rag so you won't saw through your fingers. These pearls of wisdom, by the way, are just random thoughts. We'll get deeper into these and many other tidbits in a moment.

Serious Fix-Its—What we're really talking about here are *emergency* repairs. If your license-plate light burns out or your truck develops an annoying rattle somewhere beneath the upholstery, forget about it. Minor inconveniences like these can be attended to when you're safely at home. But sally forth prepared to wrestle with the more serious problems like a fuel pump that's gone belly-up, knowing what to use as a substitute for lost brake fluid or radiator coolant, and even understanding that a picnic basket and your toilet kit hold the cures for a leaking radiator and a punctured fuel tank. This is what's meant about being resourceful and using your noggin to come up with a temporary cure so you can at least cripple your way, if not homeward, to safe haven.

Over the years and countless thousands of miles of professional and recreational off-roading, we have pretty much learned what's necessary in the way of handtools, extra parts and extra equipment when out in the wild blue yonder. Collectively, and here we're complaining rather than boasting, we've had almost every conceivable part of an off-road vehicle fizzle out at the worst possible time. So we've worked up a check-over list of things for you to consider; not a *checklist* of things you positively *must* take, but a check-*over* list to prompt your thinking. You needn't take tire chains to Baja in August, as an example, but they are listed for your skiing trip to Vermont next December.

We cannot make recommendations for personal things such as your cot, sleeping bag, a stove and its fuel, drinking water, and extra gas for your snowmobile, dirt bike, trailered boat or model airplane. And don't overlook the volleyball net. These are up to you to remember, along with a well-stocked ice chest and preferred food and drink, maps for the area you plan to explore, a sand pail for the kiddies and dog food for the mutt. All of these are strictly your business.

But if you chanced to peek into one of the authors' 4X4s, here's pretty much what you'd find. First, though, it's a good idea to create a toolbox to keep in your vehicle permanently—one that lives in the truck all the time. If this means duplicating some of your master tool set, so be it. It will mean not having to load and unload the vehicle's toolbox every time you're preparing for an off-road weekend. It keeps your chores simpler, in other words.

Screwdrivers—Take some small, medium and large screwdrivers, straight-slots as well as Phillips heads. About six should do.

Combination Wrenches—Determine if your vehicle is held together with standard-thread (SAE) fasteners or the metric variety. A 3/16-in. wrench is not the proper substitute for a 10mm wrench. Combination wrenches are the most ver-

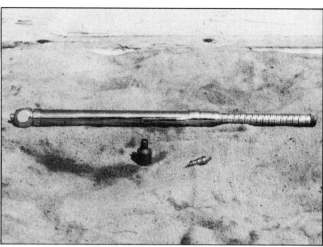

Star-wrench sees more use than wimpy jack handle that came with your truck. Arms provide leverage for really tight nuts and bolts. And, of course, no off-roader should be without a shovel.

If you don't have a regulation valve-stem-core remover, at least have one valve cap like this. A spare core is a good idea and, naturally, you should have an accurate tire gage.

satile, the type with an open-end on one end and a box-end on the other. A full set should run from 3/16 in. to 1 in. (or metric equivalents) in 1/16-in. increments. Because combination wrenches have same-size ends, you'll also need an adjustable, or Crescent, wrench in the event you have to work on opposing jam nuts of the same size.

Socket Wrenches—Socket wrenches might seem to be extraneous tools as long as you have a set of combination wrenches, but a socket wrench and a ratchet handle, as well as a breaker bar, will do the job faster. And sometimes speed is of the essence, because a rising tide won't wait while you're trying to tighten a U-bolt nut.

Get a socket set with 3/8-in. drive in sizes from 3/16 in. to 1 in. (or metric equivalents) and in increments of 1/16 in. If you can't find the larger sizes with 3/8-in. drive, settle instead for 1/2-in.-drive sockets and get a 3/8-in.-to-1/2-in. adapter. Also, get a short and a long extension and a swivel or universal for those hard-to-reach nuts and bolts. Socket wrenches can be of standard depth, but check your rig for critical fasteners that might require a deep socket—spring or exhaust-system U-bolt nuts, for example. An ordinary deep socket will work on most sparkplugs, but the special rubber-lined plug sockets are a better choice. We've seen one grizzled off-road veteran friend reduced to tears after breaking a sparkplug while trying to re-

move it to hook up his chuffer-type tire pump. And we wouldn't want that to happen to you.

Pliers—There are as many different sizes and types of pliers as there are screwdrivers, but you don't need them all. Take along the ordinary home-type pliers, medium-size needle-nose pliers, and water-pump pliers. It's unlikely you'll need the water-pump pliers for working on your rig's water pump, but their wide-jaw adjustment makes them useful for many other purposes.

Vise-Grip pliers can be very important for vehicle survival. Use them like pliers, but lock them tightly down on a really stubborn or rounded-off fastener. Or, use them as a temporary clamp or "third hand" to hold things together. Remember, never use a long screwdriver or other lever to release them; the overcenter lever can snap open with a vengeance.

Hammers—Often, you'll need to hammer things apart or back together again on your outings. There are assorted types, but trim them down by just taking a carpenter's hammer. The claw end makes a fine prybar. Or use it to pull a nail out of a tire. A soft-nosed mallet would be useful for tapping on delicate objects, but you can make your own by wrapping the business end of the claw hammer with a rag.

Cutters—The basic cutting tool is the indispensible Swiss Army Knife, but there are other cutting instruments you should add to your kit. A utility or

linoleum knife is a must; the kind with a retractable blade to save your fingers when groping in the toolbox. Also get a pair of wire, or side, cutters for electrical repairs or getting past a barbed-wire fence. We noted a hacksaw blade earlier, good for countless things besides hacksawing. Use one to saw wood or as a sparkplug gapper. A file is also a cutting tool. Take a fine-tooth file of medium size.

Miscellaneous—A star-, or four-way, wrench is better for removing and replacing wheel lug nuts than the meager little wrench that came with your rig. The star-wrench has four sizes of socket ends so you can loan it to someone with different-size lugs than your rig uses. Because of the considerable leverage that can be exerted with an star-wrench, loosening other large fasteners is a breeze as long as there's room to spin the arms. It'll make a fine base for your off-road jack, too, if you forgot to bring a board.

Don't overlook a tire-valve-core removing tool. Or be sure that at least one of your valve stems has a cap that doubles as a core remover. Ever try to unscrew or replace a core without one? But don't get carried away and use it every time you air-down your tires. It's too easy to lose the core in the sand. Also toss into your toolbox an awl and a small pipe wrench. You never know when you might need them.

Toolbox—You will need a good toolbox to carry all of the items mentioned. Get

Spare parts are a must, but you can't tote replacements for everything. Fan belt, two sparkplugs, box of fuses and hose clamps can be essential. But you can do without extra air cleaner and antifreeze solution. A quart of oil is a good measure of insurance.

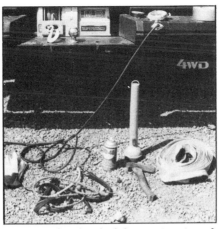

For heaven's sake, don't forget a towstrap. A flashlight can be a life saver, a hand axe has many uses, bungee cords are always needed, and a spray can of WD-40 or similar product can repel moisture from electrical system. If you have a winch on your vehicle, don't forget the hand controller, snatch block and gloves.

one that is neither too large to stow in a handy place on your truck or utility vehicle, nor too small to hold all of the above necessities. You might want to consider a permanent installation as noted earlier. There are some good-quality plastic boxes on the market that won't rust, corrode or be easily scarred. But whatever material yours is made from, trim thin pieces of foam rubber for lining the toolbox drawers and trays to keep rattling to a minimum.

SPARE PARTS

We cannot be too specific here because we have no way of knowing what make or year of off-road vehicle you own. If we told you to take an extra fan belt for your Blazer, but yours is a Bronco, you wouldn't have much respect for us. So it's up to you to choose the spare parts for your vehicle.

Just be sure to gather up one each of all your engine accessory-drive belts and hoses. Toss in two extra sparkplugs, a spare fuse for each one on your panel, and a spare fuel filter (check your vehicle closely; it may have more than one). Add one quart each of engine oil and, if your vehicle has an automatic transmission, ATF. Some people insist on loading themselves down with extra gear lube and even spare antifreeze, but these aren't absolutely essential for your off-road well-being.

It will be a good idea to get an assortment of worm-type hose clamps to match each of the different sizes under your hood, including the heater hoses. And that's it. If you think these spares aren't enough, maybe you'd better not go off-roading by yourself.

OTHER STUFF

In this catchall category is some really important equipment. One essential is a heavy-duty towstrap, because you never know when you might become either a *yanker* or a *yankee*. These are much more useful than a long length of chain, which has no resilience or "give," or a length of hawser-quality rope which will always break at the most inopportune time.

Other stuff you won't want to be caught without, and which require no explanation, are a set of jumper cables, a pair of skid chains that fit your rig, assorted lengths and gages of electrical wire and a selection of terminal ends, a small roll of black electrician's tape and a neoprene siphon hose. Far and away, the best panacea for a vehicle with mechanical shortcomings is duct tape, better known as racer's tape. One roll is absolutely essential for even the most trivial outing. Better yet, take two of them.

Add a small coil of baling wire, a good-quality air-pressure gage, an air-thief for stealing air from other tires as well as the overinflated spare, a *good*

jack, a shovel, a flashlight and an armload of bungee cords. If you want to add a small trouble light, go ahead. Get one that plugs into the cigarette-lighter socket and has enough cord to let you reach the four corners of your rig.

Toss in a square of plywood, which won't split as readily as a similar-sized length of plank, to use under your off-road jack. If your vehicle is equipped with a winch, for heaven's sake, don't forget the hand controller, a snatch block, a sling for hooking up to a tree without damaging it, and a pair of workman's gloves. Winch cables fray and can do nasty things to your hands.

Another indispensible item is a can of WD-40, or equivalent, not only for loosening corroded fasteners or getting rid of a squeak, but for spraying ignition wires to help repel moisture. A small can of LocTite or similar product might come in handy for bolts, screws and nuts that have lost their ability to "bite," and the same firm offers Form-A Thread which is a substance useful for fasteners that have stripped.

Take along a can of starter fluid, too, if you're going where it's cold. You squirt this aerosol ether into the air intake to get the engine to fire when it's too cold for gasoline to readily vaporize. But *don't* squirt ether while the engine is running because it's very explosive!

The pile of stuff is growing, but there's more you can add. Consider a small hand axe, a box of wooden matches, and don't forget spare ignition and door keys racer's-taped to the chassis or under a fender. It used to be easy to hot-wire older vehicles, but in these days of theft-deterring ignition switches and steering-wheel locks, a slide-hammer is about the only way to get going if you lose your key or lock it in the vehicle. Some rags and a roll of paper towels will also come in handy. Did we mention a tire patching kit? If not, take one that's suitable for your tires—tube-type or tubeless.

Last, but not least, gather up an old-fashioned wire coat hanger. Of all the single objects ever used to repair a vehicle on the trail, the coat hanger probably holds the record. It has, in fact, just about replaced baling wire as the genuine, all-purpose, fix-anything material. And it will hold things that racer's tape won't.

Indispensible coffee can is filled with nuts, bolts, washers, screws, nails, odd clamps, small rubber grommets and wide assortment of other odds and ends. This one has seen countless thousands of off-road miles.

Breakfast makings? Could be, but cereal or egg whites will stop or slow a radiator leak. Soap seals many a fuel-tank leak. Pour can of baking soda into radiator if coolant level is low. Potato might fix a serious radiator hole. Baking soda has a lot of uses, including brushing your teeth after you used toothbrush for cleaning your points.

Coffee Can—Right now, here in the middle of this chapter, get up and go to the kitchen. Take the one- or two-pound coffee can, the kind with the replaceable plastic lid, and find a suitable container for the contents. Now, take the can into the garage and fill it with loose nuts, bolts, washers, screws, cotter pins and even a few nails. Throw in a clothespin or two and hunt around for anything small that's even remotely automotive-oriented: odd fittings, short lengths of rubber or metal hose, *anything*. Keep at it until the can is full, snap on the lid, then cram it under your front seat. Some time, somewhere in the hinterlands, you're going to really *need* something from that can that we have so thoughtfully suggested. You'll thank us for this.

Taking It With You—Carrying spare parts, equipment and the other stuff we've suggested can be a headache. Even though our list of items doesn't add up to too formidable a pile, some of the things are relatively large and others are very small. Perhaps you feel like Noah before the Great Flood, gathering two of everything for your ark's trek. Regardless, you have to work up a plan for carrying these things in sensible order. Otherwise, the floor of your vehicle and bed of your pickup will be littered with odds and ends. Not only will they be annoyingly underfoot, you won't be able to find something in a hurry. And that's always when you need it.

If you simply dump everything into one large container, the smaller and, usually, more delicate pieces will eventually filter down to the bottom where they'll be smashed by the bulkier items on top. Or, at the very least, they'll be hard to retrieve. It is far better to sort the items by size and weight, packing smaller bits into one container and weightier things into another. For convenience, you might consider breaking the cargo down even further: spare engine parts here, electrical supplies there, and so forth. It's also a good idea to keep these things in the vehicle at all times, even during your commuter trips to work. This way, you won't be loading and unloading your vehicle's survival gear every time a back-country weekend rolls around.

Containers—Cardboard containers, while easy to come by, aren't very satisfactory as storage boxes. The bumps and grinds of off-roading will eventually cause them to split at the seams or, if they chance to get damp, the glued flaps will separate and leave you with a jumble on your hands. The heavy-duty plastic carriers for milk cartons have been popular as catchall containers, but the dairy companies who own them have seen fit to label them illegal for any but their intended use. Besides, they don't have tops and goodies carried therein can jump out all over the place.

As was noted in Chapter 17 on camping, it's a good idea to make up some

wooden storage boxes from scrap lumber and plywood. You can size them to fit the peculiar nooks and crannies in your vehicle and also tailor them to suit their contents. Equip each with a hinged lid that can be fastened down and your load-toting problems will be solved.

If your off-roader is a pickup truck with limited in-cab storage room, consider one of the commercial cross-bed toolboxes. These are constructed of heavy plastic or metal and fit between, and rest on top of, the bed side rails just behind the rear window. They don't stand on the bed floor, but rest six or more inches up so you can still slide longish things like 2x4s and a ladder into the bed. They bolt in place, are lockable and weather-resistant to protect the contents, and some have inner compartments or trays for sorting small items from large ones. With one of these conveniences, your stuff will be out of the weather, kept neatly sorted, and you don't have to remove the contents or the entire box when using your truck as an about-town vehicle. We're surprised that manufacturers of cross-bed toolboxes seldom tout them as useful for recreational purposes. They tend to be a secret held only by plumbers, electricians and wire-fencing people.

One of us has used one of these cross-bed boxes for some time and has transferred it between several vehicles. Observers helped out of a back-country dilemma swear that the box holds *every-*

thing one could possibly use in times of need. This includes the High-Lift jack and a long-handled shovel, which always present storage problems on a truck.

Sacks & Tackle Boxes—Stowing essentials in some utility vehicles presents another set of problems. You don't want cardboard cans of oil, which will easily chafe through, or other potential leakables endangering your upholstery or new jeans. One solution is to store fluid containers in one or more heavy-duty plastic bags. These range in size from 35-gallon jobs to wastebasket liners to resealable sandwich bags. With the larger sizes, put in the contents, twirl the open end closed and secure it with a tie-wrap. If available, buy oil in plastic containers with the built-in spouts and screw-on lids.

Several small bags might be a better answer than a single large one. And surely there's someplace in your rig to stow them. If your vehicle has a lift-up rear cargo floor to house the spare tire, there's often room in there to stuff a small bag or two. Or, there might be space behind the upholstery inside the quarter panels. These cubbies are often made to open for access to the jack and other tools, and there's usually space in there for more.

Better than sacks for spillables such as oil is to find them in square plastic containers. These will store easily in a wooden box and their shape will let them nestle firmly and not be so subject to harm. If such a container has been opened and closed again, make a tight seal around the lid with racer's tape. Get it to stick by first cleaning the lid and neck with fingernail-polish remover.

Jacks, shovels and other ungainly objects have a great proclivity for eating holes in upholstery. Try wrapping these in burlap sacks or scraps of left-over carpeting. Then work out some way to secure them in the cargo bay with bungee cords or adjustable straps.

The small, easy-to-lose items will fit well in two or more small fishing-tackle boxes, either plastic or metal. These are inexpensive and most have compartmented trays so you can sort things into handy categories. We've seen tackle boxes and similar containers bolted down under a hood and there is often room to do this over the wheel wells.

This photo wasn't staged. Spencer has just plugged a fuel-tank leak by rubbing it with bar soap. Photo by James T. Crow.

When you get right down to it, storing your off-roading odds and ends is mostly a matter of common sense coupled with a little inventiveness. Almost all vehicles have a sneaky *somewhere* to store the accouterments that should be aboard when you head out. Finding them, then determining what to put where, takes only a little patience and fortitude. And it will prove to be time and trouble well spent.

HELPFUL HINTS

So there you are. You've equipped your off-roader with the tools, spare parts, equipment and the other stuff to assure that you'll get safely home no matter what breaks, wears out or goes *blooey*. No walking for help for you. No problem replacing a fan belt because you brought along a spare. Everything's going great, then … *blam!* At first, you don't know what's happened. Then, you smell gasoline. You stop, get out, look underneath and, sure enough, there's a dribble coming from your fuel tank and that precious commodity is spilling uselessly onto the ground. It's 100 miles to pavement. You and your vehicle are alone. And the authors of this book didn't suggest that you bring along a spare fuel tank. So, what do you do?

Dig into your toilet kit, of course. Fish out a bar of soap. Deftly stroke it over the tear in the tank, watch the drip for a moment until it stops, then casually proceed on your way. Petroleum and most bar soaps create a chemical reaction that causes the soap to swell, then harden. The sliver wiped into the fracture seals the leak then sets up like cement. We have used, and seen used, this trick for years and it has never failed yet. This, of course, is providing the tank was ripped or split where you can get at it rather then in a crease or wrinkle you can't reach, or not punctured by a huge hole. On one memorable occasion deep in we've forgotten where, one of us opened a fuel tank seam on a Wagoneer. The fix was handled as explained and today, years later, the soap is still doing its job.

This is just one of countless fix-its, temporary or otherwise, that can get you home after you've had a setback in the outback. Did you know that the whites from a couple of raw eggs will often stop a radiator leak? Or that when the fuel pump gives up, you can pour fuel into the windshield-washer bottle, replumb a few lines, and feed the carburetor with the washer-pump switch?

On the following pages, we list some of the more common off-road mechanical problems and some rather improbable, but generally workable, cures. These are problems that will bring your back-country wanderings to an unexpected halt if you don't know what to do next.

But be aware that there are two kinds

Add any non-volatile liquid to your coolant supply if it is low. The meltwater from the ice chest has to be poured out eventually anyway. Or use the cooler to tote water from a distant source.

You say you can't lead a radiator to water? These intrepid off-roaders removed their battered radiator, soldered it on the spot and filled it with sea water. Photo by Jim Hanyen, courtesy of Road & Track magazine.

of mechanical ailments. The first is that something that goes haywire gradually will let out signs of distress well before the ultimate failure itself. Squeaks, groans, wailings, pounding, and severe engine or drive-line whirrs and clunks should be closely investigated when the annoyance is first noticed. If a U-joint is deteriorating, there's a rod knock in the engine, or smoke is wisping out of the differential, turn toward home immediately. The fishing can wait for another time and there'll surely be an even better day for camping some time next month. The farther you can cripple along toward civilization, the better your chances of making it out unscathed or the shorter the walking distance for help if you can't effect a cure.

Second is the sudden failure. The first thing to do when your mechanical beast of burden gives up the ghost without warning, is to think about it. Don't panic. Light up a smoke if that's your leaning. Or take a cool one from the ice chest. Walk around for a few minutes until the panic subsides and your head clears. Assure your fellow travelers that everything is going to be all right and that the untoward development is merely part of the fun of off-roading.

Try and diagnose the cause. Be systematic. Do nothing until you've thought the situation all the way through and considered every consequence. Give the problem your finest mental efforts.

We are going to group the potential problems and alternative cures into automotive systems and subsystems. This way, you can take this book with you and when your only widget suddenly snaps in two, the solution will be right at your finger tips. Maybe.

We cannot truthfully admit to having seen *all* these things work firsthand, or even tried all of them ourselves. But those that are new to us, and there aren't many, have been sworn to by friends and acquaintances that we can more or less trust. Understand that trying something is better than doing nothing. Also keep in mind that this is a situation where your creative imagination and the ability to improvise under pressure is going to be of more value to you than all of the book-knowledge in the world.

BRAKE SYSTEM

Stopping a vehicle is as important as going. You simply cannot drive safely without brakes. And these can sometimes fail during serious off-roading. The brake lines that twine through the chassis are often vulnerable to attack by rocks and other snags. Luckily, modern vehicles are required by law to have dual braking systems with separate systems for front and rear, or diagonal pairs of wheels. If one of these fails, you can drive along using the other. But do it cautiously. Stopping may be erratic and will certainly require a greater distance than you're accustomed to.

If the brakes become soft or spongy,

stop, get out and investigate. If there's fluid leaking from any of the lines, fittings or wheel cylinders, try to plan a repair before doing anything else. You can limp along on one brake system if the other fails, as already noted, but this requires heading toward home and giving up the rest of the weekend.

To pursue your travels safely, try to make an on-the-spot repair. Check the master-cylinder reservoir to see if the brake-fluid level has dropped seriously below the full mark. If there's a loose connection, simply tighten it. But if there's a split in a brake line, or if one has been torn away, you may want to attempt a fix. Fold the broken ends of a steel line back over themselves with a pair of pliers, then crimp them hard. Fold again and hammer the tubing shut if the leak persists. This will cancel the braking effort of the one wheel but you can proceed carefully on three brakes after bleeding out as much air as possible if all of the fluid in the one system hasn't leaked out. Or, forget about that system and head for civilization on the other one.

If you've damaged the lines to both pairs of wheels and all of the brake fluid has run out, you still have the service, or parking, brakes. Because these operate the rear wheels only, you can continue to drive, but with caution. Applying the service brakes when you must stop or slow down will call for some hand or foot dexterity, depending upon how these brakes are actuated on your vehicle. And you'll need a little familiarization with how the vehicle responds when they are applied.

If your brakes feel strange after splashing through a stream, it's probably just wet linings. Brakes work by friction and water is a lubricant. Continue driving, but slowly and with one foot lightly on the brake pedal. Heat buildup in the brakes will dry them out in no time.

If you've lost all of the brake fluid, but have found and fixed the problem, remember that fluids are non-compressible and almost anything can be used as a substitute if the emergency is dire enough. Water, oil, automatic transmission fluid, whiskey—anything that is non-carbonated will work for at least long enough for you to reach some sort of haven.

Replacing a large quantity of brake fluid with anything, even more brake fluid, will probably mean air has gotten into the system. And because air is compressible, and you may not feel safe with too-soft brakes, the system should be bled. Unless you packed along one of those nifty one-man bleeder valves available today, bleeding your rig's brakes requires two people. Top up the master cylinder reservoir, then have a companion pump hard on the brake pedal—twice. Have him or her hold the pedal down hard, even if it goes to the floor, after the second pump. Go to each wheel, in turn, and open the little valve on the wheel cylinder or caliper. You'll probably get an erratic spray of air and fluid at first, but when the stream becomes steady, close the valve and have your friend release the brake pedal. Between the bleeding of each wheel, check the reservoir and refill it to the mark.

If you have to put anything into the brake system other than proper brake fluid, it is absolutely essential to drain, flush and refill it as soon as possible. Any substitute fluid is likely to damage the master- and wheel-cylinder seals, the cylinder bores and other close-tolerance parts. Take your vehicle to a qualified brake specialist and explain what you've done. You might also want to explain why, to save face. A proper brake-system overhaul may seem expensive, but it's imperative. And it's better than walking 50 miles for help.

COOLING SYSTEM

A radiator leak can be stopped, or at least slowed down, by adding rolled oats or other fine-ground, dry breakfast cereal to the coolant that remains. The whites of two or three raw eggs have also been used for this purpose and Mexican chili powder is said to work, as well. The theory with cereal is that as the water goes out through the leak, the foreign substance will collect at the orifice and stem the leak. The egg whites will also find the leak and clot there as they cook in the hot coolant.

If the leak is really severe, say from having a rock go into the core and break one or more of the tubes, you may be able to cut the fins to isolate the damaged tubes, then roll them back on themselves, sealing off the leak or at least slowing it.

A raw potato may also plug a radiator leak. Find the leak, then jam the halved potato into the radiator from both sides. What should happen is that the hot coolant will cook the potato and it will swell, thus plugging up the problem. Of course, if you'd brought along some brand of stop-leak, you wouldn't have to go through all of this. But what we're doing is trying to show how to make a fix when you haven't the right thing to fix it with.

Remember that if you've lost a considerable quantity of proper coolant, and either don't have any extra or have used it all up, the meltwater from an ice chest, soda pop, orange juice, that last splash of gin, even urine will work. Or mix any combination together to make a larger quantity. Just don't forget to flush the system when you get home and refill it with the proper rust-inhibiting antifreeze solution.

How to get distant water to a radiator? Fetch it in your hat, the ice chest, any empty container, even the kid's beach ball. Use a hubcap if you have to. One of us actually *saw* a badly holed radiator soldered up by a chap who thought to bring this equipment along. Trouble was, the only water was in the ocean at the base of a bluff a quarter of a mile away. Undaunted, the man removed the radiator, carried it to the beach, laid it flat in the water until it was filled, then he carried it back, with rags plugging the spouts, and reinstalled it!

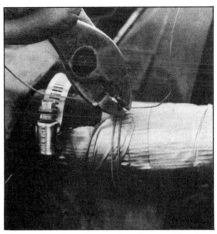

Fix a ruptured cooling-system hose with a couple of wraps of racer's tape, then cinch down with wire.

When you have a radiator leak problem, and even after jury-rigging a fix, don't replace the cap tightly. Cooling systems work under pressure and you don't want to aggravate the situation by forcing the leak. Leave the cap off or twist it on only until the tangs first engage. But watch your temperature gage and check the coolant level frequently as you cruise along toward the sunset.

Overheating has other causes, too. If the temperature-gage needle is pegged on a hot day, or the red warning light has winked on, ease off the throttle, but keep moving ahead if you can. Airflow through the radiator helps dissipate heat. Is the air conditioning on? This increases engine load, which promotes underhood heat. Turn on your heater. It may get hotter than blazes in the cab, but it's helping to further dissipate some of that high engine temperature. If you must stop, at least leave the engine at idle. The fan will draw air back and over the engine and the coolant will continue to circulate.

If the fan belt, or any accessory-drive belt, breaks and you don't have a spare, there are a couple of things to try. One is tying a lightweight rope around the proper engine and fan pulleys. If this doesn't work because the knot jumps out of the pulley grooves, borrow your wife's or girlfriend's nylons or pantyhose. No. Don't put them on! Twist them into rope form. The material will tie with a finer knot than rope and, hopefully, will work satisfactorily as long as you don't run the engine much above an idle. If even this fails, trim your belt or a length of rubber cut from the spare-tire inner tube, and "sew" the ends together with baling or electrical wire and an awl or ice pick. Be sure to loosen the adjustment pulley before you secure the ends, so you can take up the slack in your makeshift drive belt after it's in place.

A radiator or heater hose that has split from age is the fault of improper maintenance. But we won't leave you in the wilds with the wolves closing in because of an oversight. Wrap the hose heavily with some good old racer's tape, then wrap wire around the ends of the patch and tighten it down. If a split has occurred at the end of a hose under a clamp, remove it, trim off the offending inch or so, then put it back on. There is generally enough surplus length to let you do this. If a heater hose goes south, cut it off short of the leak and double it back on itself, outlet to inlet. Or, simply remove it altogether and plug the nipples with pegs whittled from branches.

DRIVE LINE

Other than a smashed transmission, transfer case or differential, about the only thing that will go wrong in the driveline department is a U-joint. If this happens and you're in a 4WD, you're in luck. Just remove the offending U-joint and its drive shaft. So what if it's the rear one? You still have front-wheel drive. Or vice versa.

This brings up the story of when one of us was conducting some fuel consumption tests with a 4X4 pickup. For no accountable reason, the rear U-joint broke and the drive shaft rolled off into a Utah gutter. Retrieving the pieces, our intrepid tester continued his voyage in front-wheel drive. The funny thing about it, though, was that the truck delivered two-mpg *better* mileage in front-wheel drive than it had in rear-wheel drive. No one has offered a solution for this.

ELECTRICAL SYSTEM

The electrical system of the modern vehicle is not only complex but has a lot of black-box wizardry about it that's virtually impossible to overcome when

there's a problem. Luckily, though, you can forget about everything but the ignition and starting circuits. Any failure with the lights or accessories doesn't rate as an emergency. You can always get home if the lights fail by waiting for daylight. What we're really concerned about is that fire reaches the sparkplugs, that the battery is up to snuff, and that the starter works. Dirt, corrosion and water are the enemies here.

If the points in an older distributor are gummed up and too dirty to work, you may be able to clean them with your toothbrush dipped in gin or aftershave lotion. To file pitted points to some semblance of a flat surface, use a nail file or the striking strip from a match folder. To reset the points, a business card will be about 0.010-in. thick or a match folder about 0.015-in. thick. Sparkplugs can be cleaned and gapped, at least close enough to fire, in the same way. If your vehicle is older and has a breaker-type ignition, it would be wise to carry a spare distributor rotor, coil and condenser. If your engine dies or won't start, replace one of these at a time.

If you think the battery has a full charge, but the starter won't spin the engine, chances are there's corrosion on the posts. You can find out for sure by jamming a screwdriver blade between the clamp and the battery post and trying it again. If the starter now operates, clean off the corrosion. Remove the cable clamps and, if you didn't pack your trusty battery-terminal brush, sand, file or scrape the posts until they're shiny. Scrape the insides of the terminals with a knife or screwdriver. Replace the cables and give the starter another try. If one of the cable-clamp bolts is corroded in half or broke while you were loosening it, borrow a similar-size bolt from some non-essential place on the vehicle. Or, work the clamp off the end of the cable and hold the bared cable to the post with Vise-Grip pliers. If it turns out that the cable has broken inside the insulation, remove the cable entirely, and make the reconnection with half of your jumper cables.

Dirt or water in the distributor can be blown out with air from the spare tire and the air-thief hose we told you about earlier. If you don't have one of these, un-

A fire extinguisher is an off-roading must. Mount one permanently in the cab where it is immediately accessible.

screw the valve core from the spare tire and feed air to the distributor with your fuel siphon hose. Water can also get into the plug-wire terminals at the plugs or at the distributor. Remove them one at a time so you won't louse up the engine firing order, and blow air here, too.

Moisture can play havoc with the high-tension sparkplug leads, but resist the temptation to remove and dry them over an open fire. Just spray them with WD-40 or an equivalent. This handy substance repels water and, as it soaks into the pores of the insulation, it will drive the water out.

If the battery charge is too low to fire the engine after an evening with the stereo or lights left on too long, you're in trouble if your rig has an automatic transmission. With a manual transmission, you can always push- or jump-start your vehicle.

However, if there is no helper vehicle or down-slope nearby, try this: Jack up the right rear wheel—both rear wheels if you have a limited-slip differential. Shift out of four-wheel drive. Now, wrap your towstrap or a hefty rope around the perimeter of the tire. Shift into second gear, let the clutch out and turn the key to start, and have someone pull as hard as they can on the rope. Sometimes, the impetus of the spun tire together with the last gasp of the starter will light the engine off. But then, sometimes it won't. And this is all

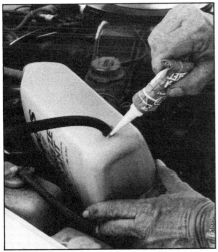
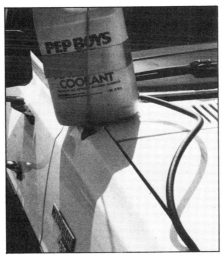

Good old gravity will let fuel run into a carburetor without fuel pump. Rig a container with a drain line and seal it with some sort of goo, connect it to carburetor, then mount container up high somewhere and fill with fuel.

to no avail with an automatic transmission, of course.

Then there's the story of a person who got his vehicle to run when the battery was dead flat from a short circuit, by using 12 volts worth of flashlight batteries. These were wired to the coil and he got coast-started on a downgrade. This might also work if the alternator goes bye-bye.

Although a blown fuse or a broken electrical wire is seldom a cause of total immobility, these can usually be overcome. First, determine the cause, like a short circuit, and fix it. Then, if you don't have a spare fuse, pop a small screw, a bolt, or a strip of metal cut from a can into the fuse holder. But tie a piece of string or wire to it so you can yank it out in a hurry if you smell smoke— before you burn your truck to the ground. As for a broken wire, replace it with a length of similar gage pirated from somewhere else. The first thing to do when you get home is replace the bolt or screw with a fuse of the proper resistance.

FUEL SYSTEM

Damage to a fuel tank or any of the myriad lines that comprise the fuel system is not an uncommon off-road occurrence. Rocks have a tendency to find a non-skidplated fuel tank in a hurry. The lines between the tank and the engine compartment are sometimes vulnerable

to being squashed, split or torn away. And fittings can unwind after long stretches of vibration-inducing washboard roads. The real danger here, other than losing all of your supply, is *fire*. This is especially true if there's a leak in the engine compartment or near the exhaust system. To minimize the danger of fire from a fuel leak or any other cause, carry a fire extinguisher. It should be maintained in apple-pie working order and be conveniently located in the cab where it can be grabbed in an instant.

It's always a good idea, after you've heard or felt a rock or other obstacle contact any part of the chassis, to get out and look underneath for telltale drippings. Vehicle liquids are identifiable by color or smell. And the pungent odor of gasoline is unmistakable.

As mentioned on page 159, if there's a small tear in the fuel tank or a seam has ruptured, rub a bar of hand soap over the damaged area a few times. The soap will swell and harden, stopping or at least slowing the leak. A hole too large for soap can sometimes be plugged with a strip cut from your belt or spare tire and held in place with sheet-metal screws after coating the surfaces with anything gooey and unaffected by gasoline.

If a steel or neoprene fuel line has split or is broken, you can probably fix it by cutting the line in two at the point of the leak. Force something cylindrical into or

over the cut ends, like a ballpoint-pen barrel, a hose from somewhere else, or even a pencil that you're removed the lead from with a red-hot ice pick or nail. If fuel leaks from the connections, wrap them with a couple of turns of wire and cinch down hard with pliers.

Vapor lock has stopped many an off-roader. Wrap the hottest section of fuel line, usually near some part of the exhaust system under the hood, with a wet rag. This will cool and help return the vaporized fuel to a liquid.

One of the authors once found himself and a companion 40 miles at sea in an inboard cabin cruiser when the fuel pump quit, just like that. No amount of twiddling, or replacement of the unit with the spare brought along for just such an emergency, would right the wrong. And being 40 miles at sea off of mainland Mexico is a bit more serious than being stuck beside a road. Several trial-and-error hours later it was discovered that the camshaft lobe which drove the pushrod that operated the mechanical fuel pump had worn down to a nub. The pump simply wasn't getting the action it needed from the engine. The eventual solution was to re-rig a few lines, run one from a fuel tank directly to the carburetor, and pressurize the tank with air from the foot-operated air-mattress pump. Enough fuel was force-fed to the engine for the craft to make it to port. Only mind over matter had kept the duo from drifting to Peru, or worse.

That's one way to bypass a dead fuel pump. There's another. We've heard of one stalwart who rigged a line between the carburetor and the windshield-washer bottle. By filling the container with fuel, then turning on the washer pump at regular intervals, he was able to limp along, stopping now and then to replenish his fuel supply by siphoning more from the main tank.

Gravity feed to a carburetor works the best and is also the safest. What you have to do is get the fuel-supply outlet higher than the carb inlet. Siphon fuel from your tank into a portable container that you've rigged with an outlet hose. Racer's-tape or wire the container somewhere under the hood so the fuel can run downhill. Or, tape the container to the radio antenna and leave the hood ajar so the hose can

You can break a tire bead loose by using your jack like this.

run into the engine compartment without being pinched. Take the hood off if you have to. You can always come back for it later. Or, do what a friend once did. He laboriously removed the fuel tank from under his Wagoneer and wired it to the top of the cowl. Then, to provide a hole through the hood for the fuel line, he simply blew one with his .45 automatic. Good thinking!

But before the fuel pump is suspected as the culprit, be sure all filters are clean and that line blockage isn't stopping fuel flow, or slowing it sufficiently that the engine is starving and only runs intermittently. Don't bother removing the fuel-filler cap and applying some lung power or air from your tire pump. If there is a fuel blockage, you'll only force it more tightly against the restriction. Instead, remove both ends of the line between the carburetor and the fuel pump. Blow upstream through it. If the plug isn't there, replace that line and remove the end of the input line to the pump from the tank. Blow upstream through this one, too, and have someone put an ear to the filler pipe and listen for gurgling. If this line is also clear, then the much-maligned fuel pump is probably at fault after all.

Don't forget that any rubber or plastic substitute for a flexible fuel line may not be impervious to gas. Small flakes may come from inside and wash downstream to eventually plug the line or muck up the filter. Flush the system when you're safely home and make sure all filters are cleaned or replaced.

LUBRICATION SYSTEM

If you've punched a hole in your engine or automatic transmission pan, shame on you. You must have skipped Chapter 13 on skidplates. But if the tear is small, you may be able to plug the leak with bar soap or chewing gum. Failing that, cut a suitably sized piece of anything tough but pliable, goop it with silicone sealer or grease, and run some metal screws through it. Drive these into the rip or punch holes in the pan with an awl or nail.

One of us took part in a curious fix-it on a lengthy desert sojourn. The automatic-transmission pan was ripped by the inevitable Baja rock. The pan was removed, the jagged tear was hammered flat—luckily no metal was actually missing—and the seam was repaired by using the vehicle's battery and its cables. The ground strap was left on its battery post and the other end was clamped to the pan with Vise-Grip pliers. Then, the remaining cable was clamped to its post. When the free terminal end was wiped over the seam, there was enough juice from the resulting short circuit to deposit some of the soft terminal and allow it to "weld" the rip shut. Maybe solder is a better word. Believe it or not, this worked well enough for the group to continue their travels.

Usually, considerable fluid will be lost before an oil leak can be stopped. Consider quickly plugging the hole with a hastily whittled stick until a better cure is planned. Try and catch as much leaking oil as you can in anything that's at hand. To replenish the supply after the fix-it has been accomplished, there's always the single quart of oil we suggested that you bring along. If this isn't enough—and you don't have to fill the crankcase completely, anything over the "Add" mark is sufficient—dump-in the automatic transmission fluid we told you about. Add either one or a mixture of the two to either the engine or transmission. For a larger quantity, you can afford to drain off some engine oil (if the dipstick shows "Full") to add to the trans, or vice versa. Need still more? Add a little siphoned gasoline, but not too much because it will thin the lubricant. If worst comes to worst, drain some gear lube from a manual transmission, the transfer case on a

4X4, or even differential lube. Gear trains will last longer with a low lubricant level than an engine or automatic transmission will.

Many of the photographs in this book were taken by our off-roading photographer friend, Jim Brokaw II. One dark and dreary night on the Mojave Desert, at 2:00 A.M. and with the thermometer hovering around 28F, good old Jim heard an ominous growling in the rear of his truck. A frigid investigation showed he'd unaccountably lost the drain plug from his differential and the last vestiges of gear oil were dribbling silently into the sand. Even though the threads of the lost drain plug and the upper fill plug were different, Jim "convinced" the fill plug into the drain hole with a pipe wrench. Then he poured his one spare quart of 10W-40 engine oil into the differential, hammered a stick into the opening, and blithely picked up the trail where he'd left off.

ODDS AND ENDS

Following is a very random list of fix-its and other hints that don't qualify for a particular category.

If you need a *bolt* or a *screw* for a more serious purpose, borrow one from an unimportant place on your vehicle.

If the *shift linkage* gives up on a column-shifted manual transmission, put it in gear by manipulating the linkage from under the hood or at the transmission itself.

If you have to *dismount a tire* from a rim and don't have a bead breaker, lay it flat on the ground under a bumper and use your jack. Or, drive over the tire but not the rim.

When a *spotlight* or *searchlight* is called for, remove one of your headlights. Usually there's enough surplus wire to let you aim the light where you want it. Or borrow more wire from another part of the vehicle.

Remove the outside door mirror to flash a *signal* in the daytime.

Douse your *deflated* spare tire with fuel and burn it as a *nighttime signal* or for a smoke signal during the day. Or simply remove your rear seat and burn it.

If you lose your *fuel-filler cap*, stuff a rag or handkerchief, even a piece of shirt, into the opening to keep dust and other grit from entering the tank.

Broken throttle linkage can often be fixed with twine and a few rubber bands. Or run a stiff wire through a fire-wall hole so you can operate the throttle by hand.

Bungee cords are useful for more than holding things down. Hold things together or apart with them.

Baking soda has many uses. A handful will put out a small fire. Mix some with water for cleaning corroded battery terminals. Or, mix some with salt to make a passable toothpaste. Use it as an underarm deodorant. Drink some with water for an upset stomach.

If you need to make a *gasket*, use the cardboard from a cereal or cracker box.

If a *door lock* freezes in winter, hold the key with pliers over a fire then put it into the lock.

If the *clutch linkage* with a manual transmission acts up, get started in low gear on the starter then shift without using the clutch, carefully but not timidly.

When you're *stuck* in snow, sand or mud, build your own road using your hood, doors and tailgate.

You can also use these same parts of your vehicle for building a makeshift *shelter*.

In cold weather, keep the *windshield* from icing up, or snow from clinging to it, by rubbing it with wet salt.

Snuff out an *engine fire* with handsful of dirt, if you've used up all of your baking soda for something else. But try not to let any get down the carburetor.

Keep a *tie-rod end* in place, when you've lost the cotter pin and nut, by crisscrossing bungee cords around the tie rod and arm.

Repair a small hole in a *tire* by running a sheet-metal screw into it after smearing it with grease or anything gooey.

To make something *long and elastic*, cut strips from your spare-tire inner tube.

If your wife or girlfriend wouldn't loan you her pantyhose or nylons to make a fan belt, see if she'll at least give them up as a *filter*.

We haven't probed under the seat in our current 4X4, but some vehicles use light-duty *coil springs* to keep the seat covering taut. These might prove useful elsewhere.

When the fuel gage has dipped dangerously low and it's still a long way to a service station, pirate some *extra fuel* from your dirt bike, snowmobile or trailered boat. Two-stroke fuel mixture will work just fine in an automobile engine.

Did you know that a *low battery* can sometimes be encouraged by heating it up?

If a *leaf spring* breaks near the shackle end, a short length of chain and some nuts and bolts from that coffee can we suggested you bring along, may hold things together temporarily.

If a *broken spring* cannot be fixed, consider wedging your spare tire, and wiring it in place, between the axle and the frame to keep the body up off of the tire and wheel.

It's a good idea to carry a *factory repair manual* for your make and model of vehicle. When something goes haywire, the book may show a cutaway or exploded view of the component so you can see exactly how it works and is put together. Knowing this may prompt a temporary fix.

CAUTIONS

These ideas, hints and suggestions ought to hold you for a while. We cannot possibly list all things that might *possibly* go wrong when you're a dozen or more miles from nowhere, nor suggest cures for every glitch that might arise. However, we hope these will stimulate your brain waves so that the next time you run into a mechanical problem on the trail, you'll be able to work out a suitable solution yourself.

But heed a few sage words of caution. *Never* attempt to mix gasoline with diesel fuel to stretch the supply. The American Petroleum Institute warns that gasoline vapors alone are too rich to burn (and which is why it's mixed with air), and that diesel vapors alone are too lean to ignite. But mixing the two can pick up enough air to fall within explosive range. To raise the ignition point of diesel fuel to help cold-weather starting, but never to increase the quantity, add a small amount of kerosene. The amount of kerosene added should *never* exceed 20 percent of the quantity in the tank.

Be absolutely sure to properly repair any temporary fix just as soon as you can. This is especially true with

A small sidewall puncture can often be "patched" with a sheet-metal screw daubed with a gooey substance and run into tire. Reinflate tire to very low pressure.

brakes. Liquids other than the prescribed brake fluid will ruin your system in short order. Use suitable replacement parts for any jury-rigged hoses, lines, connections, or whatever. Flush out a cooling system in which anything but the proper mixture of antifreeze has been substituted. Ditto for automatic transmissions into which unspecified hydraulic fluids have been added. Drain and flush all fuel lines if you suspect that anything but the correct fuel has gotten into the system. Replace the filters, as well. Replace fuses with those of proper resistance and get spares for the next trip while it's on your mind. Replace any fasteners that you had to borrow for use someplace else.

To close on a cheerful note, many temporary fixes that have taxed your imagination and brought out your native resourcefulness, not only build upon your off-roading confidence but will make terrific campfire stories. Just imagine amazing your friends by explaining how you levered yourself out of a snowbank with a tree limb and an old CJ for a fulcrum. Or how, as a friend once did when he was mired down in mud one wintry afternoon, you waited until dark and the night's freeze then drove blissfully home on ice.

And now that you reflect back on your recent off-road problems, they weren't all *that* bad, were they?

20

Off-Road Trailering

With careful driving and by remembering there's a trailer back there, off-roading can be great fun with a load hitched up behind. Courtesy Trailer Boats magazine.

Small utility trailer used to tow off-road gear has plywood cap to keep duffle in and dust out.

The best way to begin this chapter is to explain that only Class I trailers should be considered for off-road trailering. Period. This is the classification for trailers weighing no more than 2000 lb when fully loaded and a 200-lb maximum hitch weight. Medium-duty Class II trailers up to 3500 lb, and heavy-duty Class IIIs up to 5000 lb, are not recommended for off-pavement use unless it's only a

smooth, short hop over a dirt road from a highway to an RV park.

Large trailers have excessive overhang at both the front and rear, plus they have delicate undersides. The up and down motion of the tow vehicle can easily scrape the bottom of the trailer or bring you to a stop if it encounters an obstacle. Large trailers tend to be rather fragile, too, and while they are engineered to follow a car or truck docilely along highways, they cannot stand the kinds of abuse off-roading is apt to dish out. Pitching, swaying and the rattling vibrations caused by unmaintained byways will swing cabinet doors open, and cause the drawers to slide out and dump your household goods on the floor, to say nothing of the eggs lobbed unceremoniously from the refrigerator.

Utility Trailers—Into the Class I category fall all sorts of useful trailers. These can be small traveling or folding-tent trailers, designed to provide a cozy home away from home for two people, or three if push comes to shove. We suggest

limiting these to about 12 feet of overall length including the tongue and coupler.

Then there are special flat-bed or rail-type trailers intended to haul motorcycles, three-wheelers, snowmobiles, and the like. Add to these box-type cargo trailers and, of course, boat trailers.

Weight—Besides the relative fragility of larger trailers, their sheer weight is a deterrent with today's smaller vehicles and reduced-horsepower engines. It takes muscle to drag a trailer over a trail and up steep hills, to say nothing of the need to stay up with traffic on the highway and in town. Most modern off-road vehicles just don't have the pulling power that heavy trailers require.

Small trailers, then, are the answer for downsized vehicles. Most can swallow just about anything that won't fit in a pickup or station wagon. When four people go weekending in a small utility vehicle, there is seldom sufficient space for all of the paraphernalia they'd like to take along. And, a pair of three-wheelers or trail bikes will just about fill the bed of a small truck and leave no room for an ice chest, cots and sleeping bags.

A trailer to handle the overflow is the answer, of course. But before you hitch up and head for the outback, there are certain things you should know.

Tow Vehicle—Your vehicle must be equal to the demands of towing, and legally equipped to do so. When shopping for a new truck or wagon, ask the dealer about an optional towing package. See if it includes a hitch, wiring, two large outside mirrors, and proper gear ratios for the weight you're planning to tow. Trailering options often add heavy-duty rear springs, shock absorbers and radiator, and an auxiliary oil cooler for the automatic transmission.

If the vehicle manufacturer doesn't offer a towing package, or if the rig you already have isn't equipped for towing, don't despair. Look in the telephone *Yellow Pages* under Trailers, Equipment and Parts for an RV center. Larger RV cen-

A Class I hitch for trailers weighing up to 2000 lb requires only a simple, but sturdy, mount for the ball.

Front-mounted hitch ball can come in handy for spotting a trailer in a difficult spot or working it through questionable terrain. Courtesy Trailer Boats Magazine.

ters will have most of the necessities, and if they can't do the installations for you they'll recommend someone who can.

Check with your vehicle dealer if you find that engine performance is down when you're towing. Optional axle ratios are available for more low-end pulling power. On 4X4s, you'll need to change the gearsets in both the front and rear axles.

Trailer Brakes—If you prefer using trailer brakes or the law in your area dictates that you must have them, there are several choices. First are electric brakes. Trailer brakes are the internal-expanding drum-type, similar to the rear brakes of most cars and trucks. But they are activated by a solenoid instead of hydraulic pressure. In some systems, the solenoid is energized by the driver and the controller can be a small lever on the steering column. Another type uses an electronic sensor that detects the slowing motion of the tow vehicle and applies the trailer brakes with no effort on the driver's part. These have sensitivity adjustments, and you'll have to experiment with your own vehicle-trailer combination to determine the proper setting. A lighter or heavier trailer load requires readjustment of the setting, so it's a good idea to do this whenever you hook up to your trailer.

Many trailer towers prefer hydraulic trailer brakes. The best systems are self-contained and are referred to as *surge* brakes. That means they have their own wheel cylinders, master cylinder and connecting lines separate from the towing vehicle. Activation is by a sliding ram designed into the coupler. The harder you apply the vehicle brakes, the harder the trailer wants to push against the hitch and this imparts the impetus to the trailer brakes. There used to be hydraulic systems which could be tapped into the towing vehicle's brakes, but these are no longer in favor, are illegal in some cases, and may void your vehicle's warranty.

The problem with surge brakes, however, comes when trying to back the trailer up a slope, a common situation off-road. Reversing the vehicle, especially on a hill, applies the trailer brakes precisely when you don't need them. The vehicle is trying to go and the trailer is trying to stop. About the only way to avoid this is to anticipate when and how you back up.

Good trailer-brake systems, whether electric or hydraulic, have a tether tied to the rear of the tow vehicle. If the tethered trailer becomes disconnected while traveling, its brakes will be automatically applied.

Hitches—If you enjoy working around

your truck and want to add trailer wiring, heavier shocks and other towing equipment yourself, fine. But we must tell you about hitches. First of all, RV centers sell hitch assemblies ready-made for specific vehicles. Buying one is far easier and safer than trying to fabricate one yourself. Some hitch assemblies can be bolted in place, but many require welding. Let a pro do the installation to ensure it is done properly and safely, or see HPBooks' *Welder's Handbook* for tips on this. If you have a vehicle for which a hitch isn't readily available, RV stores or good welding shops can fabricate one for you.

If you have a pickup truck with a step bumper, you're in luck. They are factory-drilled for a hitch ball. Sometimes, there are two (or three) alternate holes so you can permanently mount hitch balls of different diameters and be able to tow various trailers without having to replace one ball with another. Two popular hitch-ball diameters are 1-7/8 and 2 in.

Always *be sure* the coupler on the trailer and your hitch ball are the same size. A small coupler obviously won't fit on a large ball. But the larger coupler will drop down over the smaller ball and though it will seem to latch properly, you can easily lose the trailer.

Hitch Balls—Ready-made hitch assem-

Military-type pintle-hook hitches are rugged enough for serious off-roading but are illegal in some states on civilian vehicles.

Common off-road trailering problem: When negotiating steep ramp angles, rear end of tow vehicle goes up, causing rear end of trailer to go down. Small trailers frequently have little ground clearance.

blies rarely include the hitch ball itself. This is because the manufacturer has no idea what size coupler your trailer has. For that reason, shops that sell and install hitches also sell balls.

One type is a steel or iron ball with a separate bolt that drops through it and through the hitch plate or bumper. Sometimes, a low-grade bolt will shear off, especially under the strain of serious off-roading. For this reason, the two-piece hitch ball is illegal to use in California.

Better to use is a one-piece, forged-steel ball with an integral, threaded shank. Regardless of the type ball used, it's imperative that the hole in the hitch or bumper be no larger than the hitch-ball bolt or shank.

Tongue Weight—As a rule of thumb, 10 percent of the total loaded weight of the trailer should rest on the hitch. This means a 2000-lb trailer should have 200 lb on the hitch. Actually, some trailerites prefer 12—15 percent on the tongue, but it should never be more than this or less than 10 percent. A trailer will yaw and sway if there is too little weight on the hitch. And a too-heavy condition will give the trailer a nose-down attitude, point your headlights at the sky and adversely affect steering.

Trailer Loading—Take your trailer, loaded the way you'll tow it, to a public scales or large grain scales to weigh it and check the tongue loading. If yours is a very light trailer, bathroom scales will work just fine.

Before weighing, disconnect the trailer. If it has a dolly wheel or stand at the tongue, place this on the scale platform. If it doesn't, use a board or some other prop to hold the trailer level and put this on the scale. Read the weight and write it down. Now, roll the trailer onto the scales, or slide small scales under each wheel, and weigh the whole thing—including tongue load. If the tongue weight is less than 10 percent or more than 15 percent of total weight, rearrange the load.

If your trailer carries bikes or similar back-country playthings, load them differently to shift their weight forward or backward, depending upon whether you want more or less tongue weight. With a camping trailer, shift around anything that's not nailed down—camping equipment, water, tools, groceries, and so on—until you achieve a balance. Most boat trailers have hull-carrying bunks or rollers that can be shifted on the trailer chassis (or offer alternate mounting points for the axle springs) so you can carry the boat farther forward or aft. If you still can't get the desired tongue weight this way, remove the outboard engine from the transom—it's not a good idea to carry it there on rough roads anyway—and lash it down nearer the bow or carry it in your vehicle.

Center of Gravity—Trailers, even lightweight ones, can get very tippy on rough roads, especially if there's any side-hilling to do. Get the trailer's center of gravity down as low as possible by placing the heavier cargo as near to the floor as possible. If your camping trailer is of the self-contained type and has a built-in water tank for the sink or head, consider carrying the water in a portable container on the floor. You can then add the contents to the built-in tank when you arrive at your destination.

Trailering and the Law—Each of our 50 states has its own set of trailering regulations. As with the auxiliary lights you read about in Chapter 11, every state has its own ideas about what's legal and what isn't. And these rules are frequently changed, it seems, just to keep everyone confused. For example, some states require brakes on trailers weighing over 1500 lb while others will let you go brakeless up to 2000 lb. Also, some vehicle manufacturers recommend brakes on trailers over 1500 lb because they apparently fear that vehicle brakes are marginal when asked to stop an additional 3/4 ton. Then there are states which ask you to demonstrate that your coupled-up combination can stop within a certain distance from a certain speed. This may mean that your particular trailer must have brakes even though it weighs less than 1500 lb.

Common sense says a safety chain is a trailering must. If the hitch becomes dis-

Trailer should always have between 10 and 15 percent of total weight on hitch, sit level when coupled up, and be matched to size and capabilities of tow vehicle.

Lightweight boats can be trailered to out-of-the-way launching sites in really rugged territory. Four-wheel-drive is a prerequisite when trying to negotiate sand or mud with a trailer.

connected while you're towing, a safety chain assures that the trailer and tow vehicle will stay together while you stop instead of the trailer heading off by itself into opposing traffic. But here again the rules vary. Some states say a single safety chain is permissible. Others say you must have two arranged any way that's convenient, while still others insist they be connected in specific ways.

Stop-, tail-, clearance-, and turn-indicator lights all have to meet certain criteria, but again, every state has its own ideas on what this is. Trailer fenders, though, are mandatory throughout the country—for trailers above certain weight limits, that is.

Trailer height, width and length also come under the legal crossfire, but Class I trailers almost automatically fall within these parameters because of their small size. Towing speed on major highways is the same 55 mph required of all traffic, but some states, even individual counties, may post slower speeds on secondary roads.

Checking Legalities—The best thing to do for your own trailering safety and to make certain you meet all rules and regulations, is to check with your local highway patrol, department of motor vehicles or your automobile club. They will have printed information spelling out exactly what you need to know. If you're about to head for a distant state, however, write or phone for its trailering requirements. Remember, what's legal in your home state might land you in the pokey in another state.

On the Level—A trailer should sit level when it's connected to a tow vehicle. It can sway all over the road if it's too low in front or back. And, the towing vehicle should sit as level as possible, too. Off-roader 4X4s with large tires and a lift kit, as well as some standard 4X4s, stand taller than the average cars most trailers are designed to fit. Consequently, the height of the hitch ball above the ground is a major consideration. Even if your RV dealer has a prefabricated hitch for your Bronco or Blazer, this doesn't mean your Coleman tent trailer can be hitched up properly. Readjustment of the hitch, the trailer coupler, or both, might be necessary before you can go trailering safely and legally. In some cases, the entire trailer can be raised on its suspension, but we'll get into that later.

In Dirt—The foregoing has pretty much concentrated on the requirements for paved-road trailering, which is what the off-roader must do to reach his favorite jumping-off place. But while you may leave the long arm of the law behind on an unmaintained dirt road or trail, there are common-sense requirements to follow just the same.

First, your vehicle is now effectively longer and cannot negotiate the same sharp turns as before. Remember that the trailer wheels will follow a tighter arc on a bend. It's easy to swing around a stump or boulder with the tow vehicle only to have the inside trailer tire go "blooey" when it strikes an obstacle. The average trailer tire is far more prone to damage than the rubber on your car or truck.

To adjust trailer to level stance behind 4X4, 4-in. square steel section (arrow) was inserted between trailer tongue and coupler.

Clearance—Trailer-axle ground clearance is another thing to watch out for. Most axles are a square tube or channel iron that runs straight across between the wheels, though some have a dropped center to provide a low center of gravity. An obstacle or sharp bump that your vehicle clears might impede the trailer. A bent axle or broken trailer spring is about the least damage you can expect. If you are really serious about off-road trailering, think about adding oversize wheels and tires to it for added ground clearance. Or you may want to see if it's possible to move the trailer axle *under* the springs which should give you about 3 in. of lift.

Don't forget that your trailer is back there when you're running in the rough. Drive slowly and purposefully. Your

Killing two birds with one stone: Trailer spare-tire carrier swings down to double as dolly wheel for rolling boat trailer in and out of water.

This ex-military trailer has limber leaf springs properly fitted with swinging rear shackles and securely-mounted fenders.

trailer isn't nearly as rugged as the 4X4 you're towing it with, it probably doesn't have the clearance, and the trailer tongue and your hitch assembly are points that can become high-centered. Just take it easy and you'll eventually get to your favorite campsite, though it may mean extra hours on the trail.

Proper Off-Road Trailer—Builders of commercial trailers won't like us saying so, but the ideal off-road trailer has yet to be built. You *cannot* buy a factory-built trailer intended specifically for serious off-roading. Trailers are designed for use on pavement, and tires, wheels, axles, springs, the chassis, tongue and coupler are of marginal strength in the world of slam-banging.

Of course, the little military trailers built for towing behind wartime Jeeps are virtually, no pun intended, bulletproof. But they are not easy to come by anymore. A rugged, versatile trailer could be built by a specialist who knows what he's doing or who will follow your instructions to the letter. The authors know of several enthusiasts who have done just this. However, it's also possible to upgrade an existing utility trailer if you're handy with tools and a welding torch or know of a shop who'll do it for you.

We once asked a trailer specialist why trailers don't have shock absorbers. They do have suspension, of course, so the wheels can work up and down. But why not shocks like motor vehicles? His answer was an honest one: because trailers don't carry people to complain about the

lurching and harsh ride. A trailer is mute and must soak up the abuse of rough roads while the tow vehicle's driver and passengers ride blissfully along.

Someday, though, the trailer will complain about its treatment. Some, if not all, of its light bulbs will fail if the lamp housings don't come adrift first. Flat tires, collapsed wheels and burned-out bearings are familiar occurrences to drivers who don't give a trailer the consideration it deserves. In very rough conditions, fenders can break away from their moorings, frame members and spring hangers can break or be racked out of shape, wires can snag on brush and be pulled loose from connections or be torn away altogether.

During one memorable occasion, one of the authors towed a 1200-lb boat/trailer combination over a 130-mile trail with the severest washboard surface you ever saw. And when he got to where he was going and did a little fishing, he had to retrace his route over the same 130 miles to get home. The following damage to the trailer was later tallied: lost license plate, light and bracket; one lost fender with the other held in place by just one of its four attaching rivets; and no electrical connections between the hitch and rear lights except for a rat's nest of wire tangled around the axle. The boat fared little better: the battery came adrift and spilled acid in the bilge; the portable outboard-engine fuel tank gouged holes in the stern; the screws holding the console to the decking backed out; and the

trailering bracket that holds the engine in an upright position had disappeared.

It was the trailer that was at fault. That is, if you discount the fact the author shouldn't have tackled that road with a trailer too skimpy for the job.

Trailer Shortcomings—The biggest problem with trailers lies with their suspension systems. As noted, they don't use shock absorbers to damp off-road hammering. Most trailers have semi-elliptical leaf springs with too few leaves of inadequate length. This is a cost-cutting measure on the manufacturer's part and simplifies construction. These springs are most often mounted in front by an eye rolled onto the main leaf, fitted with a bushing, and bolted to a flimsy frame bracket. In the rear, few trailers have a swinging spring shackle, as motor vehicles do, to allow the spring's arch to vary as the wheels jounce and rebound over bumps. Instead, the main spring leaf simply rests against the underside of the frame side rail, where it slides back and forth. A small guide keeps the free end of the spring from sliding off sideways.

Better Springs—The proper trailer leaf spring should be long and comprised of several thin leaves in order to be supple. Spring rate should match the weight of the loaded trailer. A spring shop could make a set of custom springs for you, but it will mean revamping the spring hangers and should include fixing a swinging shackle at the rear of each spring. A pair of light-duty shock absorbers could be added to damp the springs and reduce trailer sway. The end product should resemble the rear suspension of a small pickup truck.

Larger Tires—We have already mentioned adding larger wheels and tires to a trailer to increase its ground clearance, or moving the axle to a position under the springs if it was above them to begin with. Standard tires, wheels, bearings and hub assemblies are generally too light for the off-roading trailer. And tires rarely lay down a sufficient footprint, which can make pulling a trailer through sand or mud a real headache. If your Class I trailer came with 13- or 14-in. wheels, go up to 15- or even 16-in. In fact, why not match the trailer tires and wheels to those on your tow vehicle? This will eliminate the need to haul different-size spare tires.

Investigate replacing the trailer's original wheel-hub assemblies with something of better quality, such as those from a small pickup truck. This may mean a trip to a specialist for fabrication and welding. But the reward will be worth the effort and expense, and let you tow virtually anywhere with peace of mind.

Other Suggestions—Fenders should be formed of steel, not aluminum or fiberglass. Weld them to solid brackets instead of bolting or riveting them. Choose good-quality accessory lights with metal housings and bolt or weld these directly to the trailer chassis instead of using fancy brackets. Route wiring inside the frame channels of the trailer rather than alongside or underneath the frame where it can get snagged. Bundle or tie-wrap the wire loom securely or, better, run it through steel tubing or electrical conduit.

A friend of ours who is an advocate of boating away from the crowds does a lot of off-road trailering. He's been over some of the roughest trails ever to feel a trailer wheel. Yet his trailer is as tight and rattle-free as the day he bought it. When he first got the trailer, he dismantled it and threw all the nuts, bolts and other fasteners away. Then, he put it back

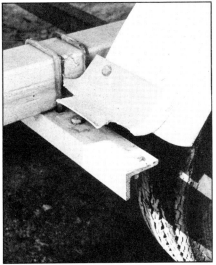

Most commercially-built trailers cannot stand abuse of heavy off-roading. This flimsy aluminum fender bracket self-destructed from continuous hammering.

Here's a trailer designed specifically for off-road travel with steel fenders welded to sturdy brackets and taillight assembly firmly mounted.

together with grade-8 aircraft-quality bolts and locknuts, liberally dousing them with Loc-Tite. Overkill? Maybe, but he's never had a problem with anything coming loose or falling off.

The tow vehicle for a proper off-road trailer should have a set of mud flaps or shields behind the rear wheels. This is so stones and gravel won't ding up the front of the trailer or eat through the gel-coat of a fiberglass boat. The flaps can be removable, of course, so if you don't like their looks you can take them off when you unhitch the trailer.

Airing-Down—Back on page 115, we told about airing-down tires for a better footprint when the going's soft and to help soak up vibrations and jolts from unpaved surfaces. Consider doing this to the trailer for the same reason. It will reduce the incessant jiggling of the trailer, and whatever you carry on or in it, and make for an easier ride all around.

However, you'll have to apply more throttle to maintain a given speed due to the added rolling resistance of the softer tires. This can lead to overheating in hot weather, so experiment and use your own judgment whether to air-down the trailer tires or not.

And Finally—So you see, there are problems with off-road trailering. But with the proper fixes, observing the precautions, minding the rules and using your own common sense, it's possible—great fun, even—to tow a trailer to a really out-of-the-way place. If yours is a camping trailer, you can get away from the often-crowded, always noisy improved campgrounds. If you tow an off-road toy, you can trailer it farther into the outback before unloading. Or, if yours is a simple box trailer to handle your weekending overflow, you can chug along the trail with more impunity than you ever imagined.

Suppliers List

Suppliers and products are listed alphabetically. If you are looking for a particular product, refer to the product list. The number next to each product refers to a company(ies) in the supplier list.

It's obviously impossible for us to include all suppliers of off-road equipment and accessories.

Other sources can be found through advertisements in the various off-road publications, your local newspaper as well as the Yellow Pages.

SUPPLIERS

1. Adbrook
   2013 W. Commonwealth, Suite N
   Fullerton, CA 93633

2. Advance Adapters
   P.O. Box 247
   Paso Robles, CA 93447

3. Airguide Instrument Co.
   2210 W. Wabansia Ave.
   Chicago, IL 60647

4. Air Lift Co.
   P.O. Box 12150
   Lansing, MI 48901

5. Airshox
   P.O. Box 38
   Newton, PA 18940

6. All Fours
   5742 S. Westnedge Ave.
   Kalamazoo, MI 49002

7. American Indian Travel Agency
   10403 W. Colfax Ave., Suite 550
   Lakewood, CO 80215

8. Appletree Automotive
   Box 310, Silver Lake
   Mears, MI 49436

9. Appliance Industries
   1333 S. Bon View Ave.
   Ontario, CA 91761

10. Armstrong Rubber Co.
    500 Sargent Dr.
    New Haven, CT 06536-0201

11. Arrow Tanks
    1031 S. Melrose Ave., Unit B
    Placentia, CA 92670

12. Autopower Industries
    3424 Pickett St.
    San Diego, CA 92110

13. John Baker Performance Products
    4304 Alger St.
    Los Angeles, CA 90039

14. B&M Products
    9152 Independence Ave.
    Chatsworth, CA 91311

15. Berrien Buggy, Inc.
    U.S. 31 South
    Berrien Springs, MI 49103

16. Bilstein Corp. of America
    11760 Sorrento Valley Rd.
    San Diego, CA 92121

17. Robert Bosch Sales Corp.
    2800 S. 25th Ave.
    Broadview, IL 60153

18. Bug Parts
    1533 Truman St.
    San Fernando, CA 91340

19. Burbank Suspension
    8341 Canoga Ave.
    Canoga Park, CA 91304

20. Bureau of Indian Affairs
    U.S. Dept. of Interior
    1951 Constitution Ave.
    Washington, DC 20242

21. Bureau of Land Management
    U.S. Dept. of Interior
    1800 C St. NW
    Washington, DC 20240

22. Bushwhacker
    9200 N. Decatur St.
    Portland, OR 97203

23. California Mini Truck
    7640-46 Sepulveda Blvd.
    Van Nuys, CA 91405

24. Carovan Products, Inc.
    22123 S. Vermont Ave.
    Torrance, CA 90502

25. Center Line Wheels
    13521 Freeway Dr.
    Santa Fe Springs, CA 90670

26. Dick Cepek, Inc.
    17000 Kingsview St.
    Carson, CA 90746

27. Charley's Off Road Center, Inc.
    14190 E. Firestone Blvd.
    Santa Fe Springs, CA 90670

28. Chenowth
    943 Vernon Way
    El Cajon, CA 92020

29. Brian Chuchua Jeep
    777 W. Orangethorpe
    Placentia, CA 92670

30. Cibie Division
    Valeo Automotive, Inc.
    34360 Glendale Ave.
    Livonia, MI 48150

31. Coleman Co.
    250 N. Francis St.
    Wichita, KS 67214

32. Con-Ferr Mfg., Inc.
    123-211 S. Front St.
    Burbank, CA 91502

33. Control Masters
    2968-N Bunsen Ave.
    Ventura, CA 93003

34. CustomFab Mfg. & Auxiliary
    Fuel Systems, Inc.
    Hanger 3, Ryan Field
    Hemet, CA 92343

35. Derwin Diversified
    130 E. Santa Maria St.
    Santa Paula, CA 93060

36. Desert Dynamics
    P.O. Box 1464
    Victorville, CA 92392

37. Desert Rat Off-Road
    3645 S. Palo Verde
    Tucson, AZ 85713

38. Dico
    323 E. Ball Rd.
    Anaheim, CA 92805

39. Dirtline Products, Inc.
    4359 State St.
    Pomona, CA 91766

40. Donaldson Co., Inc.
    P.O. Box 1299
    Minneapolis, MN 55440

41. Don's Off-Road Specialties
    18545 Topham
    Reseda, CA 91335

42. Downey Off-Road Mfg.
    10001 S. Pioneer Blvd.
    Santa Fe Springs, CA 90670

43. Draw-Tite
    14857 Martinsville Rd.
    Belleville, MI 48111

44. Dune Buggies & Hot VWs
    P.O. Box 2260
    Costa Mesa, CA 92626

45. Dune Buggy Supply Co.
    717 E. Excelsior Ave.
    Hopkins, MN 55343

46. Durakon, Inc.
    2101 N. Lapeer Rd.
    Lapeer, MI 48466

47. Duramex/Zelmot
    414 W. Rowland Ave.
    Santa Ana, CA 92707

48. Dusty Times
    5331 Derry Ave., Suite "O"
    Agoura, CA 91301

49. Bosch Lights
    364 N. Diamond Bar, Suite 127
    Diamond Bar, CA 91765

50. East/West Creations
    1626 N. Wilcox, No. 428
    Hollywood, CA 90028

51. Edelbrock Equipment Co.
    411 Coral Circle
    El Segundo, CA 90245

52. Empco Industries
    900 Allen Ave.
    Glendale, CA 91202-2820

53. Faas Wheels
    6695 Amah Parkway
    Claremore, OK 74017

54. Fey Manufacturing Co., Inc.
    15854 Omelas
    Irwindale, CA 91706

55. Flex-A-Lite Corp.
    4540 S. Adams
    Anderson, SC 29624

56. Firestone Tire & Rubber Co.
    1200 Firestone Pkwy.
    Akron, OH 44317

57. U.S. Forest Service
    U.S. Dept. of Agriculture
    14th St. & Jefferson Dr.
    Washington, DC 20250

58. 4-Way Suspension Products
    5760 Chesapeake Court
    San Diego, CA 92123

59. 4-Wheel & Off-Road Magazine
    8490 Sunset Blvd.
    Los Angeles, CA 90069

60. Four Wheeler Magazine
    6728 Eton Ave.
    Canoga Park, CA 91303-2813

61. Four Wheel Parts Wholesalers
    1900 West 135th St.
    Gardena, CA 90249

62. Fullerton Sand Tires
    11900 Beach Blvd.
    Stanton, CA 90680

63. Funco Race Cars
    8847 E. 9th St.
    Cucamonga, CA 91730

64. Gabriel Mfg. Co., Inc.
    P.O. Box 1488
    Nashville, TN 37202

65. Garvin Industries
    316 Millar Ave.
    El Cajon, CA 92020

66. General Electric Co.
    Lighting Business Group
    Nela Park
    Cleveland, OH 44112

67. General Tire Co.
    1 General St.
    Akron, OH 44329

68. Giant Off Road Centers
    3422 W. Whitton
    Phoenix AZ 85017

69. Gleason Power Systems
    2 Jetview Dr.
    Rochester, NY 14692

70. Golden Wheel Corp./Enkei
    1250 Mahalo Pl.
    Compton, CA 90220

71. B.F. Goodrich Co.
    500 S. Main, Bldg. 24-D
    Akron, OH 44318

72. Goodyear Tire & Rubber Co.
    1133 E. Market St.
    Akron, OH 44316

73. Haulamatic Corp.
    195 Anthony St.
    E. Providence, RI 02914

74. Heckethorn Mfg. Co.
    P.O. Box 310
    Dyersburg, TN 38024

75. Hella, Inc.
    42 Jackson Dr.
    Cranford, NJ 07016

76. Hellwig Products Co.
    16237 Avenue 296
    Visalia, CA 93291

77. Hickey Division of American Indust.
    4566 Spring Rd.
    Cleveland, OH 44131

78. High Desert Racing Association
    (HDRA)
    961 W. Dale Ave.
    Las Vegas, NV 89124

79. Hi-Lift Jack Co.
    PO Drawer 228
    Bloomfield, IN 47424

80. Hobrecht Enterprises
    15662 Commerce Ln.
    Huntington Beach, CA 92649

81. House of Steel, Inc.
    3552 Fowler Canyon Rd.
    Jamul, CA 92035

82. Intercompressor, Inc.
    Culver City, CA 90230

83. Interdynamics
    Brooklyn, NY 11232

84. Jackman Wheels
    1035A Pioneer Way
    El Cajon, CA 92020

85. JT Machine Products
    Star Rt. 2, Box 49
    Boulevard, CA 92005

86. K&N Engineering, Inc.
    P.O. Box 1329
    Riverside, CA 92502

87. Kargo-Master
    11261 Trade Center Dr.
    Cordova, CA 95670

88. Kayline Mfg. Co.
    20-C E. 64th Ave.
    Denver, CO 80221

89. K Bar S
    2121 Western Ave.
    Las Vegas, NV

90. KC HiLites, Inc.
    P.O. Box 155
    Williams, AZ 86046

91. Kelsey-Hayes Co.
    38381 Huron River Dr.
    Romulus, MI 48174

92. Kentrol, Inc.
P.O. Box 3304
Youngstown, OH 44512

93. Koni America, Inc.
P.O. Box 40
Culpeper, VA 22701

94. KYB Corp. of America
901 Oak Creek Dr.
Lombard, IL 60148

95. La Mar Industries
P.O. Box 2589
Long Beach, CA 90801

96. Lucas Industries
5500 New King St.
Troy, MI 48098

97. Man-A-Fre
5076 Chesebro Rd.
Agoura, CA 91301

98. G. H. Meiser & Co.
Posen, IL 60469

99. Mercury Tube
3628 San Fernando Rd.
Glendale, CA 91204

100. Monroe Auto Equipment Co.
1 International Dr.
Monroe, MI 48161

101. Mr. 4 Wheeler
118 S. Miller
Farmington, NM 87401

101A. Northwest Metal Products
3801 24th Ave.
Forest Grove, OR 97116

102. Northwest Off-Road Specialties, Inc.
1999 Iowa St.
Bellingham, WA 98226

103. Novak Enterprises, Inc.
13321 Alondra Blvd., Unit C
Santa Fe Springs, CA 90670

104. Offenhauser Sales Corp.
P.O. Box 32218
Los Angeles, CA 90032

105. Off-Road Advertiser
P.O. Box 340
Lakewood, CA 90714

106. Off-Road America
6637 Superior Ave.
Sarasota, FL 33581

107. Off Road Magazine
P.O. Box 49659
Los Angeles, CA 90049

108. Off Road Performance
P.O. Box 518
Lynwood, CA 90262

109. Off Road Unlimited
13001 N. Cave Creek Rd.
Phoenix, AZ 85002

110. On-Dirt Motorsports
P.O. Box 8938
Calabasas, CA, 91302

111. Alfred B. Patton, Inc.
P.O. Box 857
Doylestown, PA 118901

112. Per-Lux
1242 E. Edna Pl.
Covina, CA 91724

113. Perma-Cool
671 E. Edna Pl.
Covina, CA 91723

114. Pos-A-Traction Industries, Inc.
2400 Wilmington
Compton, CA 90220

115. Pro-Tech Engineering
707 South 10th
Blue Springs, MO 64015

116. Pro-Zap
P.O. Box 4023
Sonora, CA 95370

117. Quickor Engineering
6710 SW llth Ave.
Beaverton, OR 97005

118. Ramsey Winch Co.
P.O. Box 581510
Tulsa, OK 74158

119. Rancho Suspension
P.O. Box 5429
Long Beach, CA 90805

120. Randall Racing, Inc.
1121 W. Birchwood St.
Mesa, AZ 85202

121. Rapid Cool Division, Hayden Inc.
1521 Pomona Rd.
Corona, CA 91718

122. Reflexion Industries
P.O. Box 1032
West Memphis, AR 72301

123. Reider Racing Enterprises
4112 13th St.
Wyandotte, MI 48192

124. Rosser Jeep Sales
P.O. Box 709
Bessemer, AL 35021

125. Rough Country, Inc.
19007 S. Reyes Ave.
Compton, CA 90221

126. Rule Winch Co.
Cape Ann Industrial Park
Gloucester, MA 01930

127. Rugged Trail Suspensions
231 W. National Pike
Uniontown, PA 15401

128. Russell Performance Products
20420 S. Susana Rd.
Carson, CA 90745

129. SCORE Canada
390 Chemin Du Lac
Lery, Quebec, Canada J6N IA3

130. SCORE International
31356 Villa Colinas, Suite 111
Westlake Village, CA 91362

131. SCORE News
31356 Villa Colinas, Suite 111
Westlake Village, CA 91362

132. Marchal Division
Valeo Automotive, Inc.
34360 Glendale Ave.
Livonia, MI 48150

133. Skyjacker Suspensions
P.O. Box 1878
West Monroe, LA 71291

134. Smittybilt, Inc.
2118-2124 N. Lee Ave.
South El Monte, CA 91733

135. Superwinch
Winch Drive
Putnam, CT 06260

136. Surplus City
11794 Sheldon St.
Sun Valley, CA 91352

137. Stull Industries
1501 Pomona Rd.
Corona, CA 91720

138. Sway-A-Way Corp.
7840 Burnet Ave.
Van Nuys, CA 91405

139. Tensen Winches
304 SE 2nd Ave.
Portland, OR 97214

140. Mickey Thompson Performance Tires
P.O. Box 227
Cuyahoga Falls, OH 44222

141. Tire America
1 Bryan Dr.
Wheeling, WV 26003 or
540 Greg St.
Sparks, NV 89431

142. T-Mag Products
1320 E. St. Andrews, Unit 1
Santa Ana, CA 92705

143. Totally Toyota
9136 E. Firestone Blvd.
Downey, CA 90241

144. Trail Master Products
649 E. Chicago Rd., U.S. 312
Coldwater, MI 49036

145. Ultraseal International
1100 N. Wilcox Ave.
Los Angeles, CA 90038

146. Universal Security Instruments
Owing Mills, MD 21117

147. U.S. Topographic Maps
USGS, Eastern Distribution Center
1200 S. Eads St.
Arlington, VA 22202

148. U.S. Topographic Maps
USGS, Western Distribution Center
P.O. Box 25286, Federal Center
Denver, CO 80225

149. Warn Industries
19450 68th Ave. South
Kent, WA 98032

150. Weiand Automotive Industries
P.O. Box 65977
Los Angeles, CA 90065

151. Weld Racing, Inc.
933 Mulberry
Kansas City, MO 64101

152. Western Auto Supply Co.
2107 Grand Ave.
Kansas City, MO 64108

153. Western Wheel
14500 Firestone Blvd.
La Mirada, CA 90638

154. J.C. Whitney & Co.
1917-19 Archer Ave.
Chicago, IL 69680

155. Yokohama Tire Corp.
1350 Church Rd.
Montebello, CA 90640

Metric Equivalent Chart

Multiply:		by:		to get:	Multiply:	by:		to get:

LINEAR

inches	X	25.4	=	millimeters(mm)	X	0.03937	=	inches
miles	X	1.6093	=	kilometers (km)	X	0.6214	=	miles
inches	X	2.54	=	centimeters (cm)	X	0.3937	=	inches

AREA

inches^2	X	645.16	=	millimeters^2(mm^2)	X	0.00155	=	inches^2
inches^2	X	6.452	=	centimeters^2(cm^2)	X	0.155	=	inches^2

VOLUME

quarts	X	0.94635	=	liters (l)	X	1.0567	=	quarts
fluid oz	X	29.57	=	milliliters (ml)	X	0.03381	=	fluid oz

MASS

pounds (av)	X	0.4536	=	kilograms (kg)	X	2.2046	=	pounds (av)
tons (2000 lb)	X	907.18	=	kilograms (kg)	X	0.001102	=	tons (2000 lb)
tons (2000 lb)	X	0.90718	=	metric tons (t)	X	1.1023	=	tons (2000 lb)

FORCE

pounds—f(av)	X	4.448	=	newtons (N)	X	0.2248	=	pounds—f(av)
kilograms—f	X	9.807	=	newtons (N)	X	0.10197	=	kilograms—f

TEMPERATURE

Degrees Celsius (C) = 0.556 (F - 32)   Degree Fahrenheit (F) = (1.8C) + 32

°F −40   32   98.6   212   °F
       0   40   80   120   160   00   240   280   320

°C −40   −20   0   20   40   60   80   100   120   140   160   °C

ENERGY OR WORK

foot-pounds	X	1.3558	=	joules (J)	X	0.7376	=	foot-pounds

FUEL ECONOMY & FUEL CONSUMPTION

miles/gal	X	0.42514	=	kilometers/liter(km/l)	X	2.3522	=	miles/gal

Note:
235.2/(mi/gal)=liters/100km
235.2/(liters/100km)=mi/gal

PRESSURE OR STRESS

inches Hg (60F)	X	3.377	=	kilopascals (kPa)	X	0.2961	=	inches Hg
pounds/sq in.	X	6.895	=	kilopascals (kPa)	X	0.145	=	pounds/sq in
pounds/sq ft	X	47.88	=	pascals (Pa)	X	0.02088	=	pounds/sq ft

POWER

horsepower	X	0.746	=	kilowatts (kW)	X	1.34	=	horsepower

TORQUE

pound-inches	X	0.11298	=	newton-meters (N-m)	X	8.851	=	pound-inches
pound-feet	X	1.3558	=	newton-meters (N-m)	X	0.7376	=	pound-feet
pound-inches	X	0.0115	=	kilogram-meters (Kg-M)	X	87	=	pound-inches
pound-feet	X	0.138	=	kilogram-meters (Kg-M)	X	7.25	=	pound-feet

VELOCITY

miles/hour	X	1.6093	=	kilometers/hour(km/h)	X	0.6214	=	miles/hour

Index

Index